CATHOLIC SOCIAL THOUGHT, THE MARKET AND PUBLIC POLICY

St Mary's University Press is an imprint of St Mary's University. Its publications further the University's mission and values, including excellence in research and scholarship. All publications are peer reviewed. St Mary's University Press is a registered trademark. Further details can be found at www.stmarys.ac.uk/press/about.aspx.

CATHOLIC SOCIAL THOUGHT, THE MARKET AND PUBLIC POLICY

Twenty-First-Century Challenges

Edited by Philip Booth and
André Azevedo Alves

ST MARY'S UNIVERSITY PRESS

Copyright © 2024 by St Mary's University Press

Published by St Mary's University Press
www.stmarys.ac.uk/press/about.aspx

Published in association with
London Publishing Partnership
www.londonpublishingpartnership.co.uk

Second impression

All rights reserved

ISBN: 978-1-916786-00-4 (hbk)
ISBN: 978-1-916786-01-1 (ePDF)
ISBN: 978-1-916786-02-8 (ePUB)

A catalogue record for this book is available
from the British Library

Typeset in Adobe Garamond Pro by
T&T Productions Ltd, London
www.tandtproductions.com

Printed and bound in Great Britain
by TJ Books Ltd, Padstow

Cover photo: Salamanca Cathedral (Adobe Stock)

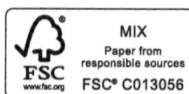

MIX
Paper from
responsible sources
FSC
www.fsc.org   FSC® C013056

Contents

Forewords

Perhaps one of many hallmarks of Pope Francis's papacy is his openness to critical dialogue and wide-ranging encouragement to raise important questions. Addressing the International Theological Commission in 2019, the Holy Father affirmed the theologian's vocation to be that of facing things which are not clear and taking risks in discussion. Of course, this can never be at the expense of the Church's faith. There are clear parameters in matters of both faith and morals, as specified by the Church's Magisterium, and these should not be breached. Some areas, however, leave a genuine space for legitimate and prudent diversity of interpretation. This is true in the application of the principles of Catholic social teaching, not least in addressing ever-changing dimensions of human and political ecology.

The encounter of Catholic teaching and tradition with contemporary social reality lends itself to a dialogical interpretive methodology. What the Second Vatican Council understood as the necessary engagement between the Church and the modern world is felt keenly in the articulation of Catholic social teaching. On such fundamental subjects as human dignity, the common good, solidarity, subsidiarity, poverty, peace, work and the environment, Catholic social teaching offers the wisdom of faith informed by reason or, as it is sometimes described, reasoning within faith.

The authors of this collection, all experts in their respective fields, trace the historical legacy of Catholic social teaching and shine its light on contemporary issues, some more contentious than others. They invite us to reflect with them, from within the Catholic tradition, considering diverse aspects of social and economic life ranging from subjects such as migration, healthcare and taxation to education and the environment. Not everyone may agree with each interpretation or conclusion set forth. The contributors' purpose, however, is to stimulate a deepened and broadened understanding of how issues facing the Church and the world might be addressed faithfully through Catholic social teaching.

The American moral theologian Thomas Shannon warned against what he called the 'fallacy of the generalization of expertise': the notion that competence in one area necessarily implies proficiency in others. To articulate properly the implications of Catholic social teaching, alongside theological voices, the Church needs the collaborative participation of those well versed in matters of economy, social and public policy, political theory and human development, at local, national and global levels. This timely and thought-provoking collection is an accessible testimony to such faithful and constructive partnership, promoting that fullness of life which Christ desires for all (cf. Jn 10:10).

MOST REV JOHN WILSON
Archbishop of Southwark

I am delighted to welcome this collection of essays on the practical application of Catholic social teaching to some of the most pressing policy tasks we face today. It is certainly the case that we urgently need to raise the quality of public discourse and inject a degree of 'wisdom' into political and economic debates which have become increasingly fractious and in which each side claims to have a monopoly on the truth. The current rise of individualism, populism and the geopolitical tensions between nations have made the job of calm deliberation based on clear values harder but even more important. Catholic social teaching, with its rich intellectual tradition, can provide an important framework for such dialogue.

Indeed, the importance of raising the quality of political and economic debate, has been emphasized by Pope Francis. In his most recent encyclical, *Fratelli tutti*, repeating a call he had made in an earlier encyclical, *Laudato si'*, Pope Francis demanded 'a politics which is far-sighted and capable of a new, integral and interdisciplinary approach to handling the different aspects of the crisis' *(Fratelli tutti*, 177). Later, the encyclical continues, again repeating a message from *Laudato si'*: 'True statecraft is manifest, when, in difficult times, we uphold high principles and think of the long-term common good. Political powers do not find it easy to assume this duty in the work of nation-building, much less in forging a common project for the human family' (178).

The notion of the 'common good' is much used in the Catholic tradition. Its particular understanding of human anthropology and the inherent dignity of human beings is not always well understood, despite its importance in tackling contemporary challenges. This book is important in that it brings together scholars with both an understanding of theology and an expertise in public policy, an unusual – but necessary – combination to examine some of these questions.

Of course, the reader may not agree with all the views expressed in this book. We may well interpret both the facts, and the best policy choices differently. The chapter authors largely favour a smaller state and a bigger role for civil society in the delivery of public services, but they recognize clearly that policy conclusions are matters for 'prudential judgement' on which 'two reasonable and faithful Catholics can disagree'. But it is certainly true, as the authors argue, that we need to think seriously about the challenges of the twenty-first century in a more considered way, based on a better understanding about where we are today and a richer application of the fuller Catholic understanding of the ideal of the 'common good' in which the state puts the conditions in place for human flourishing. It is also the case that we need to avoid knee-jerk calls for greater government intervention at every turn.

Many of the views in the book will be challenging, particularly to practising politicians concerned not just with policy but with re-election prospects. In particular, the insight that civil society has gradually been 'crowded out' by increasing government intervention – well-intentioned as that government intervention may be – is an important point on which all those concerned with public policy should reflect. For those on the left, it is worth seriously considering the argument that stronger labour protection laws have been accompanied by weaker trade unions and labour organizations. Is one the cause of the other? Or did the state need to step in as organized labour was weakened? For those across the political spectrum, the book challenges politicians to justify the differing treatment of health and education services by the state. Faith schools, specialist schools and schools with their own charisms and ethos are all provided with state funding on a similar basis in Britain. Diversity is encouraged, and parental choice over how to bring up children is at the centre of the approach. The National Health Service, however, is set up to favour uniformity of provision, with little space for faith-based or diverse provision within the public funding model.

The book also provides an important corrective, noting, despite the tendency of many to catastrophize the current global economic situation, the staggering improvements in basic measures of human welfare over the past 30 years as well as the sharp decline in inequality. As the authors note, it is important to recognize the reality of the situation, before using deciding the best course of action.

There is no doubt that politicians of all parties who wish seriously to put human dignity and the promotion of the common good at the centre of their policy approach would do well to consider the arguments presented here. This is an important contribution to the debate.

RT HON RUTH KELLY
Member of the Council for the Economy of the Vatican

Acknowledgement

The editors thank the Templeton World Charity Foundation for making this publication, and the associated website (www.catholic socialthought.org.uk), possible through their financial support. The materials on the website as well as this book will also be translated into Portuguese and made available in a number of Portuguese-speaking countries.

CHAPTER 1

Introduction

Philip Booth and André Azevedo Alves

PRUDENCE IN APPLYING THE PRINCIPLES OF CATHOLIC SOCIAL TEACHING

The main purpose of this book is to promote a better under-standing of the link between Catholic social thought and public policy. A subsidiary purpose is to examine the relationship between public policy, business and civil society. These are difficult themes to address. Experts on public policy do not generally have the theological background to ensure that Catholic social thought is considered in an appropriately scholarly way. At the same time, it is relatively rare for theologians to have the specialist knowledge to cross the empirical and theoretical bridge to subjects such as economics and political economy so that they can make appropriate prudential judgements. However, as interest in Catholic social thought grows, the number of people with the necessary breadth of intellectual experience has been increasing. This book brings together a number of those scholars.

The Catholic Church has always expressed views on issues to do with political, economic and social life. *Rerum novarum*, issued in 1891, is often identified as the starting point of that teaching from a formal standpoint. However, Catholic social thought, teaching and witness are as old as the Church herself.

There are important links between public policy in the economic sphere and objective moral matters. These may relate to issues such as fraud, theft, lying, physical oppression of workers and so on: our authors explore some of those links. However, there are additional criteria by which much of economic and social policy should be judged. This process of judgement requires the virtue of prudence. As such, the issues discussed in this book are often described as 'matters for prudential judgement' and they are matters on which two reasonable and faithful Catholics can disagree. This distinguishes these issues from the moral and theological teaching of the Church which is to be held by all faithful Catholics.

Prudence is the virtue that disposes practical reason to discern our true good in every circumstance and to choose the right means of achieving it (Catechism of the Catholic Church,[1] paragraph 1806). In the realm of public policy, prudence is important for a number of reasons.

Firstly, it helps us to determine our objectives. This is important given that, in economic matters, there are trade-offs. We might regard it as desirable that we move from a situation in a poor country in which there is universal primary education to one in which all children have secondary education – but how do we achieve this if families cannot afford basic healthcare or a reasonable standard of living in other respects?

The second area that requires prudence is in relation to how we achieve certain goals. Here, the principles of Catholic social teaching add richness to secular philosophies. A utilitarian economist, for example, might argue that we should use the policy instrument that achieves a given goal most efficiently and which therefore uses fewest economic resources for a given outcome. A student of Catholic social teaching would weigh up other things too. So, a Catholic would not sacrifice the life of the unborn in pursuit of greater economic growth or a higher standard of living for a family. A Catholic would not promote euthanasia to free up more hospital beds for younger sick people. A Catholic may support family autonomy in education, even if that led to poorer educational outcomes as measured by test scores

---

1   Referred to as 'Catholic Church (1994)' in the list of references.

(though this is unlikely), because it would allow parents to exercise their conscience in choosing a school for their child. All social and economic decisions have moral dimensions and should not just be seen through utilitarian and materialistic lenses. The Catholic social teaching perspective has something to add to public policy debates.

A third area that requires prudence is the consideration of the legitimate role of government. And this is often where there is most controversy between Catholics. The authors of most of the chapters of this book could be described as supporting a large role for a free economy and civil society and a more limited role for government than is common in many Western societies. They would also, in general, prefer government to be local and decentralized rather than power lying at the highest level of government. Some commentators, taking a somewhat reductionist approach, have described these positions as 'libertarian' and 'neo-conservative' while also confusing the two terms, which mean different things (see Finn 2011). But this is a most unhelpful and inaccurate approach which creates more heat than light (see Mueller 2011). We hope that readers will consider the perspectives in this book with open minds and with generosity of spirit.

There are good reasons, to do with our human nature, why government action to address problems within the economy and society is necessary. However, there are also good reasons to suppose that attempting to tackle problems by resorting directly to intervention by the central government is not always the best approach (see Booth 2021). No human person has been blessed with the omniscience to be able to centrally plan aspects of economic and social life confident of success. Civil society institutions, and others acting within a free economy, can use decentralized knowledge and their intimate understanding of the problems they are trying to solve and of the individuals with whom they have relationships when trying to resolve social problems. Local knowledge of specific circumstances of time and place as well as personal and communal involvement with the issues at stake are often essential requirements for successful action. In this spirit, all our authors would be in favour of less state and more society. Pope John Paul II made this distinction between state and society in *Centesimus annus*, as did Pope Leo XIII in *Rerum novarum* and Pope Benedict XVI in *Deus caritas est*. In Catholic social teaching this approach is embedded in the principle of subsidiarity.

Of course, any approach to thinking about problems of political economy in a Catholic context has to take account of our sinfulness. In this context, the question of the pursuit of self-interest is often raised. This is not an entirely straightforward issue. In a market economy, self-interest pursued in the context of a sound institutional framework can often be a constructive force (see *Centesimus annus*, 25) because market transactions require mutually beneficial exchange between parties. However, when self-interest is disordered and turns into selfishness, things can go badly wrong. A wide range of corporate scandals can be laid firmly at the door of unethical and selfish behaviour by those in positions of power in business. The Catholic Church has proposed that economic activity is regulated in order to address such problems (see *Caritas in veritate*, 65). However, there is also legitimate concern that selfishness and dishonest practice can manifest themselves in government action. We cannot, therefore, simply turn to government to solve problems that arise within market economies and expect them to be automatically resolved. Indeed, the nature of government is such that selfishness, greed and dishonesty can be catastrophic when expressed through the structures of the state. The estimated fortune of Muammar Gaddafi, of Libya, for example, was $75 billion when his assets were frozen. That of former President Mubarak of Egypt was $1.2 billion. There are many more examples that could be quoted. These fortunes were certainly not amassed through mutually beneficial transactions between the dictators and their peoples! Corruption can unite harmful business and political interests against the common good and against the interests of the people as a whole. Both Pope Francis and Pope John Paul II raised this specific question in encyclicals and other letters (Alves and Booth 2022).

We could sum this argument up by saying that one imperfect institution (government) should not be expected to perfect other imperfect institutions (the market and civil society): in some instances it may even make things worse. Once again, the virtue of prudence can help us navigate these problems. Furthermore, if we accept that we cannot deal with all the imperfections arising within economic and social life by the use of government alone, it heightens the need for ethical practice – not just in business, but in civil society and in political life.

Prudence is not just necessary in making public policy judgements, it is also necessary in economic life. Business owners and managers often face very difficult decisions. For example, making employees redundant when employment opportunities are scarce may be catastrophic for the families of the affected workers. On the other hand, if not making employees redundant leads to the bankruptcy of the enterprise, the impact on others and on the community as a whole could be much worse. To take another example, how should a company proceed when considering the building of a mine that will provide cheaper fuel, plentiful jobs, damage local fauna and flora and produce carbon emissions?

In every area of economic and political life, we need ethical decision-making as well as a technical understanding that will enable prudent decisions to be made. This need was made clear by Benedict XVI, when Cardinal Ratzinger (1986):

> It is becoming an increasingly obvious fact of economic history that the development of economic systems which concentrate on the common good depends on a determinate ethical system, which in turn can be born and sustained only by strong religious convictions. A morality that believes itself able to dispense with the technical knowledge of economic laws is not morality but moralism. As such it is the antithesis of morality. Today we need a maximum of specialized economic understanding, but also a maximum of ethos so that specialized economic understanding may enter the service of the right goals.

THE AUTHORITY OF CATHOLIC SOCIAL TEACHING AND THE NEED FOR DIALOGUE

Prudence, combined with humility, often involves admitting that we do not have the expertise to make recommendations on a particular policy issue. Catholic social teaching documents are written in that spirit. They do form part of the teaching of the Church. But the Church accepts that it is not her role to make definitive, formal statements on economic, social and political matters that carry the same weight as her teaching on moral and theological questions. The Church's teaching on economic, social and political matters can evolve and even change.

This way of thinking was expressed by John Paul II in *Centesimus annus* (3):

> The present Encyclical seeks to show the fruitfulness of the principles enunciated by Leo XIII, which belong to the Church's doctrinal patrimony and, as such, involve the exercise of her teaching authority. But pastoral solicitude also prompts me to propose an analysis of some events of recent history. It goes without saying that part of the responsibility of Pastors is to give careful consideration to current events in order to discern the new requirements of evangelization. However, such an analysis is not meant to pass definitive judgments since this does not fall per se within the Magisterium's specific domain.

And, as Rodger Charles states in his book, *Christian Social Witness and Teaching* (Charles 1998, vol. II, p. 15), the magisterial authority of the encyclicals extends to matters of moral principle and their implications only. On those matters, social encyclicals are binding on the conscience of members of the Church. Practical and other related matters, according to Charles, can be judged on the basis of the arguments presented.

It is therefore important for the Catholic Church to nurture a rich intellectual tradition that generates new contributions to Catholic social thought that can, ultimately, be reflected in her teaching. In this spirit, Pope Francis has raised many questions in social encyclicals while calling for dialogue. He uses the word 'dialogue' 24 times in his social encyclical on the environment, *Laudato si'*, and 48 times in his later encyclical *Fratelli tutti*. The purpose of this book is to contribute to that dialogue. Dialogue can often bring people together in surprising ways. Dialogue between people who disagree can not only help people to come closer to agreement, it can help people appreciate that their interlocutor is approaching the problem from a position of goodwill. When people realize that others who make different prudential judgements are acting in goodwill it can help the development of a civilized and fruitful political and intellectual culture. Dialogue can often bring people together on particular issues who have quite different philosophies in general. To give just one example, it is often those on the left of the political spectrum and those who strongly support free markets who are the most vociferous advocates of allowing asylum seekers and refugees the right to work.[2]

PRINCIPLES OF CATHOLIC SOCIAL TEACHING

Chapter four of the *Compendium of the Social Doctrine of the Church* identifies the promotion of human dignity as the first principle of Catholic social teaching. In the first place, government does this by protecting life, property, peace, the right to economic initiative and by ensuring that all have access to basic economic goods and services such as food, clothing, shelter, education and healthcare. Ensuring that all have basic goods does not mean, of course, that they should be provided by the government directly: normally, people obtain access to goods and services through earnings from work or from family members. However, the state should step in, in the name of human dignity, to ensure that, one way or another, all have the basics to live in dignity.

Another crucial pillar of Catholic social teaching is the promotion of the common good. This is not just Catholic language for 'the general welfare' or for 'thinking about the whole community rather than yourself'. Specifically, according to the Vatican II document, *Gaudium et spes* (74), the common good embraces 'the sum of those conditions of the social life whereby men, families and associations more adequately and readily may attain their own perfection.' Sometimes the quotation ends with the word 'fulfilment', which is used in the English translation of the document in another paragraph. There is a danger, when using the word 'fulfilment', of

---

2 This debate between Ronald Reagan and George Bush in 1980 might surprise some readers (https://www.youtube.com/watch?v=YsmgPp_nlok). The clip is about migration and is 2 minutes 50 seconds long.

applying a modern secular meaning to the term rather than under-standing the common good in all its richness which involves living a fulfilled and virtuous life close to God.

The common good relates to what is both 'good' and 'common'. As such, it encompasses those conditions that relate to the common life of a particular society that are indivisibly shared. In chapter six, Martin Schlag uses the example of nice conversation at a dinner party being part of the common good. If we are not keen on the food at the dinner party, then this will undermine our individual enjoyment (our private good), but not the common good. But, if somebody destroys the conversation in some way, it undermines that part of the evening that is both good and common.

This example also illustrates how the promotion of the common good is the responsibility of all individuals and institutions in soci-ety: for example, schools, businesses, families, parishes, charities, local and central government. Politics is only part of our common life which is shared at many levels.

In promoting the common good, the Catholic Church promotes the role of the family and social relationships as opposed to atomis-tic individualism; independent civil society institutions in education, labour markets and healthcare as opposed to an overbearing state; the right to economic initiative as opposed to central control and planning of economic life; and charity and justice as opposed to greed and selfishness.

The Church is aware that the need for the dignity of each and every human person to be upheld, together with the reality of human imperfection, gives rise to the need for government. At the same time, the Church wishes to ensure that government serves the human person and society and does not dominate them. Sometimes these requirements are regarded as being held in tension and this tension is often described as involving the balancing of the Catholic social teaching concepts of solidarity and subsidiarity. This is a potentially misleading simplification.

Solidarity is a virtue which involves acting upon a deep-seated concern for others. The preferential option for the poor is, of course, an aspect of the virtue of solidarity. In addition, ever since Pope Paul VI's encyclical, *Populorum progressio*, on the development of

peoples, nearly every Catholic social teaching document has emphasized that the bonds of solidarity go beyond national boundaries
and require the bringing to fulfilment of a universal brotherhood.[3]
Solidarity should also transcend the generations. This is a point Pope
Francis emphasized in *Laudato si'*, but, in fact, was also introduced
in *Populorum progressio* (17):

> We are the heirs of earlier generations, and we reap benefits from
> the efforts of our contemporaries; we are under obligation to all
> men. Therefore we cannot disregard the welfare of those who will
> come after us to increase the human family. The reality of human
> solidarity brings us not only benefits but also obligations.

Solidarity demands action at every level in society. *Sollicitudo rei
socialis* (38) puts it like this:

> [Solidarity] is not a feeling of vague compassion or shallow distress
> at the misfortunes of so many people, both near and far. On the
> contrary, it is a firm and persevering determination to commit one-
> self to the common good; that is to say to the good of all and of each
> individual, because we are all really responsible for all.

As with the common good, it is an error which impoverishes society
to assume that expressions of solidarity are only the responsibility
of the state: 'Solidarity is first and foremost a sense of responsibility on the part of everyone with regard to everyone, and it cannot
therefore be merely delegated to the State' (*Caritas in veritate*, 38).
Pope Benedict explained in an earlier encyclical why that is the case:
'The State which would provide everything, absorbing everything
into itself, would ultimately become a mere bureaucracy incapable of
guaranteeing the very thing which the suffering person – every person – needs: namely, loving personal concern' (*Deus caritas est*, 28).

Indeed, we can see that the virtue of solidarity is closely linked
to the virtue of love. How could we delegate love to the political

---

3   Of course, this theme was not absent from earlier documents.

order? Though, out of love, we may ask the political order to perform certain functions.

Subsidiarity explains how and when the state should act. The principle of subsidiarity helps us to see how different institutions in society have their different functions in promoting the common good. Subsidiarity means 'to help'. The state should help individuals, families, the community and civil associations achieve their legitimate objectives and not take responsibility from them. From a proper understanding of subsidiarity many direct policy implications follow.

The principle of subsidiarity is explained effectively with reference to health and education in chapters twelve and thirteen, by Russell Sparkes and Leonardo Franchi respectively. In the case of education, the Catholic Church teaches that the state exists to provide the framework within which parents, including Catholic parents, can obtain education for their children of the sort that parents desire. The state exists to *help* families obtain an education for their children. The implicit – and sometimes explicit – message of Church teaching in this field is that the state should provide the same support to parents to have their children educated in a private or Church school as is provided in state schools. In other words, the parent and the family should be at the centre of decision-making, together with the school and possibly the parish community. This could also lead to an effective application of the principle of solidarity at all levels, with the state ensuring that all are able to obtain an education. At the same time, the family, the school, the parish and the wider Church provide a loving environment for the intellectual formation of the children. The principle of subsidiarity is applied as parents are helped to obtain an education in accordance with their conscience and their autonomy is respected. Russell Sparkes addresses the question of whether we should apply similar principles to healthcare in the UK, perhaps taking lessons from how healthcare is currently provided in countries such as Germany.

Social justice is also a virtue that lies at the heart of Catholic social teaching. The use of this phrase can create more heat than light between people approaching the tradition from different political philosophies because of the debates set alight by Hayek in *The Mirage of Social Justice* (Hayek 1976). However, social justice in

Catholic social teaching is an entirely different concept from that discussed by Hayek and thus his dismissal of the idea is irrelevant to debates within Catholic social teaching.

In Catholic social teaching, social justice is that form of justice by which all individuals and institutions in society direct their conduct towards promoting the common good of the community.[4] It has sometimes been called 'common good justice'. It is a different type of justice from commutative justice, whereby we receive our dues set out in contractual obligations. Social justice also differs from distributive justice. The latter describes the principles by which the goods of the world should be allocated.

A topical example of the domain of social justice would be in relation to discrimination. For example, an employer who decides not to take on a male worker because he is black would be undermining social justice. The employer probably does not offend commutative justice because no contract is broken. There might not even be any offence against distributive justice if the man is able to get a job with another company at the same wage (which in a well-functioning labour market might well be possible). But the act of discrimination undermines the common good. It makes society less perfect and undermines the common life of society.

THE ECONOMIC CONJUNCTURE:
A PRUDENTIAL ASSESSMENT

Many social encyclicals begin by discussing what might be described as the economic and political conjuncture. It is worth examining that here. It is fair to say that the authors of this book would generally be more positive about the past few decades than official Catholic social teaching documents have been.

There is much discussion in Catholic Church communications about the need for new economic models that will reduce inequality, increase economic security and ensure that there are continuing reductions in poverty. An important purpose of this book is to contribute to the debate about economic models, from the perspective

---

4   See Booth and Petersen (2020) for a fuller discussion.

of Catholic social thought and teaching. It does that in the context of late-twentieth-century and early-twenty-first-century economic and cultural trends. These trends include a significant development of the phenomenon of globalization, at least until the beginning of the second decade of the twenty-first century; an improvement in many aspects of governance in substantial parts of the world; and a reduction in wars. Some of these favourable trends were slowing or reversing at the time the Covid crisis hit in 2020. Most obviously, there was a rise in protectionist measures coming from various sources, including from the US. At the time of writing, the Russian invasion of Ukraine continues.

Pope Francis suggested that inequality is the root of social ills in *Evangelii gaudium* (202) and that inequality was becoming increasingly in evidence (52). Pope Benedict suggested that inequality was increasing in *Caritas in veritate* (32). The Vatican's letter on the financial system of 2018[5] expressed similar sentiments. Indeed, it is often said or implied that extreme poverty is increasing and that globalization has failed to reduce poverty and may lead to it increasing (*Caritas in veritate*, 42). These are important issues: the common good will not be achieved until all have sufficient material goods and services to live a dignified life. At the same time, it is important to recognize the enormous progress that has been made over the last 30 years. If we do not, there is a danger that we will make imprudent political judgements and reject the policies that have led to these achievements.

It is worth looking at recent developments in economic welfare: see table 1.1.

These data suggest staggering improvements in basic measures of human welfare and such improvements are unprecedented in human history. These data are not 'cherry picked': they are genuinely representative. The fall in global inequality is especially notable. If a

---

5   Congregation for the Doctrine of the Faith and Dicastery for Promoting Integral Human Development, 2018, Oeconomicae et pecuniariae quaestiones: Considerations for an ethical discernment regarding some aspects of the present economic-financial system (https://press.vatican.va/content/salastampa/en/bollettino/pubblico/2018/05/17/180517a.html).

fall in inequality of similar magnitude were to happen in the single country of the US (which is generally regarded as being an unequal country), it would become the most equal developed country in the world. Of course, this does not mean that inequality is not becoming increasingly evident: it could be falling while becoming more visible. The social encyclicals are not necessarily wrong to point out that inequality is increasingly in evidence.

Table 1.1. Selected measures of welfare: late twentieth century to before Covid

	1980 (except where stated)	2000 (except where stated)	2019 (except where stated)
Gini coefficient for world incomes (higher means more unequal)	0.8 (1988)	0.72 (2003)	0.65 (2013)
Literacy rate	68%	81%	86%
Maternal mortality rate per 100,000 live births	385 (1990)	341	216 (2015)
Share of world population in extreme poverty	42.6%	27.8%	9.3%
Food deficit kilocalories per person*	172 (1990)	135	88 (2016)
Death rates from air pollution per 100,000 people, age standardized	111.3 (1990)	94	64 (2017)

The data from this table are from Our World in Data and the OECD. *This measures the average number of calories needed to ensure that all malnourished people have sufficient food. It is an indicator of the extent to which people are in extreme poverty.

The period since 1980 has been unique in many ways. It is the first period in human history during which the number of people living in extreme poverty has fallen in a meaningful way. Up to 1980, the proportion of people living in poverty had fallen so slowly that the number of people living in poverty continued to grow. Indeed, it is reasonable to say that, despite the challenges that remain, more progress was made in reducing extreme poverty between 1980 and 2020 than through the whole of the planet's previous economic history combined. In addition, the period since 1980 is the first time in history that global inequality has fallen in a sustained way. It has fallen because large numbers of people previously earning below the absolute poverty line have moved into the global middle class while incomes in richer countries have grown very slowly or not at all. Given the global perspective of the Catholic Church, this should be celebrated. As can be seen from the malnourishment statistics, the much smaller number of people in extreme poverty also have a lower gap between their daily food requirements and the amount of food they have available to eat.

Covid, on its own, has not changed this picture dramatically. Indeed, in some ways, Covid has hit rich countries harder than poorer countries. In addition, in many countries, the nature of the emergency measures that have been put in place has been such that inequality has fallen during the pandemic. It is important to note, however, that the poor have a smaller income cushion than the better off so that, when a crisis does hit, it will push the poor further towards and possibly into absolute poverty. So, in absolute terms, the rich may have taken the greatest hit, but, for those just above or below the poverty line, the impact will have been more dramatic. Of course, one of many reasons why we should try to understand the right economic and political conditions for economic development is to increase the resilience of the poor when there is a crisis.

It should be a matter of serious concern that some of the conditions that led to the fall in inequality and poverty are now reversing. Wars are increasing; some indicators of governance are deteriorating; and globalization seems to be in reverse. Recent data suggest that some of the global indicators that have improved in the last few decades are now going into reverse.

Notwithstanding this, it is interesting that so many commentators, as well as the Church herself in official documents, focus on bad news. One reason for this is that good news is normal and is rarely covered in the media. In addition, Steven Pinker, has written about the 'psychology of moralization' whereby people compete for moral authority.[6] Those who argue that the world is improving can look apathetic.

---

6   https://www.cato.org/sites/cato.org/files/pubs/pdf/catosletterv13n1.pdf

Pinker may be right about why people are reluctant to suggest that the position of the poor is improving. But there are, of course, many problems remaining in the world, and some that are increasing. Pope Francis and other religious leaders genuinely are concerned about problems such as human trafficking, modern slavery, environmental challenges, the treatment of prisoners, loneliness, geo-political tensions in some parts of the world, as well as large pockets of poverty that still remain and now seem to be growing. Such moral concern can then spur us into action. There is nothing wrong with the use of hyperbole to encourage the faithful. Furthermore, the common good requires a continual striving for a better common life and better material conditions for the destitute. Given this, the focus on problems in Catholic social teaching is understandable. We are a long way from achieving, in the words of recent popes, 'a universal brotherhood of man' – something that also requires more than economic progress. And we are now moving backwards with the rise of populism and conflict. At the same time, the virtue of prudence demands that we should stand back and examine the progress that has been made in recent decades and try to understand its causes.

Any prudent assessment should not look only at measurements of present conditions. When it comes to the environment, for example, it is true that, despite the fall in deaths from pollution and natural disasters, the effects of climate change may worsen in the future as a result of our lifestyles today. There has also been a deterioration in other environmental indicators which might well store up trouble for the long term.

Another part of the current conjuncture relates to the political-economic environment in which globalization has taken place. In the last 40 years, in many Western countries, there has been a removal of many direct controls on economic activity. Such controls involved the regulation of prices and incomes and of foreign exchange and investment. This has partly been facilitated by the European Union, including through the single market programme. However, in many areas, such as finance, labour markets and education, there has been a huge growth in detailed government regulation. It could be said that more things are permitted (because of the removal of the direct controls), but that those things that are permitted are more heavily regulated.

Alongside these trends, we have seen a transfer of responsibility for regulation from professions and other independent bodies to state regulatory agencies. And, as the role of trades unions in labour market negotiations has waned, government regulation of the labour market has increased.

Overall, there seems to have been a transfer of authority for the regulation of economic life from civil society and market institutions, including professions and unions, to the state. At the same time, in the last 25 years, government spending has increased as a proportion of national income in most G7 countries: Germany and Canada are the exceptions.

These trends could be thought contrary to the principle of subsidiarity. Catholic social teaching is sympathetic to the regulation of economic activity, but it often suggests that non-state bodies should take primary responsibility in this area. In *Caritas in veritate* (39), Pope Benedict XVI wrote about how an increasingly binary model of 'market-plus-state' was corrosive of society while other forms of solidarity, that had their origin in civil society, build up society. On balance, the authors of this book would take the perspective that the state has crowded out civil society and that civil society institutions involved in economic regulation emerge out of the market and help civilize it. Not everybody would agree with that analysis. However, there is widespread agreement among Catholic thinkers that civil society has been eroded and needs to be revived – or that it should be allowed to revive.

LINKING THEORY AND PRACTICE

The authors in this book return to the foundations of Catholic social thought while discussing their topics in a practical context. They examine how we should think about migration, the environment, finance, healthcare, government debt and taxation, education and business ethics while drawing on the tradition of Catholic social thought and teaching. As noted above, they largely conclude that there should be a bigger role for civil society and a smaller role for the state; that ethics is essential for the development of a healthy business culture and cannot be replaced by regulation; that the development of an ethical society has to be bolstered by an education system based on religious values where religious schools can be free of state interference; and that healthcare should not be a state monopoly but, rather, it should include large elements of provision by Catholic institutions. These conclusions do not come from new economic models, along the lines the pope has asked us to investigate, but they derive from a practical application of the tradition of Catholic social teaching to pressing policy problems.

The book begins with a chapter by André Azevedo Alves, Hugo Chelo and Inês Gregório which explores the tradition of Catholic social thought from St Thomas Aquinas to the late scholastics and its influence on the early social encyclicals. The chapter also examines Catholic social thought and teaching on just wages and private property in a Thomistic context.

The late scholastics developed Catholic social thought in a period of rapid economic and social change and globalization. The following chapter, by Philip Booth, examines that phenomenon of globalization. The Church herself is universal and she regards human rights as universal and indivisible. This provides a justification for international law and governance which are discussed in that chapter. The goal of a universal brotherhood of man demands that we do not see the world purely through the lens of individual nation states.

This broader international vision should also influence how we address the subject of migration. Andrew Yuengert discusses this complex subject on which Pope Francis has spoken on many occasions. Yuengert agrees that we should be sympathetic to those seeking to migrate. However, he points out that, in addition to the migrants, it is relatively well-off owners of capital who benefit from migration. If there are losers, they are likely to be the native poor. Yuengert argues that Catholic social teaching should consider their concerns even if it is concluded that borders should remain open to, or become more open to, migration.

The following chapter is also on a subject close to the heart of Pope Francis – that of the environment. The author places *Laudato si'*, Pope Francis's encyclical on ecology, in the wider tradition of Church teaching and emphasizes the importance of the issue for Christians. He also responds to Pope Francis's call for dialogue by arguing that Catholic social thought can unite our long-held concern for the environment with the traditional positive teaching of the Church on the role of private property. The importance of good governance and peace for environmental outcomes are also discussed. Finally, the community management of natural resources, which was surprisingly omitted from consideration in *Laudato si'*, is raised as a fruitful way to manage the natural environment in many contexts.

There then follow three chapters that directly discuss the role of business. Martin Schlag, in his first chapter in this book, discusses how the common good should always take priority over individual interest in business decisions. At the same time, the Church views business positively – indeed, as a 'noble vocation' in the words of Pope Francis. Because of the importance of business in economic and social life, it should be conducted ethically at all times. Jay Richards reminds us that government should also be conducted ethically. He discusses the problem of 'crony capitalism', where parts of government and business pursue their own interests corruptly or via lobbying, in ways that seriously undermine the common good. He expresses concern that Church teaching has not fully understood the problem of crony capitalism and that some of the specific economic policies proposed in Church documents might actually encourage it. There is then another short chapter by Martin Schlag examining the biblical and patristic roots of Catholic social teaching on business.

The following three chapters focus on questions that cause a huge amount of controversy among Christians. Robert Kennedy looks at the issue of taxation. Modern Catholic social teaching is often thought to have begun in 1891 with the publication of *Rerum novarum*. Even at that time, 1,900 years into the Church's history, taxes were only about 10 per cent of national income. Today, they are typically between 35 and 50 per cent of national income in developed countries. The nature of government has changed dramatically. Nevertheless, argues Robert Kennedy, the vision and tradition of the Church can help us understand the role of government and taxation in a good society. The following chapter, by Philip Booth, Steve Nakrosis and Kaetana Numa, considers the problems caused when governments choose to fund spending by borrowing rather than by taxation. The authors draw parallels with Pope Francis's concern for inter-generational justice expressed in *Laudato si'*. Samuel Gregg then considers the financial sector and Catholic social teaching. This has long been a controversial topic. Gregg looks at the way in which the Church's teaching on usury has evolved. He also examines the history of the Church's engagement with moral and practical questions arising from the financial sector. He suggests that the Catholic Church can learn from this history and, thereby, move from the sidelines of modern debates.

The following two chapters are on topics no less controversial. Russell Sparkes writes about healthcare and Leonardo Franchi discusses education. It is interesting that governments have approached the provision of these services in different ways. In England and Wales, albeit within a highly regulated system, the Catholic Church has been able to establish schools which do not face discrimination in relation to their funding as compared with state schools. The same applies to universities, though there are only three Catholic universities in Britain.[7] On the other hand, healthcare is totally financed and provided by the state unless patients wish to pay the entire cost themselves in addition to paying taxes to fund government provision. Germany has a health system which is rather like Britain's schooling system: it allows people to choose from a range of providers, including Christian providers, funded in similar ways.

Russell Sparkes makes the case, on both ethical and performance grounds, for a healthcare system in the UK that is rather more like that in Germany. Decisions in relation to the provision of healthcare often involve ethical questions and therefore, he argues, the Church must be involved in its provision. This would involve reviewing the post-war settlement, which is, in fact, unusual in the Western world. Leonardo Franchi makes related points about the importance of autonomy for Catholic schools, though the basic structures of the post-war settlement here are less open to question, at least in England and Wales. Recalling Catholic Church teaching, he reiterates that parents are the primary educators of children. Teachers assist parents in that role. Schools, argues Franchi, should be allowed to vary their curriculum rather than have it dictated by the state. It is also important that parents are able to

---

7   There is also one interdenominational (Anglican/Catholic) university.

exercise their conscience and choose a school which is appropriate for their children. This requires that moves to discriminate against Catholic schools when it comes to funding, or to tighten controls on their admissions policies or curricula, must be resisted. Where such discrimination or controls exist, they should be reversed. We end with a chapter, designed for reference, on the sources of Catholic social teaching. A full list of the Church documents referred to in the book is presented at the end of that chapter.

The authors of this book provide an important contribution to thinking about how Catholic social teaching can address contemporary challenges. A renewal of Christian culture in business and civil society and a revival of the participation of Catholic institutions, movements, associations and individuals in education and healthcare is required. As discussed above, the authors would agree with those thinkers in the field of Catholic social thought who believe that there needs to be a renewal of civil society: in the main, the emphasis of the authors of this book would be on government allowing civil society to thrive so that there can also be a renewal of culture within the market economy. The authors would agree with Pope Francis that business is a noble vocation but, in the main, go further in stressing the benefits of a well-ordered business economy and the importance of globalization in promoting prosperity and reducing global inequality. At the same time, many authors of chapters in this collection stress the need for ethics in business – including in its relationship with the state.

There are of course topics missing from this book. This is inevitable. There is no sustained treatment of climate change, development aid or the provision of welfare, for example. Given current trends and political challenges, there is also room for a modern restatement of the importance of the family and its relationship to public policy. There are also less obvious gaps which the writing and editing of this book has led us to feel require a more systematic treatment in Catholic social teaching. These gaps include ethics in political and civic life. Catholics write and talk a lot about business ethics, but they do so less about ethics in public life. Another issue that deserves a more systematic treatment is that of 'illegal markets'. How should we deal with prostitution, drugs and human trafficking in the public policy arena? St Thomas Aquinas considered questions related to the prohibition of prostitution 800 years ago. We should be thinking about these problems in a modern context.

There will always be more to say, both about the topics covered and questions not discussed. There is no doubt, however, that the authors of this collection make an important contribution to Catholic social thought applied to public policy in the context of late-twentieth-century and early-twenty-first-century global trends.

REFERENCES

Alves, A. A., and Booth, P. M. (2022) Virtues, vices and the responsibilities of business: an application of Catholic social teaching to the problems of corruption and lobbying. *Religions* 13: 1070 (https://doi.org/10.3390/rel13111070).

Booth P. M. (2021) A Catholic understanding of economics. In *Reclaiming the Piazza III: Catholic Culture and the New Evangelisation* (ed. L. Franchi, R. Convery and J. Valero). Leominster: Gracewing.

Booth, P. M., and Petersen, M. (2020) Catholic social teaching and Hayek's critique of social justice. *Logos: A Journal of Catholic Thought and Culture* 23(1): 36–64.

Catholic Church (1994) *Catechism of the Catholic Church.* London: Geoffrey Chapman.

Charles, R. (1998) *Christian Social Witness and Teaching,* vol. II. Leominster: Gracewing.

Finn, D. (2011) Nine libertarian heresies tempting neoconservative Catholics to stray from Catholic social thought. *Journal of Morality and the Market* 14(2): 487–503.

Hayek, F. A. (1976) *The Mirage of Social Justice.* University of Chicago Press.

Mueller, J. D. (2011) Finn's 'nine libertarian heresies' and Mueller's first lemma economists complain exactly insofar as they are unable to explain. *Journal of Morality and the Market* 14(2): 519–33.

Pontifical Council for Justice and Peace (2005) *Compendium of the Social Doctrine of the Church.* London: Burns & Oates.

Ratzinger, J. (1986) Church and economy: responsibility for the future of the world economy. *Communio* 13: 199–204.

PAPAL ENCYCLICALS AND OTHER CHURCH DOCUMENTS

Francis (2020) *Fratelli tutti*, encyclical letter (http://www.vatican.va/con tent/francesco/en/encyclicals/documents/papa-francesco_20201003 _enciclica-fratelli-tutti.html).

Francis (2015) *Laudato si'*, encyclical letter (https://www.vatican.va/content/ francesco/en/encyclicals/documents/papa-francesco_20150524_enci clica-laudato-si.html).

Francis (2013) *Evangelii gaudium*, apostolic exhortation (http://www.vatican .va/content/francesco/en/apost_exhortations/documents/papa-franc esco_esortazione-ap_20131124_evangelii-gaudium.html).

Pontifical Council for Justice and Peace (2011) Towards reforming the inter national and financial monetary systems in the context of global public authority (https://www.vatican.va/roman_curia/pontifical_councils/jus tpeace/documents/rc_pc_justpeace_doc_20111024_nota_en.html).

Benedict XVI (2009) *Caritas in veritate*, encyclical letter (https://www.vati can.va/content/benedict-xvi/en/encyclicals/documents/hf_ben-xvi_enc _20090629_caritas-in-veritate.html).

Benedict XVI (2005) *Deus Caritas est*, encyclical letter (http://www.vati can.va/content/benedict-xvi/en/encyclicals/documents/hf_ben-xvi_enc _20051225_deus-caritas-est.html).

John Paul II (1991) *Centesimus annus*, encyclical letter (https://www.vati can.va/content/john-paul-ii/en/encyclicals/documents/hf_jp-ii_enc _01051991_centesimus-annus.html).

John Paul II (1987) *Sollicitudo rei socialis*, encyclical letter (http://www.vati can.va/content/john-paul-ii/en/encyclicals/documents/hf_jp-ii_enc _30121987_sollicitudo-rei-socialis.html).

Paul VI (1967) *Populorum progressio*, encyclical letter (http://www.vatican .va/content/paul-vi/en/encyclicals/documents/hf_p-vi_enc_26031967 _populorum.html).

Vatican II (1965) *Gaudium et spes,* Pastoral Constitution on the Church in the World (https://www.vatican.va/archive/hist_councils/ii_vatican_co uncil/documents/vat-ii_const_19651207_gaudium-et-spes_en.html).

Leo XIII (1891) *Rerum novarum,* encyclical letter (http://www.vatican.va/ content/leo-xiii/en/encyclicals/documents/hf_l-xiii_enc_15051891_re rum-novarum.html).

CHAPTER 2

Thomas Aquinas, the late scholastics and their influence on the tradition of Catholic social teaching

André Azevedo Alves, Hugo Chelo and
Inês Gregório

INTRODUCTION

This chapter links the contributions to Catholic social thought of Thomas Aquinas and the late scholastics with the development of contemporary Catholic social teaching. The first part explains the relevance of Aquinas for Catholic thought in the context of his own time. The second part addresses the developments of the late scholastics, particularly those in the School of Salamanca, who built on Aquinas. The final part of the chapter addresses Aquinas's influence on contemporary Catholic social teaching from the encyclical *Rerum novarum* onwards. Each section of the chapter illustrates the development of the ideas through their application to the issues of private property and just wages.

THOMAS AQUINAS AND CATHOLIC SOCIAL TEACHING: CONTEXT AND RELEVANCE

Despite having lived for less than 50 years during the Middle Ages, the impact and reputation of the work of Thomas Aquinas (1225–74) has been extraordinarily influential. Six centuries after his death, Pope Leo XIII put Aquinas's thinking and work at the centre of Catholic social teaching, proclaiming him as an authoritative source of Catholic doctrine and giving rise to a new edition of his works.[1]

In the encyclical *Aeternis Patris* (1878), Pope Leo XIII appeals to the restoration of Christian philosophy and to the study of the doctrine of the Scholastic Doctors, among whom Thomas Aquinas is considered 'the chief and master of all towers … [who] collected together and cemented, distributed in wonderful order, and so increased with important additions that he is rightly and deservedly esteemed the special bulwark and glory of the Catholic faith' (17).

The importance of Aquinas and his work is reiterated some paragraphs later, when Pope Leo XIII recognizes that his masterpiece, *Summa Theologica* (Aquinas 2017), should be used as a guidance tool by the Catholic Church, alongside the Holy texts.[2]

According to John Finnis, what characterizes Aquinas's thinking and renders it so distinctive is the fact that he could benefit from the access to divine revelation – to the teachings found in the prophets of Israel, in the Gospels and other sacred scriptures – to better understand moral questions. He then combined these with the best philosophical approaches available, found in Plato and Aristotle (Finnis 2019, p. 12). Within this theoretical framework, Thomas Aquinas addressed the tension in the relationship between the whole and the parts, i.e. between the necessity of the political community to ensure its sustainability and to provide, at the same time, the conditions for all individuals to guide their own lives according to moral dictates.

From these two sources that inspired the work developed by Aquinas, one element of each is worth mentioning. First of all, there is a specific understanding of human dignity according to which each individual is an image of the divine nature and has the free capacity to choose. Apart from elevating human beings to a superior position when compared with other animals, this capacity for free

---

1   The so-called Leonine edition begun in 1882 and still incomplete (Koehler 2016, p. 56).

2   'But the chief and special glory of Thomas, one which he has shared with none of the Catholic Doctors, is that the Fathers of Trent made it part of the order of conclave to lay upon the altar, together with sacred Scripture and the decrees of the supreme Pontiffs, the Summa of Thomas Aquinas, whence to seek counsel, reason, and inspiration' (AP 22).

choice also corresponds to an important form of equality by which all persons are in the same position, not subject to the control of anyone.[3] However, in different aspects of his thinking, Aquinas follows notions originally set forth by the great classical Aristotelian philosophy. This is so both in terms of the understanding of justice as a particular virtue in the context of relationships between people, but also in the consideration of the legitimate origins of private property.

This concept of justice is fundamental to understanding the whole moral theology of Thomas Aquinas and, particularly, the treatment of economic questions, which are the main focus of this chapter. Classified as a primary or cardinal virtue (I.II 61, a. 2), justice is defined as 'a habit whereby a man renders to each one his due by a constant and perpetual will' (II.II 58, a. 1). By implying a form of equality, justice also implies a form of relationship towards another and, for that reason, it concerns external actions and rectifies relationships between individual people (II.II 58, a. 2):

> As stated above since justice by its name implies equality, it denotes essentially relation to another, for a thing is equal, not to itself, but to another. And forasmuch as it belongs to justice to rectify human acts, as stated above this otherness which justice demands must needs be between beings capable of action.

Within the community, apart from ensuring right relations between persons, justice is also vested of a legal value and requires respect for community laws which aim to promote the common good or universal happiness.[4]

---

3   'This reality and responsibility of *free choice* gives salience and solidity to the individual person, by nature nor a slave either to subrational instinct or to the instrumentalizing command of another person' (Finnis 2019, p. 13).

4   In this observance, the inspiration taken from classical philosophy is evident: 'Consequently the law must needs regard principally the relationship to happiness. Moreover, since every part is ordained to the whole, as imperfect to perfect; and since one man is a part of the perfect community, the law must needs regard properly the relationship to universal happiness. Wherefore the Philosopher, in the above definition of legal matters mentions both happiness and the body politic: for he says (Ethic. v, 1) that we call those legal matters "just, which are adapted to produce and preserve happiness and its parts for the body politic": since the state is a perfect community, as he says in Polit. i, 1' (I.II 90, a. 2).

Thomas Aquinas then proceeds with the discussion of this virtue and distinguishes between two types of justice. The first, distributive justice, concerns the sharing of goods and 'renders what is due to each person, as determined by a criterion of proportionality between individual worthiness and the goods being distributed'. The second form, commutative justice, concerns the exchange of goods. Commutative justice 'preserves equality in accordance with an arithmetical mean, that is to say, with respect to the quantity of things exchanged between persons or the benefits and burdens that accrue to each one' (Porter 2002, p. 278). When these conditions are not respected, injustices are committed. Those injustices take the form of a lack of respect for persons, in the case of distributive justice, or theft and robbery, in the case of commutative justice. Injustice may have a general character when it refers to vices opposed to the common good, or a particular character when it affects a particular relationship with another individual. In the case of particular justice, an injustice always constitutes an imbalance in relationship to others (II.II 59, a. 1), implying also a perspective of intentionality. Moreover, Aquinas considers that injustice reveals a violation of equality, because it fails to recognize the fundamental dictate of human dignity, according to which all persons are equal and an image of the divine nature (II.II 59, a. 1).

As noted above, the treatment given by Aquinas to the virtue of justice is fundamental to understanding the theoretical framework within which economic questions are examined. It is important to bear in mind that, in the Middle Ages, these questions were not subject to special reflection, but they were becoming important. Societies were urbanizing more rapidly and the proximity between producer and consumer that previously existed was becoming more stretched. The practical application of the key principles of what became known as the Thomistic way of thinking about economic questions became of huge importance.

THOMAS AQUINAS AND CATHOLIC SOCIAL TEACHING: APPLICATIONS

Private property

According to Aquinas, the emergence of private property cannot be dissociated from the divine episode of the expulsion from paradise, 'where nature provided for everything needed for survival' (Koehler 2016, p. 59). From that moment on, the survival of the human species depended on the use of natural and material resources in producing goods for the fulfilment of bodily necessities. In order to ensure the efficiency of this arrangement, it was necessary to find a mechanism that could make each individual accountable for his own task: such a mechanism was the possession of external things, or private property.[5] And Aquinas advances three reasons to justify this (II.II 66, a. 2):

> [I]t is lawful for man to possess property. Moreover this is necessary to human life for three reasons. First because every man is more careful to procure what is for himself alone than that which is common to many or to all: since each one would shirk the labour and leave to another that which concerns the community, as happens where there is a great number of servants. Secondly, because human affairs are conducted in more orderly fashion if each man is charged with taking care of some particular thing himself, whereas there would be confusion if everyone had to look after any one thing indeterminately. Thirdly, because a more peaceful state is ensured to man if each one is contented with his own. Hence it is to be observed that quarrels arise more frequently where there is no division of the things possessed.

Nonetheless, this private character of property is not understood by Aquinas in absolute terms, or as sustained by 'any metaphysical connection between the possessor and the property' (Walsh 2018, p. 200). On the contrary, it is based on the premise that the institution of private property ensures that property is used for the promotion of the common good. For this reason, after referring to the three justifications, Aquinas states: 'man ought to possess external things, not as his own, but as common, so that, to wit, he is ready to communicate them to others in their need' (II.II 66, a. 2).

---

5   Also in relation to this point, Aquinas follows the path of Aristotle in argu-
     ing that 'man has a natural dominion over external things, because, by his
     reason and will, he is able to use them for his own profit, as they were made
     on his account: for the imperfect is always for the sake of the perfect, as
     stated above. It is by this argument that the Philosopher proves (Polit. i, 3)
     that the possession of external things is natural to man' (II.II 66, a. 1).

There are two important results from this clarification. Firstly, the urge to possess external things should be moderate and should not degenerate into greed or avarice. It should be measured by what is necessary to provide for the sustenance of oneself and one's family, according to its condition of life.[6] Secondly, the condition of those in greater need constitutes another limitation on the use of private property, for persons can only possess external things if they are willing to share those things with those in need.[7] Aquinas affirms (II.II 66, a. 2):

> A man would not act unlawfully if by going beforehand to the play he prepared the way for others: but he acts unlawfully if by so doing he hinders others from going. On like manner a rich man does not act unlawfully if he anticipates someone in taking possession of something which at first was common property, and gives others a share: but he sins if he excludes others indiscriminately from using it.

This limitation derives also from one key principle of Catholic social teaching discussed in the beginning of this chapter: that all men are equal and created in God's image. For this reason, each life has the same value in the sight of God and its material sustainability should be secured and supported.

---

6   'Hence it must needs be that man's good in their respect consists in a certain measure, in other words, that man seeks, according to a certain measure, to have external riches, in so far as they are necessary for him to live in keeping with his condition of life. Wherefore it will be a sin for him to exceed this measure, by wishing to acquire or keep them immoderately. This is what is meant by covetousness, which is defined as "immoderate love of possessing." It is therefore evident that covetousness is a sin' (II.II 118, a. 1).

7   This limitation is often referred to as *superflua*: 'For Aquinas, because there are many persons in need who cannot practically be sustained from the same material resources, the individual possessor judges for him or herself how his or her property should be dispensed to those in need. However, the obligation to distribute *superflua* is a matter of justice – private ownership loses its lawful character if others who are in need are excluded from using material resources' (Walsh 2018, p. 203).

Given that it is lawful for an individual to own property, as long as the situation of the needy is respected, Thomas Aquinas considered that it would be a sin to violate or to act against this possibility of possessing material goods. The sin of theft thus has three main characteristics: it implies taking possession of something that belongs to another; it involves taking a material thing; and it also requires the item to have been taken secretly (II.II 66, a. 3). A second form of violation of the right to private property is the sin of robbery. This differs from theft as it is not practised in secret but done with violence. Regardless of this difference, both theft and robbery constitute vices against the virtue of justice, for 'they evidently involve a failure to render to another that which is her or his own' (Porter 2002, p. 280). However, and despite being a mortal sin,[8] there is a circumstance in which someone is allowed to take the possessions of another, either by secret or by force. This again relates to the case of the needy. If the reason why someone takes the property of another person is to provide for their survival or that of their family, then he shall not be considered guilty of theft or robbery (II.II 66, a. 7). John Finnis (2019, p. 24) summarizes the conditions imposed on private property by Thomas Aquinas as follows:

- For anyone in dire necessity, nothing belongs to anyone in particular; 'for anyone in that situation, all resources become *common* resources'. That is to say, people who find themselves or their dependants in such life-threatening need are morally entitled to take anything which will relieve that need, and this entitlement overrides anyone else's otherwise legitimate title or property right.
- In situations where no one confronts extreme necessity, the right of owners and other property-holders to keep their property extends just as far as their ... need to maintain themselves (with their dependants) in the form of life which they have reasonably adopted. All their *further* resources [*residuum*; *superfllua*] are

---

8 '... because it involves harming the neighbor contrary to the demands of charity, and, second, because were it to become a general practice, human society would be destroyed' (Porter 2002, p. 281).

'held in common': all these resources should be made available to those ('the poor') who, though not in extreme necessity, lack the resources to satisfy their needs ... The poor have a natural right that the whole of this *residuum* be distributed in their favour.

Summing up, private property is defined in Thomas Aquinas's thinking as belonging to the *ius gentium*: as a consequence of natural law (God grants men the right to use material goods for survival) that was added to by human reason (because the common good is better served when property is held privately rather than in common) and therefore restrained by natural law itself (due to the equal value of all individuals in the sight of God).[9] Private property has no absolute character and is always associated with the improvement of the common good. The distribution of property to the poor is an obligation in charity and justice that is not necessarily to be enforced by the state.

Just wages

Thomas Aquinas understands wages as being strictly associated with merit. They are a reward for the applied service of a human faculty and, for this reason, it is an act of justice to pay someone in return for the effort put into a specific job. As he affirms (I.II 114, a. 1):

[M]erit and reward refer to the same, for a reward means something given anyone in return for work or toil, as a price for it. Hence, as it is an act of justice to give a just price for anything received from another, so also is it an act of justice to make a return for work or toil.

An important aspect of the discussion about wages in Aquinas is the concept of the just price, *justum pretium*. The wage is the price paid

---

9   'Private ownership is a rational derivation from the law of nature's require-ment that human beings must have use of the earth's material resources for their sustenance. Accordingly, it forms part of the *ius gentium* and lies between the law of nature and positive law' (Walsh 2018, p. 203).

in return for the labour of the worker. The just price or just wage does not simply follow a mathematical formula. It takes into account the economic value of whatever is traded and the circumstances of a specific time and place.[10] When this definition is applied to the wage, we find the criteria for determining whether it is just. The wage has to assure the sustainability of the worker and of his family: in other words, the wage is just when it is proportional to the necessities of the life of the worker, which include not only everything without which it is not possible to exist, but also those things necessary to live a life with dignity according to his station in life. As Aquinas argues (II.II 32, a. 6):

> [A] thing is said to be necessary, if a man cannot without it live in keeping with his social station, as regards either himself or those of whom he has charge. The 'necessary' considered thus is not an invariable quantity, for one might add much more to a man's property, and yet not go beyond what he needs in this way, or one might take much from him, and he would still have sufficient for the decencies of life in keeping with his own position ... for no man ought to live unbecomingly.

On the other hand, the definition of a just salary must take also into account the quantity and the complexity of the labour that was hired by the worker. St Thomas does not deny that there are differences between professions and the faculties required for each one and he recognizes that not all labour has the same value.[11] For this reason, someone who works more or who performs a more complex task deserves a bigger salary: 'more laborious, more difficult and more productive labour, demands a higher remuneration' (Rocha 1992, p. 36).

---

10 For a broader discussion of the concept of just price in Aquinas and other scholastic authors, see Alves and Gregório (2021).
11 'Hence, with the construction of buildings, the designer of the building is paid more – in spite of not doing any manual labor – than the manual laborers who cut the wood and carve the stones' (Aquinas's Quodlibetal questions quoted in Rocha (1992, p. 35)).

Within this framework, the salary paid may be unjust either by defect or by excess. In the first case, it is unjust when the master or the buyer refuse to pay the worker what is due to be paid for his labour. In the second case, it is unjust when the worker receives more than he needs given his conditions of life, especially if this leaves the one who paid in a condition that is not decent. This injustice by excess is not very common in the case of manual labour. However, Aquinas draws attention to the case of professions such as lawyers or doctors, where professionals are allowed to sell their services but should establish a price considering the circumstances of those who resort to them and common practices. When this does not occur, injustices may be committed (II.II 71, a. 3):

> Now it is evident that an advocate is not always bound to consent to plead, or to give advice in other people's causes. Wherefore, if he sells his pleading or advice, he does not act against justice. The same applies to the physician who attends on a sick person to heal him, and to all like persons; provided, however, they take a moderate fee, with due consideration for persons, for the matter in hand, for the labour entailed, and for the custom of the country. If, however, they wickedly extort an immoderate fee, they sin against justice.

THE LATE SCHOLASTICS AND CATHOLIC SOCIAL TEACHING: CONTEXT AND RELEVANCE

The contributions of the late scholastics mark a significant stepping stone in the development of Catholic social thought. Although Catholic social teaching as a structured and articulated body of thought is relatively recent, its roots go back much further. As evidenced above, the work of St Thomas Aquinas is certainly pivotal in this regard. But, in relation to several applied economic and social issues, the first consistent reflection from a Catholic perspective ought to be credited to the late scholastics and particularly to the so-called School of Salamanca (Alves and Moreira 2013a).[12]

---

12 An additional reference on the late scholastics which readers might find useful is Grice-Hutchinson (1978).

The founder of the School of Salamanca, a Dominican called Francisco de Vitoria, studied in Paris where he developed a Thomist line of reasoning, combining Aristotelian foundations with a strong emphasis on the concept of natural law and the exploration of its implications. In 1526, Vitoria returned to Spain to take over the prime chair of theology at the University of Salamanca.

The School included a distinct group of Iberian late scholastics of the sixteenth and seventeenth centuries who, in most cases, applied Thomistic reasoning to deal with new problems arising out of the European expansion into the New World. In doing so, they significantly expanded the pre-existing understanding of many important issues, ranging from business ethics and economic theory to politics and international law. The rapid growth of commercial and financial activity in this period, coupled with the new problems related to international relations and the rights of indigenous populations, led to the need to address new problems from a Catholic perspective. The serious theological, political and cultural challenges posed by Protestantism further reinforced this need and so ethical reflection and discourse on a wide variety of applied subjects were a primary concern for the Iberian late scholastics.

The intellectual importance of the School of Salamanca also corresponded historically with a period in which several favourable demographic, economic, cultural and political circumstances turned the Iberian Peninsula into a focal point for commerce and diplomacy as well as for intellectual exchange. The interaction between Christian, Jewish and Muslim elements in the Iberian Peninsula was an important factor, as was the development of the printing press, which allowed mass production of literary material.

The conjunction of all these circumstances led to the late scholastics being in a position to apply long-standing pillars of Catholic thought to the new challenges presented by a new process of globalization.

This was done mostly by revisiting Aquinas and developing an analytical framework that could be applied to these new challenges in a suitable way. Even though the earlier thought of St Thomas Aquinas was firmly rooted in an association between the common good and objective right (rather than individual rights), the emphasis on the prevalence of universal natural law over positive law dependent on time, place and the disposition of the ruler, provided a favourable environment for laying a foundation for an affirmation and defence of individual rights. The emphasis on the importance of the natural law paved the way for increased protection for individuals in their relationship with civil authorities and from potential abuses in positive law enacted by the state.

Furthermore, the adaptation and expansion of the traditional Roman law concept of *ius gentium* by the late scholastics, leading to the development of a notion of international law, meant that their contributions were universal, i.e. common to all mankind and applicable to all nations and peoples. Authors such as Vitoria, Soto and Suárez all agreed that the *ius gentium* was universal and could be recognized by reason even though it was not the product of the will of any human assembly or legislator.

The late scholastics progressively added an increased understanding of autonomy of the person to the traditional Thomist conception of objective right linked with a distinct sphere of individual freedom. Building upon the universal character of natural law, these notions were then gradually – but not linearly – understood to extend to all mankind, which ultimately led most of the late scholastics to, for example, oppose forced conversions of the peoples of the New World, stressing the need to employ peaceful means of conversion.

In the following section, this approach is illustrated by summarizing key aspects in the late scholastics' analysis of property and wages.

LATE SCHOLASTICS AND CATHOLIC SOCIAL TEACHING: APPLICATIONS

Private property

The approach of the late scholastics to the right to property builds directly upon the foundations laid by Aquinas. The arguments for the legitimacy and desirability of the existence of property rights are linked to their understanding of how best to promote the common good under a realistic anthropological framework about human society and an individual's reaction to the incentives they face.

In this context, the justification for private property lies in the incentives it fosters to promote a better use of material goods while at the same time contributing to a peaceful and well-ordered community (Alves and Moreira 2013b). The late scholastics, for the most part, mounted a robust defence of private property that always had in the background an articulate understanding of the dire negative effects that could be expected of common ownership of material goods given the conditions of human nature and of human earthly existence. As expressed by Domingo de Soto (1968, book iv, q. iii, a. i):

> What the poet has said, that these words: mine and yours, lead to many disputes and fights, we sincerely recognize; but there would be many more [disputes and fights] if the things were possessed in common.

This recognition of the importance of private property was closely linked to the underlying assumptions about human nature (De Soto 1968, book i, q. v, a. iv):

> Considering also the premises that in a corrupted [i.e. fallen] state of nature, if men lived in common they would not live in peace, nor would the fields be fruitfully cultivated, men have deduced that it is more convenient to divide property.

Following Aquinas, the late scholastics did not regard private property as an absolute right. They nevertheless defended it robustly and argued that it was fully compatible and in harmony with the principles of natural law. Private property was primarily justified through its social function and importance, which, in turn, gained greater emphasis through the increased understanding of economic theory by the late scholastics.

A defence of private property based on its social function meant that it was ultimately subordinated to the common good, which, in turn, implied that, in extreme circumstances, such as dire need or imminent danger to human life, it could be deemed legitimate to make use of goods one did not own (although the late scholastics were also careful to stress that an obligation to compensate the original owner applied whenever feasible).[13]

Just wages

The treatment of wages by the late scholastics also tended to build upon a pre-existing Thomist framework. They refined it taking account of their interpretation of the economic and social circumstances of their time.

Since the wage is the price paid for labour and, in many cases, the price paid for a product is directly the wage of the seller, the understanding of the idea of a just wage by the late scholastics is necessarily heavily influenced by their just price theory. The authors of the School of Salamanca made important contributions to just price theory (Elegido 2009). Particularly important for the treatment of wages are the notions that equivalence in value is the fundamental standard of commutative justice and that the price fetched by a good in an open market is generally the best indicator of its value.

For the late scholastics, value should be associated with 'common estimation' in a regular market setting, an understanding that was close to what contemporary economic theory refers to as the subjective theory of value. A good illustration of this understanding can be found in De Molina's (1981, p. 168) definition of the concept of 'natural price':

> They call him so not because it doesn't depend to a large extent upon the esteem with which men appreciate some things more than others, as happens with certain precious objects, that sometimes

---

13 For example, the founder of the School of Salamanca, Francisco de Vitoria, wrote: 'It is enough to see the indigent prostrated in his bed, anguished by his ailments, or when tolerating hunger for an extended period reaches such extremes that, if he is not succoured, he would rapidly walk to death. It is then, when there is extreme need and, if it can be done without scandal, that it is licit to rob from the rich' (quoted in Chafuen 2003, p. 44).

are valued in more than twenty thousand gold coins and more than many other things, which, by their nature are much better and more useful; nor do they call him so because that price doesn't fluctuate and change, since it is evident that it does change; but they call him natural because it is born out of these same things, independently of any human law or public decree, but dependent on many circumstances which make it vary and on the affection and esteem that men have for things according to the several uses in which they can be employed.

Consistent with this, Molina argued that the justice of a wage should be evaluated according to the wages paid for similar functions under similar circumstances (quoted in Chafuen (2003, p. 106)):

After considering the service that an individual undertakes and the large or small number of people who, at the same time, are found in similar service, if the wage that is set for him is at least the lowest wage that is customarily set in that region at that time for people in such service, the wage is to be considered just.

As with other prices, 'common estimation' played a key role in determining if a given wage was to be considered just or not.

The late scholastics also placed great emphasis on the need to ensure that no coercion was involved. Consent and voluntary contracts were important pre-conditions that had to be assured in order for a wage to deemed as just (see Chafuen 2003, pp. 107–8).

AQUINAS, THE LATE SCHOLASTICS AND THE MODERN ENCYCLICALS

The influence of Thomas Aquinas on the doctrinal corpus through which the social dimension of the pontifical magisterium was developed is undeniable. The development of *Rerum novarum* drew heavily on this body of Thomistic thinking and, in turn, provided a 'lasting paradigm for the Church' (*Centesimus annus*, 5).

The prevalence of St Thomas's thinking was not constant or uniform. However, from Leo XIII until the first stages of the Second

Vatican Council, the impact of the Thomist doctrine was evident and abundant. This was true both in the philosophical contributions of the works of Mercier, Maritain or Gilson, and in theological developments led by priests such as Congar, Chenu, Lubac or Daniélou. Aquinas's thinking exerted its influence inside the Church (Souto Coelho 2002, p. 28) as well as in the secular world: for example, in the work of Yves Simon, Heinrich Rommen, Josef Fuchs, Mortimer Adler or Robert Hutchins (Sigmund 1988, p. xxiv).

Thomist thought was emphasized and praised by John Paul II (see, for example, *Fides et ratio*, 58). However, it could be argued that it waned in influence through and following the Second Vatican Council with a move towards the incorporation of technical and social scientific knowledge in the development of Catholic social teaching as well as the incorporation of more scriptural and patristic sources. However, in the *Compendium of the Social Doctrine of the Church* (Pontifical Council for Justice and Peace, 2005), which Benedict XVI consecrated as the organic presentation of Catholic social teaching (*Deus caritas est*, 27), Aquinas still remains the most referenced ecclesiastical author, though he has only 26 references (not all direct) while there are more than one thousand references to biblical texts, ecumenical councils, papal documents, Church documents, of congregations, pontifical councils and documents of international law.

Nevertheless, the insights of Thomistic thinking incorporated in *Rerum novarum* have infused the tradition of Catholic social teaching. We will examine this in relation to the topics discussed above: private property and just wages.

Private property

Rerum novarum is especially notable for its support of private property and includes an explicit reference to Thomas Aquinas (*Rerum novarum*, 22):

> Private ownership, as we have seen, is the natural right of man, and to exercise that right, especially as members of society, is not only lawful, but absolutely necessary. 'It is lawful,' says St Thomas

Aquinas, 'for a man to hold private property; and it is also necessary for the carrying on of human existence.'

Furthermore, the reasons put forward for the right to property explicitly use the Thomist synthesis in which, following on from the distinction between possession and use, it is affirmed that the title of the domain over things derives originally from God and that there is a primary right to the common use of goods. It is this which subordinates and conditions the right to possession and it remains unchanged in the subsequent magisterium. This does not mean that the right to private ownership is not of paramount importance. It can be the case that secondary rights are indispensable for ensuring that primary rights are realized. If property was undivided and unowned without legally enforceable title, experience suggests that one of the results is that it is exploited by the strongest or most astute and nobody cares for it.

As the Church makes clear in her encyclicals, the principle of private property puts serious obligations on its holders to act justly and charitably. Pope Pius XI emphasizes the principle of just distribution (*Quadragesimo anno*, 56–58). John XXIII highlights the social function of all property, including of productive goods (*Mater et magistra*, 19) founded on the natural order that establishes the priority of the individual in relation to society (*Mater et magistra*, 109).

The Second Vatican Council synthesized this teaching, declaring (*Gaudium et spes*, 69):

> God intended the earth with everything contained in it for the use of all human beings and peoples. Thus, under the leadership of justice and in the company of charity, created goods should be in abundance for all in like manner. Whatever the forms of property may be, as adapted to the legitimate institutions of peoples, according to diverse and changeable circumstances, attention must always be paid to this universal destination of earthly goods. In using them, therefore, man should regard the external things that he legitimately possesses not only as his own but also as common in the sense that they should be able to benefit not only him but also others.

This subordination of the right to private property to the common use of goods follows the formulation of Aquinas and the late scholastics. In other words (*Laborem exercens*, 14):

> Christian tradition has never upheld this right [to private property] as absolute and untouchable. On the contrary, it has always understood this right within the broader context of the right common to all to use the goods of the whole of creation: the right to private property is subordinated to the right to common use, to the fact that goods are meant for everyone.

It is also important to note that, in Catholic social teaching, the question of property is indissolubly linked to the topic of labour. Property, as *Rerum novarum* (5) puts it, is a working person's wages in another form and this adds resonance to the teaching on private property. This then relates, of course, to the question of the justice of wages.

Just wages

The social encyclicals have also developed teaching on just wages. *Rerum novarum* 45 and 46 state that underlying any wage agreement should be the condition that the wage is sufficient to 'support a frugal and well-behaved wage-earner'. So, free agreement is not enough to establish that a wage meets the criterion of distributive justice. There should be an additional condition that, if it is possible, an enterprise should pay sufficient so that the worker can sustain himself and his family and have some savings. This teaching was elaborated by Pope Pius XI, Pope John XXIII and Pope John Paul II.

Much of Catholic social teaching has emphasized that the payment of just wages is an essential part of the whole socioeconomic system. As noted above, wages can be linked to the right to private property – the worker should be able to keep what he is paid. At the same time, the payment of just wages is an important social use of the property that is held by the owner of a business enterprise. And, it is argued that, if enterprises pay just wages, the state will need to intervene less and social movements that demand the redistribution of property will have less traction. Furthermore, different groups of people will be able to live in harmony rather than being in conflict. Therefore, a system of just wages underlies much else, especially when it comes to the position of the poor (*Laborem exercens*, 19):

> In every system, regardless of the fundamental relationships within it between capital and labour, wages, that is to say remuneration for work, are still a practical means whereby the vast majority of people can have access to those goods which are intended for common use: both the goods of nature and manufactured goods.

In determining the justice of wages, precedence is given to the objective demands of distributive justice and giving to each what is due. Simple free, contractual agreement according to the principles of commutative justice is not sufficient to determine that a wage is just. At the same time, it should not be assumed that free agreement of wages contracts does not, in general, lead to just wages: in well-functioning labour markets it may well do so. There is, in a sense, a combination of the thinking of St Thomas Aquinas, which concluded that wages should be sufficient to support the worker while being related to the value of what is produced, with that of the late scholastics, who concluded that wages should be determined by common estimation of the value of a particular type of work, in the statement of the *Compendium of the Social Doctrine of the Church* (Pontifical Council for Justice and Peace 2005, p. 302):

> The simple agreement between employee and employer with regard to the amount of pay to be received is not sufficient for the agreed-upon salary to qualify as a 'just wage', because a just wage 'must not be below the level of subsistence' of the worker: natural justice precedes and is above the freedom of the contract.

It could be argued that these questions are more difficult in modern developed economies. A number of conditions have changed since 1930, when the principles of just wages were discussed at length in *Quadragesimo anno*. In particular, 'needs' have become more complex and difficult to define objectively in modern society. In addition, women within a family with children may well work as well as the father. Governments, of course, provide welfare payments, but they also tax low-paid workers thus lowering their disposable income. In addition, other government policies, especially in relation to housing, raise the cost of living. These things are not within the control of a business enterprise and complicate the concept of a just wage. For example, is a business to pay a different wage to an employee who is part of a two-earner family from that paid to a single-earner family? It could be argued that, given these developments, the idea of the just wage needs further reflection. There are questions, for example, about the role of welfare payments in topping up wages and whether living wages should be legislated or negotiated. Nevertheless, the original precepts remain true. Free contractual agreement is not necessarily sufficient to guarantee that a wage is just; if an enterprise exploits employees' weakness in determining their wages, this offends justice; and employers should pay a living wage, taking everything into account, if it can be afforded.

REFERENCES

Alves, A. A., and Gregório, I. (2021) Price controls and market economies. In *Christianity and Market Regulation: An Introduction* (ed. D. A. Crane and S. J. Gregg). Cambridge University Press.

Alves, A. A., and Moreira, J. M. (2013a) *The Salamanca School*. New York: Bloomsbury.

Alves, A. A., and Moreira, J. M. (2013b) Business ethics in the school of Salamanca. In *Handbook of the Philosophical Foundations of Business Ethics* (ed. C. Luetge), pp. 207–25. Heidelberg: Springer.

Aquinas, T. (2017) *The Summa Theologiæ*. Translated by Fathers of the English Dominican Province (https://www.newadvent.org/summa/).

Chafuen, A. (2003) *Faith and Liberty: The Economic Thought of the Late Scholastics*. Lanham: Lexington Books.

De Molina, L. (1981) *La Teoria del Justo Precio*. Madrid: Editora Nacional.

De Soto, D. (1968) *De Iustitia et Iure* (facsimile of the 1556 Latin edition accompanied with a Spanish translation). Madrid: Instituto de Estudios Politicos.

Elegido, J. M. (2009) The just price: three insights from the Salamanca school. *Journal of Business Ethics* 90(1): 29–46.

Finnis, J. (2019) Aquinas as a primary source of Catholic social teaching. In *Catholic Social Teaching. A Volume of Scholarly Essays* (ed. G. V. Bradley and E. C. Brugger), pp. 11–33. Cambridge University Press.

Grice-Hutchinson, M. (1978) *Early Economic Thought in Spain 1177–1740*. London: George Allen & Unwin.

Koehler, B. (2016) The thirteenth-century economics of Thomas Aquinas. *Economic Affairs* 36(1): 56–63.

Pontifical Council for Justice and Peace (2005) *Compendium of the Social Doctrine of the Church*. London: Burns & Oates.

Porter, J. (2002) The virtue of justice (IIa IIae, qq. 58–112). In *The Ethics of Aquinas* (ed. S. Pope), pp. 272–86. Washington, DC: Georgetown University Press.

Rocha, M. (1992) *Trabalho e Salário na Escolástica*. Lisboa: Editora Rei dos Livros.

Sigmund, P. E. (1988) Introduction. In *St Thomas Aquinas on Politics and Ethics* (ed. P. E. Sigmund). New York: W. W. Norton & Company.

Souto Coelho, J. (coord) (2002) *Doctina Social de la Iglesia: Manual Abreviado*. Madrid: Biblioteca de Autores Cristianos/Fundación Pablo VI.

Walsh, R. (2018) Property, human flourishing and St Thomas Aquinas: assessing a contemporary revival. *Canadian Journal of Law & Jurisprudence* XXXI(1) (February): 197–222.

PAPAL ENCYCLICALS AND OTHER CHURCH DOCUMENTS

Benedict XVI (2005) *Deus caritas est*, encyclical letter (http://www.vati can.va/content/benedict-xvi/en/encyclicals/documents/hf_ben-xvi_enc _20051225_deus-caritas-est.html).

John Paul II (1981) *Laborem exercens*, encyclical letter (http://www.vatican .va/content/john-paul-ii/en/encyclicals/documents/hf_jp-ii_enc_14091 981_laborem-exercens.html).

John Paul II (1991) *Centesimus annus*, encyclical letter (https://www.vati can.va/content/john-paul-ii/en/encyclicals/documents/hf_jp-ii_enc _01051991_centesimus-annus.html).

John Paul II (1998) *Fides et ratio*, encyclical letter (http://www.vatican.va/ content/john-paul-ii/en/encyclicals/documents/hf_jp-ii_enc_14091998 _fides-et-ratio.html).

John XXIII (1961) *Mater et magistra*, encyclical letter (http://www.vatican
.va/content/john-xxiii/en/encyclicals/documents/hf_j-xxiii_enc_15051
961_mater.html).

Leo XIII (1878) *Aeterni Patris*, encyclical letter (http://www.vatican.va/con
tent/leo-xiii/en/encyclicals/documents/hf_l-xiii_enc_04081879_aeter
ni-patris.html).

Leo XIII (1891) *Rerum novarum*, encyclical letter (http://www.vatican.va/
content/leo-xiii/en/encyclicals/documents/hf_l-xiii_enc_15051891_re
rum-novarum.html).

Pius XI (1931) *Quadragesimo anno*, encyclical letter (http://www.vatican
.va/content/pius-xi/en/encyclicals/documents/hf_p-xi_enc_19310515
_quadragesimo-anno.html).

Pius XII (1942) *Con Sempre Nuova Freschezza*, radio message (https://www
.vatican.va/content/pius-xii/it/speeches/1942/documents/hf_p-xii_spe
_19421224_radiomessage-christmas.html).

Vatican II (1965) *Gaudium et spes* Pastoral Constitution on the Church in
the World (https://www.vatican.va/archive/hist_councils/ii_vatican_co
uncil/documents/vat-ii_const_19651207_gaudium-et-spes_en.html).

CHAPTER 3

The universal Church and globalization

Philip Booth

It can be argued that there should be a natural empathy among Catholics for globalization. The Catholic Church desires to take the faith to the ends of the earth. Given this, why should commercial and cultural relationships not extend across borders? Furthermore, it could be asked whether the hostility to foreigners or instinct for self-preservation (even if misguided) which often accompanies protectionism is a healthy way to conduct political, civil and economic relationships. Pope Francis, for example, exhorted President Trump to build 'bridges rather than walls',[1] referring to the US president's desire to reduce migration from Mexico using physical constraints.

Despite this, the Church has expressed concerns about globalization in practice. The pope has said:

> I recognize that globalization has helped many people rise out of poverty, but it has also damned many others to starve to death. It is true that global wealth is growing in absolute terms, but inequalities have also grown and new poverty arisen.[2]

---

1 General audience, 8 February 2017 (https://www.reuters.com/article/us-pope-wall-idUSKBN15N1ZW).

2 Interview in *La Stampa*, 15 January 2015 (https://www.lastampa.it/vatican-insider/en/2015/01/11/news/francis-to-care-for-the-poor-is-not-communism-it-is-the-gospel-1.35302663).

There are also legitimate worries that a globalized economy will undermine local cultures and the relational aspect of economic activity. This concern was expressed in Pope Francis's most recent social encyclical, *Fratelli tutti* (100). On the other hand, globalization can lead to economic and cultural relationships developing across national boundaries and these can be fruitful and fulfilling.

Interestingly, the Victorian historian Lord Macaulay conceded that 'the Spiritual force of Protestantism was a mere local militia' in comparison with the global reach of Catholicism. 'If [a Jesuit] was wanted in Lima, he was on the Atlantic in the next fleet,' Macaulay (1856, vol. 1, p. 227) explained, 'If he was wanted in Bagdad [sic], he was toiling through the desert with the next caravan.' Unlike Martin Luther, who viewed the world outside Protestant Europe as fraught with moral danger, Ignatius of Loyola and the Jesuits (along with the resurgent mendicant orders) saw only an immense vista of opportunity for the Church.

It would seem clear that the Church's social teaching should never reject globalization as such. But, as in other areas of economic life, it may caution about particular manifestations of globalization; or practices or legal structures that are unjust. It is through this lens that this chapter will examine Catholic social thought and teaching and its relationship with globalization.

GLOBALIZATION IN HISTORICAL PERSPECTIVE

It is often assumed that globalization is a modern phenomenon and that it arises from what are described as 'neoliberal' influences on economic policy. This is ahistorical. There have been several phases of globalization. Indeed, global trade and the movement of people could be regarded as natural extensions of everyday economic and business life in the absence of physical constraints and constraints imposed by governments.

We know from archaeological finds that trade in the minerals obsidian and chert took place in New Guinea in Palaeolithic times (*c.* 17,000 BC; Smith 2009). In the Neolithic period, archaeological excavations show widespread use of obsidian for cutting utensils and tools. Obsidian artefacts have been discovered in areas of the Mediterranean where the local flint is sedimentary chert, proving the existence of trade routes (probably with southern Greek islands; Blake and Knapp 2005). Through the period of the Roman empire and the growth of Islam, trade routes grew and developed. At a later stage, the Hanseatic League developed trading relationships covering an area extending from Novgorod in what is now Russia to Boston in England. It was a highly ambitious and effective project aimed at reducing barriers to trade over land and by sea. Cod, salt, herring, fur, wood and silver were among the main items traded. But there was also an exchange of knowledge and expertise: the exercise of what would now be called 'soft power' or 'soft diplomacy'. These developments transcended existing states which often impeded economic cooperation.

To a greater or lesser extent, and often interrupted by war or disease, global economic relations have been an important part of the evolution of culture in the West. No British shopper would consider the purchase of potatoes, tomatoes, olive oil, coffee, chocolate, sugar, turkey, carrots, chicken and sweetcorn (perhaps with a bottle of wine and a packet of cigarettes) as a particularly 'exotic' selection, and yet not a single one of these goods is indigenous to Britain: most are not indigenous to Europe. As tomatoes, potatoes, corn and turkeys came from the New World to the Old, wheat, rice, barley, oats, sheep, cattle and pigs went in the other direction (the so-called 'Columbian Exchange'). Fish and chips owes its origins to the Americas (potatoes), Spain and Belgium (chips), Jewish immigration from Portugal and Spain via Holland (battered fish) and later immigration from Eastern Europe (the first fish-and-chip shop owner).

The last great era of globalization before the current one was brought to an end by World War I. Before the 1914–18 conflict, it was possible to travel through nearly every country in the world without a passport as well as trade goods on non-discriminatory terms. The current era, it could be argued, is waning under the threats of successive US presidents and the protectionist fears they represent, the dominance of the Chinese state in economic life and, as in past eras, the problem of disease.

THE SALAMANCA SCHOOL AND
INTERNATIONAL LAW

Spanish expansionism into the Americas was an important aspect of one of the waves of globalization. This, of course, was a form of imperialism on the part of a powerful nation, rather than the free interaction and integration between people, businesses and sovereign states. But it is important because it was really the first time that theologians started to wrestle with questions that touched upon the organization of a genuinely global commonwealth. The conception of humankind as a political and moral republic encompassing the whole world took shape in that Catholic intellectual cradle of early modernity: the School of Salamanca.

It was at Salamanca in the sixteenth century that the first intimations of a global theory of international law emerged, as well as the beginnings of a notion of universal human rights. 'All the peoples of the world are humans and there is only one definition of all humans and of each one, that is that they are rational ... Thus all the races of humankind are one' (De Las Casas 1992, p. 14).

This assertion by the Dominican friar and missionary Bartolomé de las Casas sounds strikingly modern. It was in Spain that the morality (or immorality) of colonialist adventures was a matter of public intellectual debate, and the disputations which took place at Salamanca had no real analogue elsewhere. The task for the Salamanca School was to reconcile Thomism with realities encountered in the New World as well as with humanism, Protestantism and religious division in Europe. As such, Salamanca functioned as a bridge between medieval and modern thought. As members of a universal Church, in an Empire claiming universal reach, the theologians of Salamanca had to adapt their frame of reference to accommodate the realities of a suddenly much larger world. Eventually, they would formulate the legal conception of a *totus orbis qui aliquo modo est una republica* in which the whole world was conceived of as a republic: a single moral and political community ultimately based upon Christian teaching, but primarily based upon reason and natural law.

Francisco de Vitoria brought about a legal turning of the tide in Salamanca. In his lectures dealing with the 'just titles' of conquest that were habitually used to justify the subjection of the New World, he reached a revolutionary conclusion: neither the Emperor nor the pope could claim spiritual or temporal authority over the whole world because the latter was populated by human beings who were the 'true owners in both public and private law' of their own land and personal property (De Las Casas 1992, p. 2). He also denied that Spain (or any other power) had any just claim or title over the Indies (or any other lands) by virtue of the right of discovery, or conquest, or the refusal of natives to accept the gospel, or the submission of their rulers to a conquering sovereign, unless with the consent of their people. This is important. In Catholic social thought, authentic globalization should be about economic and social cooperation and exchange between people who all have the same dignity and right to self-determination. It should not be imposed by coercion and peoples should not be subject to the illegitimate authority of other states.[3]

From this way of thinking developed the idea of international law which is applied in many fields, including in the governance of the trading relationships that are a feature of globalization through, for example, the European Union and the World Trade Organization. These questions of global governance are also prominent in modern debates about globalization in Catholic social thought. Vitoria argued that international law is not just a matter of temporary treaties and alliances but had to be grounded in a universal order based upon natural law in the service of the Common Good. As Vitoria puts it (Brown Scott 2007, p. 490, from *De Potestate Civili*, §21):

International law has not only the force of a pact and agreement among men, but also the force of a law; for the world as a whole, being in a way one single State, has the power to create laws that are just and fitting for all persons, as are the rules of international law.

3 Exactly what counts as illegitimate here is worthy of investigation, but will not be considered further. On the one hand, it can be argued that the involvement of the Soviet Union, modern-day China and, indeed, some actions by the US state in the affairs of other states might be illegitimate. At the same time, we should not assume that all interventions by one state in the affairs of another are not legitimate.

> In the gravest matters it is not permissible for one country to refuse
> to be bound by international law, the latter having been established
> by the authority of the whole world.

For Vitoria, the universal rights were the rights to travel, sojourn and trade in foreign lands: aspects of what one might consider 'pillars' of contemporary globalization. Added to these were the right to preach the gospel, the right to protect the baptized, and the right to depose a tyrannical ruler.

Students at Salamanca included some who would go to the New World as missionaries and they needed to be trained to hear confessions. Questions concerning large-scale property transfers, exports, loans, monopolies, price-speculation and entrepreneurship were suddenly real questions requiring real answers, not simply topics for scholastic disputation. In the confessional, for Catholic Spaniards, souls depended upon it.

The teachings of the Salamanca scholastics are often seen as providing a theological justification for the imperial ambitions of the Spanish crown. Although they did to some extent provide such a basis, those teachings also imposed limits upon the same rulers in favour of a more general view of human freedom. Vitoria, Domingo de Soto and others argued for the right of the Emperor (Charles V) and Spanish merchants to explore the New World and engage in international trade, and they did so as part of a general, global theory of trade. However, Spanish merchants did not need to be authorized by the crown because economic exchanges were part of a universal theory of *dominium* which was applicable all over the world. It was, therefore, as applicable to Protestants as it was to Catholics, and to pagans and Muslims too. Trade and commerce were protected by the natural law which recognized the essential sociability or 'natural partnership' of human beings. This formed the beginnings of a global *Lex mercatoria* in which the greater freedom belonged to the merchants themselves, not their rulers.

Sixteenth-century 'Catholic globalization' was surrounded by moral, legal and political debates which had no clear corollary in the Protestant world. It was Catholic Iberia that first established a worldwide economic system. The Protestant powers that would later

achieve global dominance and which, arguably, were more important in promoting the globalization of the late nineteenth century
did not create early modern globalization but inserted themselves
into an existing system and learned to profit from it.

GLOBALIZATION, CATHOLIC SOCIAL TEACHING AND THE HUMAN FAMILY

Despite these developments in Catholic social thought, globalization
was not addressed directly in the main sources of modern Catholic social teaching until comparatively recently. References tend to
begin in the 1960s. Pope John XXIII, for example, wrote in *Pacem
in terris* (130):

> There is also a growing economic interdependence among States.
> National economies are gradually becoming so interdependent that
> a kind of world economy is being born from the simultaneous inte-
> gration of the economies of individual States.

The term 'globalization' occurs for the first time in a social encyclical
in *Centesimus annus* (58) in 1991, though rather tentatively. Up to
this point and, indeed, for some time after, the approach to globalization in Catholic social teaching could only be tentatively extrapo-
lated from more general principles laid down in papal encyclicals
and conciliar documents.

The first social encyclicals are mainly concerned with the social
problems facing industrialized, developed nations. *Rerum novarum* was
published at the time of an intense period of globalization, but no particular attention was paid to it. The realm of concern was later enlarged
to include developing countries in *Mater et magistra* (1961). This focus
was further widened in *Populorum progressio* (1967), *Laborem exercens*
(1981) and, most notably, in *Sollicitudo rei socialis* (1987). It was after
the fall of Communism in the late 1980s that *Centesimus annus* (1991)
began to sketch out a global approach towards questions concerning a
just economic, social and political global order.

There has been a growing move in Catholic social teaching
towards a global view of social problems and, at the same time, an

increasing call for global cooperation. The Church is well-placed to address the issue of globalization as she is clearly a global actor, *par excellence*. As we read in *Mater et magistra* (178): 'The Church by divine right pertains to all nations. This is confirmed by the fact that she is everywhere on earth and strives to embrace all peoples.' The contribution of the Church to the debates around globalization is linked with her mission to preach and witness to the fundamental unity of the human family in Christ. The criterion for judging the 'success' of globalization is the extent to which it contributes to fostering true unity among all people and furthering human dignity and the universal common good.

This unity is not something to be compelled by force of arms, terror or the abuse of power. It must flow from that 'supreme model of unity, which is a reflection of the intimate life of God, one God in three Persons ... what we Christians mean by the word "communion"' (*Sollicitudo rei socialis*, 40). The Church teaches that peoples tend to unite not only for political and economic reasons, or in the name of an 'abstract ideological internationalism', but because of a free decision to cooperate, and an awareness 'that they are living members of the whole human family' (*Pacem in terris*, 296).

In his message for the World Day of Peace in 2000, Pope John Paul II repeatedly stressed a fundamental yet simple principle which may guide our reflection upon globalization, namely, that 'humanity, however much marred by sin, hatred and violence, is called by God to be a single family'.[4] The principal theme is peace, but he goes on immediately (paragraph 5) to note that:

> [T]his recognition can give the world as it is today – marked by the process of globalisation – a soul, a meaning and a direction. Globalisation, for all its risks, also offers exceptional and promising opportunities, precisely with a view to enabling humanity to become a single family, built on the values of justice, equity and solidarity.

---

4   Message of His Holiness for the celebration of the World Day of Peace (2000, p. 2).

This fundamental unity is theological in character, and this theological view must shape, indeed define, the worldview of believers even when they approach the technical questions of globalization.

In reflecting upon globalization and its effects upon the unity of the human family, the social teaching of the Church has tended to be couched in terms of the context of development and a concern that groups and individuals should not be excluded from social and economic progress. For example, when *Centesimus annus* addresses the topic of unfair competition and monopoly power it does so with concern for the poorest in society, rather than simply addressing the mechanics of the market, stating (35):

> It is necessary to break down the barriers and monopolies which leave so many countries on the margins of development and to provide all individuals and nations with the basic conditions which will enable them to share in development.

This larger context, within which 'economic globalization' must be judged, is taken up in *Ecclesia in America*, published after the Special Session of the Synod of Bishops for America, North and South (1999). In this document, it is noted (20):

> The ethical implications of globalization can be positive or negative. There is an economic globalization which brings some positive consequences, such as efficiency and increased production and which, with the development of economic links between different countries, can help to bring greater unity among peoples and make possible a better service to the human family. However if globalization is ruled merely by the laws of the market applied to suit the powerful, the consequences cannot but be negative.

A number of recent documents and statements from Pope Francis have echoed these sentiments but have also made definitive statements about factual matters. Pope Francis has talked about increasing inequalities, new poverty and exclusion. Earlier, in the 2011 document *Towards Reforming the International Financial and Monetary Systems in the Context of Global Public Authority*, it was stated that inequalities between various countries have grown significantly (1). It is, of course, reasonable, for pastors to use hyperbole to gain the attention of an audience to help it focus on an important problem. This is a frequently used device in Pope Francis's writing and speaking.[5] However, when we move from pastoral exhortation to intellectual discourse, prudent deliberation requires us to examine the data.

ECONOMIC TRENDS AND GLOBALIZATION

There is no question that, during the recent period of globalization, there has been a dramatic reduction in absolute poverty in the world. Of course, whether there is a causal link is a matter of debate. In 1820, more than 90 per cent of the world's population lived on less than $1.90 a day (adjusted for inflation and differences in purchasing power). In other words, 90 per cent of the world's population did not have sufficient food, shelter, clothing and other basics. That figure fell very slowly in the next couple of generations and was still just under 44 per cent in 1980. But, by 2019, only 7 per cent of the world's population lived beneath the absolute poverty line. In other words, about as much progress was made in reducing world poverty between 1980 and 2019 as in the whole of previous world economic history put together. In 1980, the number of people living in poverty in the world started to fall and, other than a slight blip in the 1980s, that fall has continued without a break. This was the first time in 200 years that the number of people in extreme poverty had fallen.

In addition, it is also worth noting that we are living through the first period in the modern age during which global inequality is falling and it is highly likely that this trend will continue. The economies in rich countries are stagnating (partly because of demography and the few number of young people) while poor

---

5   A particularly good example of this is in *Laudato si'* (15) in which Pope Francis states: 'The earth, our home, is beginning to look more and more like an immense pile of filth.' Very many environmental indicators are improving in most parts of the world. However, in certain parts of the world the assertion is true, and it is an effective and legitimate rhetorical device to draw the audience's attention to the problem.

countries are growing. The most important feature of the recent phase of globalization is that the previously poor have begun to catch with the rich world.[6]

It is not only indicators of material economic well-being that have improved, important as those are for the world's poorest. The proportion of the world's population of primary school age who are not in schools has fallen from 28 per cent in 1970 to 9 per cent today. Health outcomes have also improved dramatically. In Uganda, for example, the number of women who die from pregnancy-related causes while pregnant or within 42 days of the end of pregnancy per 100,000 live births fell from 687 to 343 between 1990 and 2015. Of course, the cause of these improvements is disputed. But the strong relationship between social outcomes and the elimination of poverty and the relationship between poverty reduction and the extent to which countries have taken part in the process of globalization is suggestive of globalization being an important factor.

Fratelli tutti (21) recognized this progress, but with a qualification:

> The claim that the modern world has reduced poverty is made by measuring poverty with criteria from the past that do not correspond to present-day realities. In other times, for example, lack of access to electric energy was not considered a sign of poverty, nor was it a source of hardship. Poverty must always be understood and gauged in the context of the actual opportunities available in each concrete historical period.

Of course, at face value, this is true. However, if it is economic progress and globalization that have made 'present-day realities' possible, then it would seem odd to criticize (or qualify praise) of that system on that ground alone. At the time *Fratelli tutti* was published, we were also seeing signs of the reversal of both globalization and the favourable economic trends that have reduced poverty. In addition, global conflicts have been increasing for the first time in decades. It

---

6   Our World in Data (https://ourworldindata.org) is an excellent source of objective information on these issues.

is quite likely that past progress will stall rather than poverty continue to reduce in the next few years.

In its social teaching, the Church makes judgements about political and economic issues as well as about theological and moral issues, with the former carrying less authority than the latter. Judgements about policy questions might change over time as evidence, scholarship and context changes. In the light of the above trends, it is therefore not surprising that the Church's teaching changed from what seemed to be a sceptical position on globalization in the 1960s. In *Populorum progressio*, for example, it was stated: 'trade relations can no longer be based solely on the principle of free, unchecked competition, for it very often creates an economic dictatorship' (59) and there was scepticism expressed of trade between developed and poorer countries. However, in 1991, in *Centesimus annus* (33), John Paul II wrote:

> Even in recent years it was thought that the poorest countries would develop by isolating themselves from the world market and by depending only on their own resources. Recent experience has shown that countries which did this have suffered stagnation and recession, while the countries which experienced development were those which succeeded in taking part in the general interrelated economic activities at the international level.

While more recent statements have tended to question or criticize globalization, overall there is a strong case for the Church to welcome economic globalization if the issue is to be judged by the economic prospering of the poor alone. In addition, the link between protectionism and nationalism might also suggest that a favourable disposition towards globalization is appropriate.

GLOBALIZATION: BEYOND THE ECONOMICS

Even if there is much to welcome in the economic and social trends arising from globalization, the Church will always address the signs of the times and the new problems to which economic and social trends give rise. Pope Leo XIII did this in 1891, and the Church does so today in relation to the impact of globalization.

Despite recent advances, there is still a large number of people who live poor or unfulfilled lives. Some would say that the process of globalization needs to be humanized or tamed or governed at the global level to try to address this. Others would say that the challenge is to bring development to the margins by removing the impediments to development that lie within poor countries themselves – these might include corruption, poor governance or barriers to market entry imposed by larger corporate interests. All Catholics would agree that development needs to be promoted within an environment of ethical business and ethical political behaviour and many Church teaching documents reflect this.

New developments also bring new evils and challenges. In the case of globalization these have included the migration of the poor and oppressed to unfamiliar environments and the phenomenon of large-scale human trafficking. Catholic social thought needs to address these matters and, in doing so, does not confine itself to commentary on economic statistics. The Church has taken a great interest in the problems of corruption, trafficking, forced migration and the treatment of migrants, both by providing enormous practical support and by working to improve the public policy environment which encourages these problems. In *Evangelii gaudium*, Pope Francis noted (211):

> I have always been distressed at the lot of those who are victims of various kinds of human trafficking. How I wish that all of us would hear God's cry: 'Where is your brother?' (Gen 4:9). Where is your brother or sister who is enslaved? Where is the brother and sister whom you are killing each day in clandestine warehouses, in rings of prostitution, in children used for begging, in exploiting undocumented labour? Let us not look the other way. There is greater complicity than we think. The issue involves everyone! This infamous network of crime is now well established in our cities, and many people have blood on their hands as a result of their comfortable and silent complicity.

The Church stresses that development that comes with globalization should be ethically based. With growing incomes in previously poorer countries comes the need to warn about lifestyles that see consumer goods as an end in themselves when such warnings might previously have been irrelevant. Furthermore, globalization may raise questions about culture and the extent to which we should be concerned that local cultures might be undermined by the development of more uniform global cultures. Pope Francis has warned about this, as noted above, but Pope John Paul II had also done so:

> Globalization must not be a new version of colonialism ... It must respect the diversity of cultures which, within the universal harmony of peoples, are life's interpretive keys. In particular, it must not deprive the poor of what remains most precious to them, including their religious beliefs and practices, since genuine religious convictions are the clearest manifestation of human freedom.[7]

There are also questions of governance, especially to do with the appropriateness of global governance, that are addressed in Catholic social thought and teaching.

THE UNIVERSAL COMMON GOOD

In many ways, the global nature of the Church combined with her teaching that all human persons are made in the image of God and share the same nature, leads globalization to be a natural extension of the traditional concerns of Catholic social teaching. We can move easily from thinking about the responsibilities of national governments in relation to the common good to the idea of the global common good. As *Pacem in terris* (139) puts it: 'like the common good of individual states, so too the universal common good cannot be determined except by having regard for the human person'. The same principle is found in the Catechism (1911), which notes that (Catholic Church 1994):

> Human interdependence is increasing and gradually spreading throughout the world. The unity of the human family, embracing

---

7   Address to the Pontifical Academy of Social Sciences (27 April 2001).

people who enjoy equal natural dignity, implies a universal common good. The good calls for an organisation of the community of nations able to provide for the different needs of men.

Talk of a 'global common good' is predicated upon the principle that human rights are both indivisible and universal, a theme addressed by the School of Salamanca. Pope John Paul II stressed this when addressing the question of human rights violations arising from situations of exclusion and poverty: 'the restructuring of the economy on a world scale must be based on the dignity and rights of the person, especially on the right to work and the worker's protection'.[8] And then in paragraph 36 of the same address he goes on to stress the importance of social and economic rights and states:

> [I]t is important to reject every attempt to deny these rights a true juridical status. It should further be repeated that to achieve their total and effective implementation, the common responsibility of all the parties – public authorities, business and civil society – must be involved.

This implies that special attention should be given to the promotion of the common good at the international level and perhaps special structures will be needed. But this is a natural extension of the responsibilities of political and other institutions that has been discussed in Catholic social teaching over several centuries. Enduring principles are being applied to new situations.

The call of Catholic social teaching to create new, or improve existing, multinational, transnational or supranational structures in order to promote the universal common good has troubled some because it seems to be at odds with the principle of subsidiarity. To 'anti-globalists' it seems like a call for world government. But from the time of *Pacem in terris* onwards, successive encyclicals have cautioned that the existing structures for guaranteeing the universal

---

8   Address to participants in the World Congress on Pastoral Promotion of Human Rights (4 July 1998) (4).

common good are inadequate. Two sections of *Pacem in terris* in particular spell out this concern (135, 137):

> We are thus driven to the conclusion that the shape and structure of political life in the modern world, and the influence exercised by public authority in all nations of the world are unequal to the huge task of promoting the common good of all peoples.

> The universal common good presents us with problems which are world-wide in their dimensions ... problems which cannot be solved except by a public authority with power, organisation and means co-extensive with these problems, and with a world-wide sphere of activity.

At various times, papal encyclicals and other statements have called for a strengthening of existing or the creation of new structures of governance in order to regulate global economic activity. Such structures do, of course, already exist both in the political and economic domain and a challenge for Catholic social teaching is to promote a form of governance that will genuinely promote the common good. A particular problem is that international institutions can be taken over by interests hostile to a Christian understanding of the common good, be difficult to hold to account and difficult to limit to their proper functions in accordance with the principle of subsidiarity.

The idea of international governance continues to be an important theme. In Pope Benedict's social encyclical, *Caritas in veritate*, it was stated (in the English translation) (67):

> In the face of the unrelenting growth of global interdependence, there is a strongly felt need, even in the midst of a global recession, for a reform of the United Nations Organization, and likewise of economic institutions and international finance, so that the concept of the family of nations can acquire real teeth.

Interestingly, in the other translations of that encyclical it was proposed that there should be a 'real concreteness' to the concept of the family of nations rather than that it should have 'real teeth'. These other translations are more likely to be authentic. This is a somewhat different emphasis.

Importantly, though, Pope Benedict warned (57):

> the principle of subsidiarity is particularly well-suited to managing globalization and directing it towards authentic human development. In order not to produce a dangerous universal power of a tyrannical nature, the governance of globalization must be marked by subsidiarity.

In *Fratelli tutti*, Pope Francis reflected this previous teaching but also warned of some of the dangers of international institutions, at least in their current manifestations.

One way of realizing this desire for international institutions while respecting the principle of subsidiarity is to limit their scope. Another is to focus more on cooperation between existing institutions of government rather than the creation of new, overarching institutions. Ahner (2007, p. 1), for example, argues: 'the determining forces of our lives are truly global but the institutions of support that protect and nurture human values are still local', which leads, in his view, to the need to build and develop 'mediating institutions and associations that can support this new global reality.' On the other hand, Coleman (2005, p. 14) notes that 'change in our social and economic realities has outpaced change in the political institutions and processes that once firmly embedded them.' And Hug (2005, p. 65) takes a similar view and specifically states: 'global governance institutions are essential at this stage of human development precisely to protect the common good where sovereign nations no longer can.'

Since the financial crisis, Vatican documents have increasingly called for more international regulation of finance. However, it is worth noting that there is, and was at the time of the financial crisis, a huge range of international organizations with economic or political powers. Most countries that were affected by the crisis subscribed to the Basel Accord, which dictated how banks were regulated among its signatories. Arguably, it made the crash worse by embedding regulatory errors across a wider number of countries. Indeed, academic work has called into question the approach of creating regulatory regimes at higher political levels (see, for example, Romano 2014).

The question of exactly what global governance should mean in practice is one that requires further discernment as Catholic social teaching evolves in this area. But, three things can be said for certain. Firstly, the concept of international courts, treaties and organizations restraining nation states and exercising some juridical power in order to enforce justice and human rights is one that is totally consistent with the evolution of Catholic social teaching, given the importance that teaching places upon the universality of human rights. Secondly, international institutions can be difficult to hold to account and may be captured by interests that distorts their legitimate mission and may even be hostile to the Church and the Church's teaching. Finally, it should be clear that calls for new forms of governance and political authority are not tantamount to support for a 'One World Government': the principle of subsidiarity means that this cannot be the case.

CONCLUSION

Globalization has brought enormous economic benefits. Arguably, this is especially so for the least well off. Some may fear the effect that this has had on local cultures. At the same time, however, cultures can be enriched by cooperation with communities overseas. And, while there may be legitimate concerns about the loosening of local ties as a result of globalization, it is difficult to argue that protectionism is a legitimate response given that protectionism can be borne of and give rise to a hostility to our global neighbours. Indeed, Catholic social teaching, insofar as it recognizes the fact of globalization and the challenges it brings, even to the extent of calling for new forms of global governance, should recognize that globalization is the opposite dynamic to that which takes place when we have *Balkanization*. Globalization is about the spread of cooperation between individuals, businesses, civil society organizations and governments and not the imposition of a single global standard at the local level. A genuinely global system or company must operate at a global *and* local level. In response, Catholic social teaching needs to consider what the functions and authority of the different levels of government should be.

In the author's view, the dangers of ensuring accountability and the complexity of governing at the international level are such that the functions of international institutions of governance should be limited. Functions could include peace keeping; the enforcement of rules-based systems that are agreed by governments (such as exists within the World Trade Organization); ensuring human rights are not abused by national governments (through such mechanisms as war-crimes tribunals); and coordinating solutions to genuinely global problems where bodies that transcend national governments are necessary.

There is always a balance to be struck between *subsidium* and *solidum*. In championing new forms of governance, globalization's democratic deficit must be balanced by ensuring that existing institutions are reformed and new ones designed with transparency, participation and accountability at the fore. This is more likely to happen if their functions are appropriate. As Pope John Paul II warned:

> [S]maller social units – whether nations themselves, communities, ethnic or religious groups, families or individuals – must not be namelessly absorbed into a greater conglomeration, thus losing their identity and having their prerogatives usurped. Rather, the proper autonomy of each social class and organization, each in its own sphere, must be defended and upheld.[9]

Catholic social thought does not provide a blueprint for global governance, but rather offers basic principles for governance at all levels. Responsibility for attaining the common good belongs to all organizations in society. How those organizations in the political sphere should be structured requires prudent judgement and more discernment. The Brexit debate, the role of the World Health Organization in the Covid crisis and the failure of the comprehensive systems of international financial regulation in the 2008 financial crisis suggest that such discernment is needed from those involved in the development of Catholic social thought and teaching

---

9   Pope John Paul II, *Message to the Pontifical Academy of Social Sciences* (24 February 2000).

REFERENCES

Ahner, G. (2007) *Business Ethics: Making a Life, Not Just a Living.* Maryknoll, NY: Orbis.

Blake, E., and Knapp, A. B. (2005) *The Archaeology of Mediterranean Prehistory.* John Wiley & Sons.

Brown Scott, J. (2007) *The Catholic Conception of International Law.* Clark, NJ: The LawBook Exchange.

Catholic Church (1994) *Catechism of the Catholic Church.* London: Geoffrey Chapman.

Coleman, J. A. (2005) Making the connections: globalization and Catholic social thought. In *Globalization and Catholic Social Thought: Present Crisis, Future Hope.* Toronto: Novalis Press.

De Las Casas, B. (1992) *A Short Account of the Destruction of the Indies* (ed. N. Griffin). London: Penguin Books.

Hug, J. (2005) Economic justice and globalization. In *Globalization and Catholic Social Thought: Present Crisis, Future Hope.* Toronto: Novalis Press.

Macaulay, T. B. (1856) *The History of England from the Accession of James II,* vol. I. London: Harper and Bros.

Romano, R. (2014) For diversity in the international regulation of financial institutions: critiquing and recalibrating the Basel architecture. *Yale Journal on Regulation* 31(1): 1–76.

Smith, R. L. (2009) *Premodern Trade in World History.* London: Taylor & Francis.

PAPAL ENCYCLICALS AND OTHER CHURCH DOCUMENTS

Francis (2020) *Fratelli tutti,* encyclical letter (http://www.vatican.va/content/francesco/en/encyclicals/documents/papa-francesco_20201003_enciclica-fratelli-tutti.html).

Francis (2013) *Evangelii gaudium,* apostolic exhortation (http://www.vatican.va/content/francesco/en/apost_exhortations/documents/papa-francesco_esortazione-ap_20131124_evangelii-gaudium.html).

Pontifical Council for Justice and Peace (2011) Towards reforming the international and financial monetary systems in the context of global public authority (https://www.vatican.va/roman_curia/pontifical_councils/justpeace/documents/rc_pc_justpeace_doc_20111024_nota_en.html).

Benedict XVI (2009) *Caritas in veritate*, encyclical letter (https://www.vati
can.va/content/benedict-xvi/en/encyclicals/documents/hf_ben-xvi_enc
_20090629_caritas-in-veritate.html).

John Paul II (1999) *Ecclesia in America*, apostolic exhortation (https://www
.vatican.va/content/john-paul-ii/en/apost_exhortations/documents/hf
_jp-ii_exh_22011999_ecclesia-in-america.html).

John Paul II (1991) *Centesimus annus*, encyclical letter (https://www.vati
can.va/content/john-paul-ii/en/encyclicals/documents/hf_jp-ii_enc
_01051991_centesimus-annus.html).

John Paul II (1987) *Sollicitudo rei socialis*, encyclical letter (http://www.vati
can.va/content/john-paul-ii/en/encyclicals/documents/hf_jp-ii_enc_30
121987_sollicitudo-rei-socialis.html).

John Paul II (1981) *Laborem exercens*, encyclical letter (http://www.vati
can.va/content/john-paul-ii/en/encyclicals/documents/hf_jp-ii_enc_14
091981_laborem-exercens.html).

Paul VI (1967) *Populorum progressio*, encyclical letter (http://www.vatican
.va/content/paul-vi/en/encyclicals/documents/hf_p-vi_enc_26031967
_populorum.html).

John XXIII (1963) *Pacem in terris*, encyclical letter (http://www.vatican.va/
content/john-xxiii/en/encyclicals/documents/hf_j-xxiii_enc_11041963
_pacem.html).

John XXIII (1961) *Mater et magistra*, encyclical letter (http://www.vatican
.va/content/john-xxiii/en/encyclicals/documents/hf_j-xxiii_enc_15051
961_mater.html).

Leo XIII (1891) *Rerum novarum,* encyclical letter (http://www.vatican.va/
content/leo-xiii/en/encyclicals/documents/hf_l-xiii_enc_15051891_re
rum-novarum.html).

CHAPTER 4

The right to migrate and the common good

Andrew M. Yuengert

Three principles describe Catholic social teaching on immigration (Yuengert 2004):

- There is a right to migrate – both to emigrate and to immigrate (*Pacem in terris*,[1] 21; *Populorum progressio*, 69; *Laborem exercens*, 23).
- The right to migrate is not absolute. Host countries may regulate migrant flows when the burdens of immigration threaten a nation's common good (WDM 1993; WDMR 2011).
- The right to migrate is especially strong for poor migrants and refugees; nations should not abridge their rights lightly or arbitrarily (WDMR 2013; *Evangelii gaudium*, 210).

Pope Francis has not changed the three principles of Catholic social teaching on immigration. Consistent with his apostolic vision, however, he begins with the third principle. Poor immigrants and refugees are often marginalized and vulnerable, and should be first,

---

1 In this chapter, papal encyclicals, apostolic exhortations and similar documents will be given their title in the first reference and then cited by their initials. Messages for World Day for Migrants or World Day for Migrants and Refugees will be described by the initials WDM and WDMR followed by the date throughout.

not last, in our hearts (WDMR 2019). Fraternal charity balances a healthy love of one's native land and a universal love for those in need at and beyond one's borders (*Fratelli tutti*, 142).

The current political impasse over immigration challenges the Church to be more specific about its second principle. The 1987 Immigration Reform and Control Act promised a combination of an amnesty for three million illegal immigrants and renewed enforcement. It delivered the amnesty but not enforcement, setting the stage for intractable political conflict. Thirty years later, after decades of large legal and illegal immigrant inflows, the US immigrant population stands at 42 million – 13 per cent of the US population (Blau and Mackie 2017, p. 19). The number of illegal immigrants is estimated to stand at 11 million, nearly four times higher than in 1987.

In the last three decades the opposing positions on immigration have hardened. Immigration reform movements in 2007 and 2013 promised a 'path to citizenship' paired with new enforcement initiatives. Each effort foundered on conservative suspicion that enforcement would once again fail to materialize, and the left's growing intolerance of any restrictions whatsoever on immigration from poor countries.[2] Donald Trump was elected in part on a promise of enforcement, amid ongoing chaos at the border. The impasse in Europe is equally intractable, although it is focused more intensely on questions of national identity and on the effects of Muslim and poor immigrants on homogeneous secular cultures.

Conflicts over immigration have contributed to the rise of populist nationalism in the US and Europe. Supporters of these movements (labelled 'somewheres' by Goodhart (2017)) identify more closely with place, and with those who share their community and nation. They suspect that the elites who rule them (the 'anywheres', according to Goodhart) neglect their interests in favour of global initiatives. Populists tend to be poor and working class. In the US, it is well documented that they have done poorly both inside and outside of markets. Their political concerns focus on immigration and trade, which they regard as threats to their well-being.

---

2   Many on the free-market right share the left's effectively open-border objective (Powell 2015).

As the politics of immigration has become polarized, economic research into the effects of immigration has expanded. The National Academies of Sciences recently published a comprehensive summary of recent research (Blau and Mackie 2017). The basic conclusions have not changed since the last National Academies' report in the 1990s (Smith and Edmonston 1997). Immigration has large beneficial effects on immigrants themselves and net positive effects on natives on aggregate. Although the aggregate effect on natives is positive, the effects are distributed unevenly. Immigration has small but probably negative effects on the wages of low-skill native workers, and has overall modest effects on government budgets (although the effects differ widely across states and localities, and between the state and national governments).[3]

Two bodies of research, one addressing the benefits of immigration to immigrants, and the other addressing its burdens for native workers, bring into sharp focus the conundrum posed by the populist challenge to a generous immigration policy and for Catholic social teaching. Firstly, new research on 'place effects' vividly documents the enormous benefits of migration to poor immigrants. The economic gains to migration are not a simple redistribution of material goods. They reveal a morally significant expansion of immigrant labour productivity.

A second body of research takes as given the relatively modest negative effects of migration on poor natives, but questions whether even modest burdens on this group are acceptable. Government transfers have not shielded poor and working class natives from the dysfunctions that attend even modest declines in job prospects. Populist challenges to immigration bring to the fore a crucial question: how should we weigh large economic benefits to immigrants against relatively modest but humanly significant losses to native workers and their communities? Should the fact that poor natives are 'our poor' count for something in our policy deliberations?

---

3   A new emphasis on high-skill immigrants reflects a general trend in immigration policy discussions toward 'improving' the immigrant inflow. Any shift of immigration policy toward skilled immigration and away from unskilled creates a potential conflict with the third principle of Catholic social teaching, that the rights of poor immigrants are paramount.

Catholic social teaching gives us few resources to grapple with the tension between the rights of vulnerable poor migrants and the modest negative effects of immigration on the vulnerable native poor. In theory, the popes accept the need to weigh the right to migrate against potential damage to the common good of the host country. In practice, they are quick to classify concerns about the effects of immigration on native incomes and culture as 'aggressive nationalism' (*Fratelli tutti*, 159). The explicit ethnic chauvinism of many populist movements deserves the Church's criticism. Nevertheless, we need to hear more from the Church on what an appropriate concern for the national common good looks like – about the contours of 'well-ordered nationalism'.

The discussion on the economics of immigration will be organized around the three principles of Catholic social teaching on immigration. The first section reviews the right to migrate and its ambiguities in light of the common goods of the country of origin and of the host country. The following section reviews recent research on the effects of immigration on host countries. The third section examines the Church's emphasis on solicitude for the poor, contrasting the strikingly large benefits to poor immigrants with the plight of the native working-class poor.

THE RIGHT TO MIGRATE

The right to migrate in Catholic social teaching is oddly different from other rights. It is not absolute, like the right to life. You cannot deny even yourself the right to life. The right to migrate is more like the right to enter into marriage, which does not impose an obligation to marry. We have a right to migrate, even if we do not exercise it. Still, the right to migrate differs from the right to marry in one important respect: Catholic social teaching expresses a certain *regret* when someone exercises the right to migrate; there is no similar regret when couples marry.

The ambiguity comes from the relationship of the migrant to two common goods. An international immigrant touches two nations, each with a common good. *Gaudium et spes* defines the common good as 'the sum total of social conditions which allow people, either as groups or as individuals, to reach their fulfilment more fully and more easily' (26). The common good is the shared justification and purpose of the state. It is a necessary framework for human flourishing. Its conditions include respect of the rights of the person, the family, religious communities, and civil society.

The 'social conditions' of the common good are cooperatively produced by the members of a state. Each should share in the benefit, and the joint project produces a certain fellowship among citizens. A shared common good calls forth a sense that we are 'debtors' to our communities, and generates solidarity, 'a firm and enduring commitment to the common good' (Pontifical Council for Justice and Peace 2005,[4] p. 195). We owe something to the countries in which we live and to our fellow citizens. A community which pursues its own common good identifies as a community, as a 'we'. Our contribution to the common good is crucial to our flourishing.

An immigrant finds himself between two national communities, each with a common good. He leaves behind a nation whose common good has a claim on him (unless it is oppressing his dignity) and enters a country whose common good he does not share in the same way that citizens and residents of the host country do.

The first source of ambivalence about the right to migrate is the common good of the country of origin. *Gaudium et spes* affirms a right to migrate, but the affirmation is an aside to a discussion of the 'right and duty' of all citizens in developing countries to contribute to their country's common good (65):

> [I]t is their right and duty ... to contribute to the true progress of their own community according to their ability. Especially in underdeveloped areas ... those who hold back their unproductive resources or who deprive their community of the material or spiritual aid that it needs – saving the personal right of migration – gravely endanger the common good.

---

4   That is the Compendium of the Social Doctrine of the Church, hereafter denoted by 'the Compendium'.

All citizens should employ their resources toward the common good of their countries. The countries themselves should respect and safeguard this right and duty. However, this expectation does not permit restrictions on 'the personal right of migration'.[5]

The context of the right to migrate comes with a default expectation that people will participate in and contribute to their native land's common good. When migrants exercise their right to leave, it is often because they are unable to participate in the common good there. The right to migrate exists when there are 'just reasons' to leave (*Pacem in terris*, 25), when citizens are exploited or otherwise prevented from contributing 'according to their ability' (*Gaudium et spes*, 65).

Clearly, there is some ambivalence about the right to migrate: it merits respect and urgent protection, but its widespread exercise is a symptom that something has gone wrong in the country of origin or in the international system.[6] John Paul II notes that migration is a loss to the home country, whose native sons and daughters contribute to some other country's common good instead (*Laborem exercens*, 23). Pope Francis expresses regret for the 'cultural and religious uprooting' of emigrants, and 'fragmentation ... felt by the communities they leave behind' (*Fratelli tutti*, 38). In an ideal world, fewer people would exercise the right to migrate (*Fratelli tutti*, 129).

Three arguments for the right to migrate

Yuengert (2004) outlines three arguments from Catholic social teaching that together support a right to migrate. They also highlight the relationship of the migrant to his native land's common good. The first is 'the right of a family to sustenance' (p. 12). It is

---

5   John Paul II lists the universal rights at stake in migration, each closely tied to place and community. For example, 'the right to have one's own country, to live freely in one's own country, to live together with one's family ... to preserve and develop one's ethnic, cultural and linguistic heritage' (WDM 2001, p. 3).

6   John Paul II ties the right to migrate to a 'right not to emigrate' (WDMR 2004, p. 3).

closely related to the universal destination of goods, and the right to private property (*Mater et magistra*, 45; *Populorum progressio*, 69). To flourish, families need access to productive work and this world's goods. The ability to move across national boundaries is a further guarantee of this access.

The second argument is 'the priority of the family over the State' (Yuengert 2004, pp. 12–13). This priority is clearly established by Leo XIII's defence of private property (*Rerum novarum*, 13). This principle does not forbid any restrictions whatsoever on the family for the sake of the common good. Rather, it insists that the state and its laws exist *for the sake of* the family. A state objective that requires the sacrifice of families and other basic societies does not truly promote the common good.

This second argument brings into focus the ambivalent nature of the right to migrate. Potential immigrants originate in communities and nations with common goods. It would be good and just that they seek their flourishing within their home nations and that their home nation would respect and promote their flourishing as part of the common good. Many nations, however, fail to provide conditions in which families can thrive and people can contribute to the common good 'according to their ability' (*Gaudium et spes*, 65). The popes blame this situation on a combination of imbalances and inequities in the international system as a whole, and mismanagement and oppression in countries of origin. In either case the right to migrate is a safeguard, allowing citizens to 'seek better conditions of life in another country' (*Laborem exercens*, 23) (see also WDMR 2004, p. 3; WDMR 2014; WDMR 2015).

The third argument for the right to migrate, 'the right of economic initiative', connects migration explicitly to economic agency, or to the lack of it in the home country. John Paul II describes clearly what is at stake in 'economic initiative' in the following way. It is (*Sollicitudo rei socialis*, 15):

> important not only for the individual but also for the common good ... the denial of this right, or its limitation in the name of an alleged 'equality' of everyone in society, diminishes, or in practice absolutely destroys the spirit of initiative, that is to say *the creative*

subjectivity of the citizen ... This provokes a sense of frustration or desperation and predisposes people to opt out of national life, impelling many to emigrate.

This passage reminds us that an abstract concept such as 'creative subjectivity' is closely related to work and economic activity. There is a close relationship between the right to migrate and the right to economic initiative. Although the popes give special attention to non-economic migrants fleeing violence and oppression, two of the three arguments listed above emphasize material provision and the expression of human agency through economic activity.

Human beings are both material and spiritual: the exercise of personal agency ordinarily has spiritual and material consequences. The suppression of economic agency likewise has spiritual and material consequences. The economic poverty that migrants flee is often an expression of a broader denial of the dignity of the migrant.

THE COMMON GOOD OF THE HOST COUNTRY: ECONOMIC RESEARCH

In Catholic social teaching, the right to migrate is not absolute. Large migrations may affect the common good of receiving countries. The Church recognizes these burdens and qualifies her assertion of the right to migrate accordingly. John Paul II acknowledged that indiscriminate migration may harm the receiving country and thus ought 'to be regulated' (WDM 2001, p. 3); receiving countries may fear a 'loss of identity' amid a large migrant influx (WDM 1998). Benedict XVI affirmed that 'States have the right to regulate migration flows and to defend their own frontiers, always guaranteeing the respect due to the dignity of each and every human person' (WDMR 2011).

A nation's common good is pursued at the national level; citizens contribute to it at every level, and are supposed to participate in its benefits. The primary ways in which immigration may harm the common good is through its effect on culture or through unequal economic burdens on some portion of the native population. Recent research addresses each of these aspects of immigration.

Cultural effects

Arguments that immigration is a threat to national culture are stronger in countries with stronger ethnic identities. These arguments have less purchase in the US, which has always been an ongoing social project, 'conceived in liberty, and dedicated to the proposition that all men are created equal', as Lincoln described it in his Gettysburg Address. US culture has in the past been shaped by the principles on which it was founded: equality before the law, aspirations to self-government, and the associational habits necessary for a vibrant civil society. Immigrants from very different cultures have assimilated to this culture, even those whom natives held in deep suspicion: Germans in the eighteenth century; the Irish in the nineteenth; eastern Europeans in the twentieth; and Latin Americans and Asians in the twenty-first.

There is currently a fierce debate raging in the US over what kind of nation it wants to be. Every aspect of US history, its institutions and its culture are on the table and under attack. Every policy issue is drawn into this debate and immigrants find themselves recruited to one side or the other. Even the ongoing impasse over illegal immigration is really a conflict between natives over the rule of law and immigration policy. It is not an argument between immigrants and natives.[7]

In the face of the deep disagreements over what American civic culture should become, it is unfair to immigrants to expect them to hit a contested cultural target. It is more reasonable to evaluate their assimilation to US culture by means of less disputed measures. Are they criminals? Do they learn English? Do they work hard? On all of these measures immigrants are good neighbours who eventually find their place in US society. Butcher and Piehl (2007) shows that immigrants are institutionalized (incarcerated) at one-tenth the rate of natives of the same age and education. The most recent waves of immigrants learn English more slowly than previous cohorts, but

7   This is not to deny that immigration has political effects. Giuliano and Tabellini (2020) provide evidence that large immigrations have shifted the US leftward politically in the past.

their progress is still steady, and their children speak English (Blau and Mackie 2017, pp. 114–19). Both immigrant wages and employment increase relative to native workers the longer they live in the US (Blau and Mackie 2017, pp. 98–114).

Fiscal effects

The effect of immigration on government finances is modest in the aggregate, but unevenly distributed between the Federal and state and local levels. Blau and Mackie (2017) estimate immigration's past and predicted future effects at the Federal and state and local levels. Unsurprisingly, the predicted impacts depend upon the assumptions.[8] Nevertheless, a clear picture emerges. At the Federal level, immigrants are a net fiscal benefit, especially when the contributions of second and third generation immigrants are counted (Blau and Mackie 2017, pp. 436–38). At the state and local level, immigrants are a net burden, although the effects vary substantially across states and immigrant generation (Blau and Mackie 2017, pp. 522–31).

The estimated fiscal effects are complicated by the fact that, under the current unsustainable debt path at every level of government, even the average native is a net fiscal burden, receiving more in benefits and services than they receive in taxes. Any additional person simply adds to the problem. However, in any scenario where the US returns to fiscal sustainability, immigrants and their offspring become less fiscally burdensome than natives.[9]

Effects on native workers

Economists emphasize the net positive effects of immigration: the efficiency of comparative advantage and of mutually beneficial

---

8   Blau and Mackie (2017, pp. 461–62) emphasize crucial assumptions about the long-term budget outlook, the allocation of sunk costs to the 'cost' of an immigrant, and the socioeconomic characteristics of new immigrants.

9   There is a further complex twist to this argument which is important. Migrants can reduce the current fiscal burden on the native population by sharing the debt among more people. Migration also slows the ageing of the population and the fiscal burdens that come with that process.

exchange. The biggest winners from immigration are immigrants themselves, who increase their own incomes considerably. Among natives, however, there are winners and losers and aggregate effects do not adequately capture the common good of the host country. The common good includes the good 'of each and of all.' Although in theory the winners ought to be able to compensate the losers (through adjustment assistance, retraining or income support), in practice transfers may fail to compensate for the losses.

As the share of well-educated immigrants has grown (although it is still small), more research has focused on the effects of highly educated immigration on labour markets. Blau and Mackie (2017, pp. 251–53) survey these results. Although the empirical results are mixed, there is some evidence that an influx of highly skilled immigrants increases wages across native education levels, perhaps through spillover and innovation effects.[10] Highly skilled immigrants appear to increase the rate of production of new patents, and immigrants in general have higher self-employment rates than natives. Higher rates of self-employment and technological innovation may increase economic productivity, although this research is in its early stages (Peri et al. 2015; Borjas 2019; Burchardi et al. 2020).

The 1997 National Academies Study (Smith and Edmonston 1997) surveyed the literature on the effects of immigration on unskilled labour markets, and found negative but relatively small effects. The 2017 National Academies study (Blau and Mackie 2017, p. 267) summarizes the intervening explosion of creative empirical research on this topic. New research has not modified the 1997 study's conclusion: immigration has at most modestly negative effects on unskilled native wages: 2–3 per cent slower growth over a 10 year period.

Blau and Mackie (2017, ch. 5) discuss the empirical challenge of discerning the effect of immigration in a dynamic labour market.

---

10 Some studies find a negative effect on the wages of highly skilled natives who compete most directly against the highly skilled immigrants (see Borjas 2006).

Immigrants tend to settle in areas where their economic opportunities are greatest; this (and the movement of native workers in response to labour market changes) confounds our ability to isolate the effect of an immigrant influx. Moreover, it is difficult to identify which natives compete against which immigrants. In the short run, immigrants will increase the supply of labour (and decrease wages) in markets where they are substitutes for native workers (unskilled workers and teens, mostly) and will increase demand for labour (and wages) in markets where they are complements.

Whatever the effect of immigration in the short run, in the long run capital investment responds in ways that mitigate these effects. Investors will provide more capital and new technology to take advantage of the influx; this new investment increases demand for unskilled labour, counteracting the fall in wages. When immigrants bring capital with them, or when investors increase capital in anticipation of a large immigrant influx, the negative effects of immigration on wages will be smaller even in the short run.

To summarize, in the short run (over a period of 10 years or so) an influx of unskilled immigrants is likely to have modestly negative effects on low-skilled, low-income native workers. This decline in wages benefits native owners of capital. In the long run, as capital levels increase to meet the new supply of labour, the negative effects are smaller: even the relatively small effects decrease. The long-run beneficiaries are the immigrants themselves and the owners of capital.[11]

IMMIGRANT POOR AND 'OUR' POOR

Although the right to migrate is not absolute, Catholic social teaching cautions nations against arbitrary restrictions on this right: international migrants are usually poor, and even those who

---

11 Negative effects on wages might also be reduced (or, indeed, reversed) by the influx of new, complementary entrepreneurial ideas that increase the demand for labour, reduce the cost of goods and services or increase the quality or variety of goods and services.

are wealthier often seek better conditions and rights denied them in their home countries. Pope Francis notes that Jesus calls the Church to recognize him in 'the poorest and most abandoned; among these are certainly migrants and refugees, who are trying to escape difficult conditions and dangers of every kind' (WDMR 2015). Our attitude toward poor migrants and refugees 'is not just about migrants ... The progress of our peoples ... depends above all on our openness to being touched and moved by those who knock at our door' (WDM 2019).

Although Western nations look with increasing favour on well-educated, highly skilled immigrants, Catholic social teaching urges us to keep our eyes fixed on the poor. Research confirms that the economic benefits to poor immigrants are undeniably large. They increase their incomes substantially simply by moving across borders. The fact that this benefit accrues to immigrants with relatively small short-run effects on native workers (and even smaller long-run effects) is a puzzle – a puzzle that perhaps only economists fully appreciate. By exploring it, we can see more clearly the human stakes of immigration: the large economic benefits to poor immigrants are an indicator and concomitant of the large non-economic benefits of immigration.

The place premium

Not surprisingly, over one million immigrants enter the US each year and very many more would like to come (Clemens 2011, p. 83). We take this for granted, but we should linger over this striking fact. In a dynamic, global economy, in which capital, goods and services are all mobile across borders, differences in labour income should not be so persistently large. Workers in poor countries should not have to leave their home countries to raise their incomes significantly. Markets can come to them: capital investment and technology is extremely mobile and responsive to opportunities; and free trade in goods and services allows the poor greater access to world markets than at any time in world history. This raises a crucial question: why does opportunity *not* come to them?

Consider the following statistics, from Kennan (2013):[12]

- A Filipino worker, educated in the Philippines and working in the US, earns four times more than a Filipino with the same education who remains in the Philippines.
- A Mexican worker, educated in Mexico and working in the US, earns two-and-a-half times more than a Mexican with the same education who remains in Mexico.

We find these differences across every country that sends immigrants to Europe and the US: the same person, with the same education in the home country, can earn much more in a developed country than at home.

The characteristics of immigrants relative to those who stay at home cannot explain differences this large (Clemens 2011). Education does not explain this gap, since both emigrants and those who stay are educated in the home country. Neither are barriers to trade severe enough to account for it. Perhaps differences in pay reflect something other than differences in productivity. Maybe Mexican workers are equally productive in Mexico and the US, but simply get paid a lot less in Mexico. However, this is implausible because capital investment and trade (unlike labour) move relatively easily across borders. If workers in Mexico were as productive as Mexican workers in the US, but were paid a lot less, demand for Mexican workers to work in Mexico would be large and expanding; investments in Mexico would be more profitable; and those higher profits would be as persistent as the wage differences. But this does not seem to be the case. Returns to capital are roughly equal across countries (Caselli and Feyrer 2007). There is no ongoing shortage of workers in the developing world.

Something about the home country itself makes the same worker less productive at home than abroad. The same Filipino worker is four times more productive in the US than at home. The same

---

12 Table 1, fourth and fifth columns. Kennan takes his estimates from Clemens et al. (2008).

Mexican worker is two-and-a-half times more productive in the US than in Mexico. Something about countries of origin makes workers less productive there, but does not similarly reduce the marginal productivity of capital investment in those countries. The technical explanation for this disparity is 'labour-augmenting productivity' in the developed world (Kennan 2013, p. L2). Clemens et al. (2008) call this 'the place premium', although from the point of view of the country of origin it is a 'place penalty' on labour.

What accounts for this 'penalty'? The most obvious culprits are economic policies and institutions of the sending countries that suppress labour productivity (Olson 1996; Clemens 2011). In developing countries it is difficult to start new enterprises and protect them from appropriation by the powerful and politically connected. Justice and the rule of law are applied unequally. In short, workers and entrepreneurs are unable to take full advantage of the opportunities that present themselves. Their native lands give them little opportunity to exercise their economic initiative and employ their skills.[13]

If a worker becomes more productive simply by moving to the US or Europe, then the potential economic benefits from immigration are enormous – much larger than the benefits to free trade, of increased education or of free movement of capital (Clemens 2011).[14] There are trillions of dollars of benefits for poor workers at stake.

The place premium puts human work and human enterprise at the heart of immigration policy. A worker who immigrates to the US

---

13 There is abundant economic evidence on this point. However, perhaps more compelling than the books and academic journal articles that have been written about the subject is this Ted talk, which narrates the personal experience of Magatte Wade and those she tries to employ in Senegal (https://www.ted.com/talks/magatte_wade_why_it_s_too_hard_to_start _a_business_in_africa_and_how_to_change_it).

14 Clemens (2011) estimates that 'the emigration of less than 5 per cent of the population of poor regions would bring global gains exceeding the gains from total elimination of all policy barriers to merchandise trade and all barriers to capital flows' (p. 84). See Kennan (2013, 2017) for similarly large estimated effects.

gets far more than an increase in income: he or she does not just happen to get paid more. Higher wages reflect higher productivity. He or she produces more and contributes more. In the country of origin, the worker is not robbed of his wages, but paid in accordance with low productivity. Productivity may be so low that workers in their country of origin may be working in inhumane conditions. Workers are deprived of their productivity and must emigrate to realize it.

To use the language of Catholic social teaching, by migrating to developed countries poor migrants do not just 'have' more income: this 'having' reflects their ability to 'be' more – more productive, more creative, more responsible for themselves both in and out of the labour force. Their low incomes in their native land reflects a lack of 'being' as well as a lack of 'having'. In *Laborem exercens*, John Paul II asserted that 'human work is ... the essential key to the social question' (*Laborem exercens*, 3). By work man realizes himself as a person, develops himself and contributes to his community. The great benefit of work to the human person and to human community bolsters the 'right to economic initiative', the third argument for a right to migrate discussed above. The denial of this right leads many to 'opt out of national life', and emigrate (*Laborem exercens*, 15). It generates a poverty which is not purely economic (*Laborem exercens*, 9):

> [T]he 'poor' appear under various forms ...; in many cases they appear as a result of the violation of the dignity of human work: either because the opportunities for human work are limited as a result of the scourge of unemployment, or because a low value is put on work and the rights that flow from it ...

The place premium, and the suppression of economic initiative that it reflects, puts the human stakes of immigration into stark perspective. Many think of the benefits of immigration to immigrants as a sort of redistribution of world income – of rich countries giving something of their wealth to immigrants. The economics of immigration suggest that this is not true. What is happening instead is much more morally significant. The movement of immigrants from countries where their economic initiative is suppressed to countries where they can be more productive is an expansion of opportunity, not a redistribution of income. Pope Francis urges developed countries to welcome migrants and ensure that they 'are empowered to achieve their potential as human beings, in all the dimensions which constitute the humanity intended by the Creator' (WDMR 2018). The tremendous increase in incomes is closely connected to the 'empowerment' of immigrant workers.

Gainers and possible losers from immigration

Research reviewed in the last section confirms that immigration to the US has been and still is an aggregate economic benefit to Americans. Its benefits and costs are distributed unevenly, however. Those who compete most directly with immigrants (unskilled natives) bear some of the cost. These costs are small in dollar terms: at most a 2–3 per cent decrease in earnings growth over a period of 10 years. Even this small negative effect does not appear to persist into the long run, as capital investment catches up with the immigrant influx.

Compare these dollar costs with the startlingly large benefits for the immigrants themselves. A poor immigrant sees his or her earnings grow by 200–1,000 per cent. This growth represents, more or less, an increase in productivity. By coming to the US, immigrants escape institutional and legal environments that artificially suppress labour productivity.

Dollar-for-dollar comparisons of costs and benefits clearly favour immigration, especially since immigrants do not appear to be a larger burden on government finances than natives, and they appear to assimilate steadily into US labour markets and culture. Economists are comfortable with these efficiency arguments: when the economic pie increases, those who gain can compensate those whose incomes decrease, and everyone can have more.

Should we make the comparison between the benefits to immigrants and the costs to native workers on a dollar-for-dollar basis? In Yuengert (2004) I concluded that we could only argue *against* immigration if we were willing to 'weigh the wage decrease for native unskilled workers more heavily than the significant increase in wages that is enjoyed by immigrants from much poorer countries'. In other words, we would have to be willing to count the costs to native unskilled workers more than the much larger benefits to poor immigrants. I wrote this somewhat dismissively – surely we should not prevent poor immigrants from quadrupling their incomes simply to keep unskilled natives' wages from stagnating temporarily?

In light of the well-documented plight of low-wage native workers today (Murray 2012; Putnam 2015; Case and Deaton 2020), I have found myself returning to this passage frequently. Should we care more about small predicted effects of immigration on the native poor? I am aware of the argument that immigration ought to be a win–win for unskilled natives and immigrants: a dynamic economy that is open to everyone can be good for everyone. Appropriate transfers, such as through funding for retraining or welfare payments, can compensate poor natives for lower incomes and lost work. Indeed, many government programmes have attempted to alleviate the plight of the unskilled working poor in just this way. Still, many unskilled natives do not think it has worked out in their favour. Their consumption may in fact be higher, but perhaps a better-paying job would be better than a package of transfer payments. In the US and in some parts of Europe the effects of immigration on this native population appears to be fueling the rise of nationalist movements (Moriconi et al. 2018).

The plight of the native poor has many interrelated causes. Empirical evidence points to, for example, technological change, family breakdown, a failed education system and free trade. Of these, immigration may be the least important. Moreover, a restriction on immigration would not by itself improve the lot of working class natives. Immigration restrictions are often proposed as part of a larger programme (Cass 2018).[15]

---

15 Jacks and Tang (2018) document a close connection between trade and immigration.

CONCLUSION: BALANCING OBLIGATIONS TO GAINERS AND POSSIBLE LOSERS FROM MIGRATION

Lest the empirical arguments distract us from the separate question of moral evaluation, I will state the question that we must address as a hypothetical: if we were to agree that immigration imposed costs on poor natives which cannot be adequately compensated through transfers and retraining, would we ever be justified in restricting immigration, even though the material benefits to poor immigrants were greater than the material costs to poor natives? We can only reach this conclusion if our poor, our unskilled, count for more in our deliberations than the poor and unskilled of other countries. Is it ever defensible to value the interests of our poor fellow citizens more than the interests of the poor from other places? What claims of solidarity and justice do our fellow citizens have on us and on our government relative to claims of justice and solidarity of foreigners? This is the question that goes unasked, both in Catholic social teaching and in immigration debates.

The common good of a country is not simply its aggregate income. If it were, economic efficiency would dictate open borders with appropriate transfer payments to the losers from immigration. The common good of a country includes the flourishing of all of its members, particularly the poorest. If some are struggling, the common good of the whole is not achieved. Aquinas (1948, II.II, 26) outlines an order in human charity – God first, followed by self, family and neighbour. The crucial question for citizens of developing countries is whether a neighbour who is a fellow citizen (or even a fellow resident non-citizen) is closer in the order of charity than a neighbour who lives in another country. If a country has a common good separate from some universal common good, then fellow citizens and residents should count for more. I do not know how much more, but more.

There is widespread hostility to arguments in support of policy preferences for fellow citizens: these preferences are often characterised as dangerously nationalistic, chauvinistic and bigoted. The cosmopolitan left condemns claims that there are trade-offs between the poor of different nations: they are regarded as distractions from the structural changes needed to lift up all the poor. Supporters of free trade, often characterized as being on the 'right' of politics, dismiss pleas to protect 'our poor' as mere smokescreens to mask a cynical struggle for inefficient restraints on trade. Both sides assert that the proposed trade-off between immigrant and native poor is illusory and need not be faced squarely.

Catholic social teaching offers some help in thinking through this conflict, but the tone of the teaching is highly suspicious of national common goods.[16] The *Compendium* (170) acknowledges the moral weight of a nation's common good, but warns that it must not be closed to the broader common good among nations and peoples. In *Fratelli tutti*, Pope Francis explores the conflict in some detail. He asserts that the common good balances a love for one's native land and a generous openness to those outside one's borders (*Fratelli tutti*, 142–42). Nevertheless, like his predecessors he is swift to warn against a 'xenophobic mentality' (39), 'ancestral fears' (27), an 'instinct for self-defense' (41), and 'local narcissism' (146).

There are four reasons for the ambivalence of the Catholic Church towards national common goods. Firstly, the nation state was born in conflict with the Church, and is buttressed by political philosophies in which an aggregate of individual interests or a general will supplant the idea of a common good. Secondly, there is ample ground for suspicion about the nation state. Nationalism in combination with ideology has generated wars, discrimination and untold suffering. The Catholic human rights tradition developed to defend human dignity from the state. In addition, the Catholic Church is universal: it is not bounded by any state, and has a common good that embraces all of humanity and creation. Consequently, immigrants who fall between national borders rank high among the concerns of the Church (*Evangelii gaudium*, 210).

A further reason that Catholic social teaching is somewhat mute on the trade-offs between the well-being of poor migrants and the

---

16   See, for example, Pope John Paul II's address to the People of Poland (http://www.vatican.va/content/john-paul-ii/en/letters/1978/documents/hf_jp-ii_let_19781024_polacchi.html).

well-being of unskilled natives is an implicit assumption that there need be no trade-off if host nations were fully committed to their own and the universal common good. Catholic social teaching is optimistic, assuming that people of goodwill, with converted hearts and minds, can adequately address most social problems. If developed countries were governed according to the principles of Catholic social teaching, they would be able to both welcome large numbers of poor immigrants and at the same time address the unequal burdens of immigration in a just way.

Nevertheless, finite and fallen human beings often fall short, and are unable to satisfy fully the demands of justice and charity. What if even people of goodwill can address the inequities in developed countries only imperfectly? Alternatively, what if developed countries fail to address these inequalities, through neglect or indifference? In either case, immigration may pit the interests of poor migrants against those of the native poor. Catholic social teaching offers little guidance for second-best scenarios like this.

The benefits to poor migrants of moving to the developed world are enormous. These benefits are not just material. In the face of this, it is difficult to resist the conclusion that developed countries should embrace mass immigration, even if it imposes burdens on the native poor. This is a powerful argument, but perhaps the native poor deserve more consideration from their fellow citizens. We need to hear more from Catholic social teaching on the demands of national common goods – on reasonable attachments to our fellow citizens – so we can address the challenges of choosing second-best solutions in relation to migration in an imperfect world.

The Church's suspicion of unhealthy nationalism is justified, but an instinctive rejection of all claims of the importance of nationhood and patriotism can be dangerous and destabilizing: communities are built up from the bottom, starting with the family. The Church should engage, challenge and encourage anyone making reasoned, humane arguments in favour of the autonomy of the nation state and for particular obligations towards fellow citizens (Hazony 2018; Cass 2018; Reno 2019). Such people are claiming intellectual ground from autocratic populists who appeal to nationalism and the bonds of citizenship for illiberal and inhumane ends. If the appeals of the autocrats are not balanced by reflection on a healthier respect for the nation, the autocrats may continue to gain strength. Catholic social teaching should weigh in on this debate.

REFERENCES

Aquinas, T. (1948) *Summa Theologica* (trans. Fathers of the English Dominican Province). New York: Benziger Brothers.

Blau, F., and Mackie, C. (eds) (2017) *The Economic and Fiscal Consequences of Immigration*. Washington, DC: National Academies Press.

Borjas, G. (2006) Immigration in high-skill labor markets: the impact of foreign students on the earnings of doctorates. NBER Working Paper 12085. Cambridge, MA: National Bureau of Economic Research.

Borjas, G. (2019) Immigration and economic growth. NBER Working Paper 25836. Cambridge, MA: National Bureau of Economic Research.

Burchardi, K., Chaney, T., Hassan, T., Tarquinio, L., and Terry, S. (2020) Immigration, innovation, and growth. NBER Working Paper 27075. Cambridge, MA: National Bureau of Economic Research.

Butcher, K., and Piehl, A. (2007) Why are immigrants' incarceration rates so low? Evidence on selective immigration, deterrence, and deportation. NBER Working Paper 13229. Cambridge, MA: National Bureau of Economic Research.

Case, A., and Deaton, A. (2020) *Deaths of Despair and the Future of Capitalism*. Princeton University Press.

Caselli, F., and Feyrer, J. (2007) The marginal product of capital. *Quarterly Journal of Economics* 122(2): 535–68.

Cass, O. (2018) *The Once and Future Worker: A Vision for the Renewal of Work in America*. New York: Encounter Books.

Clemens, M. (2011) Economics and emigration: trillion-dollar bills on the sidewalk? *Journal of Economic Perspectives* 25(3): 83–106.

Clemens, M., Montenegro, C., and Pritchett, L. (2008) The place premium: wage differences for identical workers across the US border. World Bank Policy Research Working Paper 4671. Washington, DC: The World Bank.

Giuliano, P., and Tabellini, M. (2020) The seeds of ideology: historical immigration and political preferences in the United States. NBER

Working Paper 27238. Cambridge, MA: National Bureau of Economic Research.

Goodhart, D. (2017) *The Road to Somewhere: The Populist Revolt and the Future of Politics*. London: C. Hurst and Company.

Hazony, Y. (2018) *The Virtue of Nationalism*. New York: Basic Books.

Jacks, D., and Tang, J. (2018) Trade and immigration 1870–2010. NBER Working Paper 25010. Cambridge, MA: National Bureau of Economic Research.

Kennan, J. (2013) Open borders. *Review of Economic Dynamics* 16: L1–L13.

Kennan, J. (2017) Open borders in the European Union and beyond: migration flows and labor market implications. NBER Working Paper 23048. Cambridge, MA: National Bureau of Economic Research.

Moriconi, S., Peri, G., and Turati, R. (2018) Skill of the immigrants and vote of the natives: immigration and nationalism in European Elections 2007–2016. NBER Working Paper 25077. Cambridge, MA: National Bureau of Economic Research.

Murray, C. (2012) *Coming Apart: The State of White America 1960–2010*. New York: Crown Publishing.

Olson, M. (1996) Big bills left on the sidewalk: why some nations are rich, and others poor. *Journal of Economic Perspectives* 10(2): 3–24.

Peri, G., Shih, K., and Sparber, C. (2015) STEM workers, H1B visas, and productivity in U.S. cities. *Journal of Labor Economics* 33(S1 Part 2): S225–S255.

Pontifical Council for Justice and Peace (2005) *Compendium of the Social Doctrine of the Church*. London: Burns & Oates.

Powell, B. (ed.) (2015) *The Economics of Immigration: Market-based Approaches, Social Policy, and Public Policy*. Oxford University Press.

Putnam, R. (2015) *Our Kids: The American Dream in Crisis*. New York: Simon and Schuster.

Reno, R. R. (2019) *The Return of the Strong Gods: Nationalism, Populism, and the Future of the West*. New York: Regnery Gateway.

Smith, J., and Edmonston, B. (eds) (1997) *The New Americans: Economic, Demographic, and Fiscal Effects of Immigration*. Washington, DC: National Academies Press.

Yuengert, A. M. (2004) Inhabiting the land: the case for the right to migrate. Christian Social Thought Series, no. 6, Acton Institute, Grand Rapids, MI.

PAPAL ENCYCLICALS AND OTHER CHURCH DOCUMENTS

Francis (2020) *Fratelli tutti*, encyclical letter (http://www.vatican.va/con
tent/francesco/en/encyclicals/documents/papa-francesco_20201003
_enciclica-fratelli-tutti.html).

Francis (2019) Message for the 105th World Day of Migrants and Refugees
2019 (http://www.vatican.va/content/francesco/en/messages/migration/
documents/papa-francesco_20190527_world-migrants-day-2019.html).

Francis (2018) Message for the 104th World Day of Migrants and Refugees
2018 (http://www.vatican.va/content/francesco/en/messages/migration/
documents/papa-francesco_20170815_world-migrants-day-2018.html).

Francis (2015) Message for 101st World Day of Migrants and Refugees
2015 (http://www.vatican.va/content/francesco/en/messages/migration/
documents/papa-francesco_20140903_world-migrants-day-2015.
html).

Francis (2014) Message World Day of Migrants and Refugees 2014 (http://
www.vatican.va/content/francesco/en/messages/migration/documents/
papa-francesco_20130805_world-migrants-day.html).

Francis (2013) *Evangelii gaudium*, apostolic exhortation (http://www.vati
can.va/content/francesco/en/apost_exhortations/documents/papa-franc
esco_esortazione-ap_20131124_evangelii-gaudium.html).

Benedict XVI (2013) Message for World Day of Migrants and Refugees 2013
(https://www.vatican.va/content/benedict-xvi/en/messages/migration/
documents/hf_ben-xvi_mes_20121012_world-migrants-day.html).

Benedict XVI (2011) Message for World Day of Migrants and Refugees 2011
(https://www.vatican.va/content/benedict-xvi/en/messages/migration/
documents/hf_ben-xvi_mes_20100927_world-migrants-day.html).

John Paul II (2004) Message for 90th World Day of Migrants and Refugees
2004 (http://www.vatican.va/content/john-paul-ii/en/messages/migrati
on/documents/hf_jp-ii_mes_20031223_world-migration-day-2004
.html).

John Paul II (2001) Message for the 87th World Day of Migration 2001
(http://www.vatican.va/content/john-paul-ii/en/messages/migration/
documents/hf_jp-ii_mes_20010213_world-migration-day-2001.html).

John Paul II (1998) Message for World Day of Migration 1998 (http://www
.vatican.va/content/john-paul-ii/en/messages/migration/documents/hf
_jp-ii_mes_09111997_world-migration-day-1998.html).

John Paul II (1993) Message for World Day of Migration 1993 (https://www
.vatican.va/content/john-paul-ii/it/messages/migration/documents/hf
_jp-ii_mes_19930806_world-migration-day-93-94.html).

John Paul II (1987) *Sollicitudo rei socialis*, encyclical letter (http://www.vati
can.va/content/john-paul-ii/en/encyclicals/documents/hf_jp-ii_enc_30
121987_sollicitudo-rei-socialis.html).

John Paul II (1981) *Laborem exercens*, encyclical letter (http://www.vati
can.va/content/john-paul-ii/en/encyclicals/documents/hf_jp-ii_enc_14
091981_laborem-exercens.html).

John Paul II (1978) Letter 'To the People of Poland' (http://www.vatican
.va/content/john-paul-ii/en/letters/1978/documents/hf_jp-ii_let_19781
024_polacchi.html).

Paul VI (1967) *Populorum progressio*, encyclical letter (http://www.vatican
.va/content/paul-vi/en/encyclicals/documents/hf_p-vi_enc_26031967
_populorum.html).

John XXIII (1963) *Pacem in terris*, encyclical letter (http://www.vatican.va/
content/john-xxiii/en/encyclicals/documents/hf_j-xxiii_enc_11041963
_pacem.html).

John XXIII (1961) *Mater et magistra*, encyclical letter (http://www.vatican
.va/content/john-xxiii/en/encyclicals/documents/hf_j-xxiii_enc_15051
961_mater.html).

Leo XIII (1891) *Rerum novarum,* encyclical letter (http://www.vatican.va/
content/leo-xiii/en/encyclicals/documents/hf_l-xiii_enc_15051891_re
rum-novarum.html).

Vatican II (1965) *Gaudium et spes,* Pastoral Constitution on the Church in
the World (https://www.vatican.va/archive/hist_councils/ii_vatican_co
uncil/documents/vat-ii_const_19651207_gaudium-et-spes_en.html).

CHAPTER 5

The environment, Catholic social teaching and public policy[1]

Philip Booth

The publication of *Laudato si'* in 2015 was hailed as a landmark by many in the Catholic Church and beyond. Indeed, it was the first social encyclical to focus on the environment. However, an examination of the Church's teaching on the environment will demonstrate that there is remarkable continuity in relation to this topic.

The first part of this chapter will focus on the continuity of the Church's teaching on the environment. The second part will respond to Pope Francis's call for dialogue and the discussion of *Laudato si'* is offered in that spirit. The analysis will be set in the context both of developments in economics and of earlier Catholic social thought on issues which might seem unrelated to the environment but which are, in fact, closely connected. It is hoped that, by contributing to dialogue, and responding to the challenge of the encyclical, we can improve the Catholic contribution to discussion of public policy issues in this field.

---

1   Although the material has been updated and changed substantially, there are overlaps between later sections of this chapter and Booth (2017).

LAUDATO SI': CONTINUITY WITH CHURCH TEACHING

When a papal social encyclical is produced, the media tend to scour the document for statements on politics and public policy.[2] In doing so, they tend to look at the document through a secular lens. Of course, statements on public policy questions are important. But even more important in a social encyclical is the way in which Catholic social teaching frames issues theologically, philosophically and anthropologically. *Laudato si'* is a good example of this. Within this document was an important discussion about our relationship with the natural environment which was consistent with earlier Catholic teaching and with the Catholic Church's understanding of natural law.

Laudato si' begins by reflecting on the harm we have inflicted on the earth. Pope Francis describes the natural environment as a 'sister'. The pope reminds us that our bodies are made up of the elements of the earth and that we breathe and drink the products of the earth. In other words, we have a relationship with the earth which is intrinsic. We should cherish and nurture the earth and not plunder it violently.

In paragraph 33, Pope Francis notes that different species are not merely resources to be exploited but also have value in themselves because they are created creatures. Of course, they have a lesser value than that of a human person, but they have value. Considering these insights should help us understand how a rightly ordered life would treat the earth, the natural environment and other creatures.

Quoting Thomas Aquinas, *Laudato si'* notes that it was through the intention of the Creator that the whole variety that we see in the creatures of the earth came about (86):

> Saint Thomas Aquinas wisely noted that multiplicity and variety 'come from the intention of the first agent' who willed that 'what was wanting to one in the representation of the divine goodness might be supplied by another', inasmuch as God's goodness 'could

---

2   The author of this chapter, for example, was invited onto the BBC programme *Newsnight* the evening before *Laudato si'* was issued to debate the pope's expected rejection of carbon trading.

not be represented fittingly by any one creature'. Hence we need to grasp the variety of things in their multiple relationships. We understand better the importance and meaning of each creature if we contemplate it within the entirety of God's plan.

Again referring to Aquinas,[3] Pope Francis points out that we are more wholesome as people if we understand our proper relationship with the rest of creation (240):

> [T]he world, created according to the divine model, is a web of relationships. Creatures tend towards God, and in turn it is proper to every living being to tend towards other things … This leads us not only to marvel at the manifold connections existing among creatures, but also to discover a key to our own fulfilment. The human person grows more, matures more and is sanctified more to the extent that he or she enters into relationships, going out from themselves to live in communion with God, with others and with all creatures.

As well as being consistent with Thomistic teaching and natural law, the encyclical is also consistent with modern Church teaching on the environment. Perhaps the first document published by the Catholic Church which addresses modern ecological problems was *Octogesima adveniens*, published in 1971. Pope Paul VI warned that we risked destroying nature and then becoming a victim of its degradation. He refers to pollution, refuse and the absolute destructive capacity of the human race that was creating an environment which might well become intolerable (21).

Paul VI's successor, John Paul II, raised the issue of the environment in his first encyclical, *Redemptor hominis*. Typically, he developed important anthropological and philosophical insights stating (15):

> Man often seems to see no other meaning in his natural environment than what serves for immediate use and consumption. Yet it

---

3   The references are in footnote 171 of *Laudato si'*.

was the Creator's will that man should communicate with nature as an intelligent and noble 'master' and 'guardian', and not as a heedless 'exploiter' and 'destroyer'.

This criticism of consumption for its own sake is a common theme throughout John Paul II's encyclicals. The importance of our being both masters and guardians of the environment arises from our nature as human persons who can reason while taking responsibility for creation.

John Paul II again related environmental questions to the problem of over-consumption and to the dangers of 'having' rather than 'being' in his encyclical *Sollicitudo rei socialis*. Interestingly, he did so in a slightly positive light, writing (26):

> Among today's positive signs we must also mention a greater realization of the limits of available resources, and of the need to respect the integrity and the cycles of nature and to take them into account when planning for development, rather than sacrificing them to certain demagogic ideas about the latter. Today this is called ecological concern.

John Paul II stressed that life itself is a gift which must be respected. He therefore joined what came to be called the 'moral ecology' with the need for respect for the environment. In other words, it does not make sense to debase the human person and not be open to the transmission of life and disposed towards the protection of life from conception to natural death while purporting to have concern for other aspects of the natural environment. In this respect, we should beware false green movements that see the environment incompletely, seemingly forgetting the human element.

And Pope Francis's immediate predecessor, Benedict XVI, referenced environmental concerns in a number of homilies and written statements as well as in his social encyclical *Caritas in veritate*. In that document he wrote (48):

> Today the subject of development is also closely related to the duties arising from our relationship to the natural environment. The

environment is God's gift to everyone, and in our use of it we have a responsibility towards the poor, towards future generations and towards humanity as a whole. When nature, including the human being, is viewed as the result of mere chance or evolutionary deter- minism, our sense of responsibility wanes. In nature, the believer recognizes the wonderful result of God's creative activity, which we may use responsibly to satisfy our legitimate needs, material or otherwise, while respecting the intrinsic balance of creation.

This raises the question of stewardship, but also the fact that our concern for the environment should result from the fact that it is God's creation for which we should care: it is a gift for us to use creatively for our benefit. But, like all gifts, we should not abuse it. Pope Francis also addresses this issue specifically in his theological treatment of ecology.

In the theological reflections in *Laudato si'*, Pope Francis raises many similar themes to those raised by his predecessors. In para- graph 67 *Laudato si'* explains how man having 'dominion' over the earth does not mean that we should be domineering and destructive, but that we should till the earth. The encyclical further states that, endowed with intelligence, we need to respect the laws of nature and the letter uses the psalms and other books of the bible to reinforce that point.

While emphasizing that man is superior to all other creatures, the document quotes the Catechism (339) which summarizes the Christian reality that (*Laudato si'* (69) and Catechism of the Catho- lic Church 1994):

> Each creature possesses its own particular goodness and perfection ... Each of the various creatures, willed in its own being, reflects in its own way a ray of God's infinite wisdom and goodness. Man must therefore respect the particular goodness of every creature, to avoid any disordered use of things.

Laudato si' does not depart from the teaching of Pope Francis's predecessors on the fundamental treatment of the theology of the environment. There is a continuity in Church teaching that we would expect. There is also a strong natural law element to *Laudato si'*. It is clear that Francis's writing is based on a starting point of how human persons, as created beings, ought to order their lives in relation to God's creation.

FROM THEORY TO PRACTICE: SOLIDARITY AND DISTRIBUTIVE JUSTICE

As with all social encyclicals, *Laudato si'* was not simply a discussion of theory. There were calls for action, both at the individual level and at the level of government policy. There was also a call for dialogue.[4] This is important. Catholic social teaching on specific issues is often contingent on time and place, especially in relation to practical details. Its development relies on the virtue of prudence, which requires deliberation, and it is often informed by other disciplines. Indeed, Bishops' conferences from around the world had an input into the document.

Laudato si' struck a very pessimistic note on climate change in general and on its impact on the world's poor in particular. Pope Francis stated (23):

> A very solid scientific consensus indicates that we are presently witnessing a disturbing warming of the climatic system. In recent decades this warming has been accompanied by a constant rise in the sea level and, it would appear, by an increase of extreme weather events, even if a scientifically determinable cause cannot be assigned to each particular phenomenon.

In a more recent apostolic exhortation, *Laudate deum* this message was repeated with even greater force. Despite criticisms from some quarters, this statement is difficult to dispute. Some would argue that the scientific consensus is wrong, but this is an accurate description of that consensus.

---

4   Including three times in the introduction. The word 'dialogue' appears 23 times in the document.

Pope Francis sees this, and other environmental questions, as issues of intergenerational justice a subject which forms a whole section of the encyclical. Intergenerational justice is a form of distributive justice. Distributive justice is that form of justice by which the goods of this world are divided according to appropriate criteria. There is no systematic treatment of how this might relate to future generations in Catholic social teaching. However, it would seem clear that there is no application of this principle that would conclude that it is just for one generation to enrich itself in such a way that it imposes costs on future generations without conferring any equivalent benefit. Or, as *Laudato si'* expresses is: 'Intergenerational solidarity is not optional, but rather a basic question of justice, since the world we have received also belongs to those who will follow us' (159). Of course, we should enjoy the fruits of the earth. However, we should restrain ourselves when enjoying them so that future generations can obtain what is justly theirs.

This is not an innovation in Church teaching. In his 2010 World Peace Day message, Pope Benedict XVI wrote: '*A greater sense of intergenerational solidarity* is urgently needed. Future generations cannot be saddled with the cost of our use of common environmental resources' (8; emphasis in original). And, rather less specifically, the Compendium of the Social Doctrine of the Church had already stated: '*Responsibility for the environment, the common heritage of mankind, extends not only to present needs but also to those of the future.* "We have inherited from past generations, and we have benefited from the work of our contemporaries; for this reason we have obligations towards all, and we cannot refuse to interest ourselves in those who will come after us, to enlarge the human family"' (467; emphasis in original).[5]

Another way in which environmental issues can be connected to distributive justice, solidarity and the common good is suggested by Pope Francis in relation environmental damage in poor countries caused by actions in rich countries. *Laudato si'* relates this both

---

5   This quotation itself quotes from *Populorum progressio* thus going even further back. This reference is listed as Pontifical Council for Justice and Peace (2005) in the references.

to natural resource use and the impact of global warming, which, argues Pope Francis, is largely caused by over-consumption in richer countries while many of the impacts are felt by poorer countries. This is described as an 'ecological debt' (51).

PRACTICAL POLICY CONCERNS

Some have criticized Pope Francis for taking a view on environmental questions, especially climate change. It is true that it is legitimate for Catholics to take different positions on the economics, politics and the science of environmental issues, including climate change: disagreement and dialogue on prudential issues is to be encouraged. However, it is also reasonable for the Church, in her social encyclicals, to apply what she regards as the best of the physical and social sciences and combine them with philosophy and theology to make statements that involve prudential judgements. Such judgements may then change over time, or at least the emphasis may change.[6] As Charles (1998, vol. II, p. 15) states, the magisterial authority of the encyclicals extends to matters of moral principle and their implications only. On those matters, it is binding on the conscience of members of the Church. Practical and other related matters, according to Charles, can be judged on the basis of the arguments presented.[7] It is in this spirit and in response to Pope Francis's call for dialogue that the remainder of the chapter proposes some additional perspective on the issues raised in *Laudato si'*.

Private property and the environment

The concept of private property has always been important in Catholic social thought. There is legitimate dispute about its place in the

---

6 Note, for example, the difference, in tone at least, between *Populorum progressio* (58) and *Centesimus annus* (33) on the question of trade and protectionism.

7 This is also pointed out clearly in *Centesimus annus* (3). It is often debated whether social encyclicals fall within the magisterium. That would be to miss the point. It is the nature of reasoning which determines whether particular statements within an encyclical fall within the magisterium.

thinking of the early Church (see Chroust and Affeldt 1951; Bergida 2020). However, in the thought of both Thomas Aquinas and the Late Scholastics there is no doubt that private property was regarded as important for promoting the common good (see Charles 1998, vol. 1, p. 207; Alves and Moreira 2010). In Pope Leo XIII's encyclical, *Rerum novarum*, the importance of private property was stressed repeatedly. Private property was connected to work and responsibility: people would be more likely to cultivate what they owned and would also be more likely to work if they could keep some of their wages in the form of property. And if ownership of property were clear, people would be more likely to take responsibility for it. In *Laborem exercens* (12), Pope John Paul II suggested that it is through taking ownership of the various riches of nature, including sea, land or space, that we are able, through work, to cultivate the natural world and make it bear fruit.

However, Catholic social teaching has emphasized that the principle of private property must be subordinate to the promotion of the common good, and the question has been raised as to whether private property might undermine the protection of the environment.

Laudato si' discussed the issue of private property rights in 93–95. In doing so, it repeated the conclusions of *Sollicitudo rei socialis* and *Centesimus annus* and gave the impression that private property rights were problematical, rather than helpful, in promoting the common good when it came to environmental resources. The more recent encyclical, *Fratelli tutti*, published in 2020, emphasized so emphatically that private property rights were subordinate to other principles of Catholic social teaching that many commentators were left with the firm impression that Pope Francis was attacking the institution of private property, though there are also some affirmations of private property in that encyclical (see below).

In *Centesimus annus*, John Paul II specifically raises what he describes as the 'ecological question' in relation to private property (37). He then suggests that 'It is the task of the State to provide for the defense and preservation of common goods such as the natural and human environments, which cannot be safeguarded simply by market forces' (40). In doing so, he seems to be calling into question the ability of private ownership to protect the environment. *Laudato si'* reiterates this statement and continues the discussion about private property and the protection of the environment with a negative emphasis. Pope Francis says that the Christian tradition has never recognized property rights as absolute or inviolable and that they must be subordinated to a social purpose. Specifically, he says: 'The natural environment is a collective good, the patrimony of all humanity and the responsibility of everyone. If we make something our own, it is only to administer it for the good of all' (95).

Laudato si' moves on not to address the subject again. So, Pope Francis leaves unconsidered the question: 'are private property rights the best way to deal with the protection of the natural environment for the good of all?' This is the crucial question.

In the period between the publication of *Sollicitudo rei socialis* and *Laudato si'* a huge amount of work has been undertaken on the importance of property rights for environmental conservation. Interestingly, this confirms the Church's general position on the importance of property rights for the promotion of the common good.

We could compare the statement in *Laudato si'*: 'The natural environment is a collective good, the patrimony of all humanity and the responsibility of everyone' with one of the justifications for private property suggested by Aquinas. He stated that human affairs are more efficiently organized if each person has his own responsibility to discharge and that there would be chaos if everybody cared for everything (Aquinas 1965, IIa, Q 66, Art 2). *Rerum novarum* (7–9) also explained how persons cultivate what they own so that it is sustainable and will provide sustenance for the future. This is confirmed by modern economic work. The absence of property rights in environmental resources leads to a situation whereby the environment is the responsibility of nobody and in which people bear no cost from destroying while obtaining no benefit from caring for the environment. On the other hand, private property rights can lead to effective stewardship.

The importance of ownership for promoting environmental conservation is illustrated by the idea of the 'tragedy of the commons'. This idea is often attributed to Garrett Hardin following the publication of an article with that title in the journal *Science* (Hardin 1968). The original work was a pamphlet by the economist William Forster Lloyd in which a situation was described whereby common land was open to grazing by all. The land would be over-grazed because a person would get the benefit of putting additional cattle on the land without bearing the cost that arises from over-grazing which would be shared by all. In the end the common land would be destroyed.

An even clearer example is that of the stewardship of fish stocks. A trawler taking extra tuna from the ocean will benefit, but the greater cost of taking the extra tuna in terms of lower levels of breeding will be shared between all trawler owners over the very long term. In practice, examples of fishing rights being tradable and privately owned, such as in Iceland, have led to fishing grounds thriving (see, for example, Gissurarson 2015), whereas the unclear definition of fishing rights has led to the devastation of fish stocks.[8]

If an environmental resource is owned, the owner both bears the cost and gains the benefit of over-exploitation. This is not to say that all environmental resources that are privately owned will always be managed sustainably or that private property rights are the only way to deal with these problems: state regulation can be used too. However, the state regulation of every environmental resource, such as fields, fisheries and forests, would be impractical and has not always given rise to good results. Certainly, private ownership and the enforcement and protection of property rights are compatible with environmental conservation. Indeed, Pope Francis himself recognized this when he noted in *Fratelli tutti* (in a section separate from the main discussion on private property (143)): 'All this brings out the positive meaning of the right to property: I care for and cultivate something that I possess, in such a way that it can contribute to the good of all.' This question is certainly worth deeper reflection within Catholic social thought and teaching, especially if we take account of the points raised in the discussion below.

---

8   See, for example, the report by the World Wildlife Fund (https://wwf.panda .org/our_work/oceans/problems/fisheries_management/).

Case study: property rights and pricing of water resources

The provision of water is a good example of the importance of private property rights and environmental conservation. There is general concern about the depletion of water resources. In *Laudato si'*, this was linked to privatization (30, emphasis in original):

> Even as the quality of available water is constantly diminishing, in some places there is a growing tendency, despite its scarcity, to privatize this resource, turning it into a commodity subject to the laws of the market. Yet *access to safe drinkable water is a basic and universal human right, since it is essential to human survival and, as such, is a condition for the exercise of other human rights.*

It is, though, under conditions of scarcity that markets and property rights are most important. When things are in abundance, we need neither markets nor property rights to allocate resources. The fact that water might be regarded as a human right and essential for survival does not change this. Food and shelter are regarded by the Church as basic human rights, but it is rarely argued there should not be markets, property rights or pricing of such goods and services.

The most important social functions of markets and property rights, when it comes to water, are to ensure that it is used with care and allocated towards its most important and valuable uses. In the developed world, for example, California has a water crisis and yet most homes in many cities do not have metered water and the government caps water charges. Furthermore, agriculture accounts for 80 per cent of water consumption in California but is only 2 per cent of economic activity, with land being flooded to grow crops such as rice and alfalfa. By one account, over the years, farmers have paid just 15 per cent of the capital costs of the federal system that delivers much of the water to farmers in California. Not surprisingly, only 4 per cent of water in the US is reused.

The situation is worse in many poorer countries. A report to the Indian Parliament suggests that the current subsidy system: 'Encourages using more inputs [in agriculture] such as fertiliser, water and power, to the detriment of soil quality, health and the environment. They also disproportionately benefit rich and large farmers.'[9]

The pricing of water resources and well-defined property rights encourages conservation, investment in preventing wastage, and the use of water for its most valuable ends in water-scarce countries. It also reduces the extent to which rich and well-connected business interests can obtain water subsidies at the expense of the population in general.

The absence of property rights in water also has the potential to sow the seeds of violent conflict in the coming century as water becomes more scarce. This takes us back to Aquinas's third point about private property: private property ensures peace, if it is divided and its ownership understood.

However, there may be an issue of semantics here. There have been significant problems with water privatization programmes, especially in poorer countries, including in countries the Bishops' Conferences of which contributed to *Laudato si'*. This has normally involved the private management of pre-existing water infrastructure in a public–private partnership, and it is true that such schemes have often been beset by corruption and inefficiency. It could be that *Laudato si'* is, implicitly, referring to the problems with such schemes when it mentions the problems of privatization. It should also be noted that the nationalization of water rights and provision is not incompatible with its efficient use as long as water is priced. Clarity of property rights may be more important than whether those rights are private or held by the state in this case.

The conclusion is not that water should always and everywhere be privately owned and priced but that:

- Pricing may well be important in ensuring that water resources are used for their most important social ends and in ensuring that they are not wasted where most scarce or appropriated by well-connected political interests.

9   https://www.thethirdpole.net/2016/02/28/government-underlines -indias-water-crisis/

- Private ownership is not intrinsically incompatible with the common good and may well promote it in this as in other areas.
- Clear ownership (even if by the state) may help prevent conflict.
- The state, in some way or other, must ensure that all have access to clean water for essential functions.
- If the state controls water resources, in most circumstances, if it is scarce, it should ensure that their use is priced.
- Good governance and the protection of property rights is important whatever the regime of ownership and some privatization schemes have been beset by corruption.

Although these may seem like economic rather than theological arguments, it is the sort of prudent reasoning that is important in Catholic social thought when making judgements about social institutions.

Good governance, the rule of law and environmental outcomes

While private ownership of environmental resources is consistent with the promotion of the common good, there may be circumstances in which state ownership or regulation is more practical either at the local or national level. Regardless of whether private or state ownership is adopted, it is vital that there is good governance and that property rights are effectively enforced through uncorrupt legal systems.

The problem of corruption is mentioned a number of times in *Laudato si'*, for example (197):

Often, politics itself is responsible for the disrepute in which it is held, on account of corruption and the failure to enact sound public policies. If in a given region the state does not carry out its responsibilities, some business groups can come forward in the guise of benefactors, wield real power, and consider themselves exempt from certain rules, to the point of tolerating different forms of organized crime, human trafficking, the drug trade and violence, all of which become very difficult to eradicate.

Corruption is problematic for environmental outcomes. It is easy to understand why that might be the case. Corruption might, for example, lead to bribes being paid to governmental authorities in return for permission to abuse environmental resources or to bribes being paid to law-enforcement agencies or the judiciary to prevent successful prosecution. It has been estimated that: 'almost half (49 per cent) of total tropical deforestation between 2000 and 2012 was due to illegal conversion for commercial agriculture' (Lawson 2014, p. 2). Sundstrom (2016) suggests that the academic evidence shows that bribery is a 'door opener' to illegal activities in forest management.[10]

The problem, however, is not just the direct relationship between bribery and environmental destruction as might happen when a corporate interest bribes law-enforcement agencies to ignore illegal logging. Good governance is important more generally. One interesting example is given by the difference between Haiti and the Dominican Republic, which share an island. Photographs of the border zone reveals a stark contrast between the Haitian and Dominican Republic sides.[11]

As the United Nations puts it, 'Environmental degradation in the worst affected parts of the Haitian border zone is almost completely irreversible, due to a near total loss of vegetation cover and productive topsoil across wide areas' (United Nations Environment Program 2013, p. 6). Haiti has around 4 per cent forest cover, a figure which is reducing. In contrast the Dominican Republic has around 40 per cent, a figure which has increased significantly over the last 20 years.[12]

---

10 For a less academic discussion see https://www.youtube.com/watch?time_co ntinue=156&v=JmNlmIM2HC8&feature=emb_logo.

11 Both sides of the border can be seen at https://www.unenvironment.org/ news-and-stories/story/haiti-and-dominican-republic-jointly-counter-env ironmental-degradation-and.

12 https://ourworldindata.org/forests#forest-cover-by-country

In effect, the Haitian side of the border is a huge, ungoverned and unowned commons. Haiti has been, for much of the recent past, a failed state. It is ranked the 12th most fragile state in the Foreign Policy Fragile State Index 2019[13] and has a terrible record of corruption (173 out of 183 in the Transparency International Corruption Perception Index).[14] In relation to Haiti, the 2022 Heritage Index of Economic Freedom states that 'legitimate property titles are often nonexistent'.[15]

Haiti and the Dominican Republic are a particularly interesting contrast because of their proximity to each other. However, there is abundant evidence that the lessons from this example can be generalized. For example, Araujo et al. (2009) argues: 'insecure property rights in land drive deforestation in the Brazilian Amazon'. They demonstrate a causal relationship which arises through several channels. Their results are strong and lead to the conclusion that an exogenous escalation in property rights insecurity brings a significant increase in the rate of deforestation.

The modern economics of this issue is really just a reiteration of the points that Aquinas makes and the points we have made regarding water. Private ownership and the institutions that surround it, provide incentives for sustainability. The value of a piece of land at any time reflects the value of all that can be yielded from the land in the indefinite future. The cost of damaging the resource is huge because it relates to all possible lost future production and not just to production over a year or two. However, people will not nurture property in a sustainable way if they believe that it is going to be polluted and plundered by others or if they believe that they are not going to enjoy the fruits of the investments and restraints necessary for sustainability.

Private property and uncorrupt juridical systems are not the only aspects of good governance which are important. Civil conflict and

---

13 https://fundforpeace.org/wp-content/uploads/2019/04/9511904-fragilesta tesindex.pdf

14 https://www.transparency.org/en/cpi/2019/results/table

15 https://www.heritage.org/index/pdf/book/2022_IndexOfEconomicFree dom_FINAL.pdf

war can both lead to the direct destruction of the environment and its plundering for short-term purposes and are not compatible with environmental stewardship. Rewilding projects in Mozambique demonstrate how a number of different governance solutions and property rights solutions have restored some of the environmental devastation of earlier wars.[16] But it should be noted that the destruction of the wildlife in the first place arose as a result of a war that rode roughshod over established property rights.

It is worth noting that, despite the pessimistic tone of *Laudato si'*, the rate of deforestation has slowed dramatically in recent years to around 0.1 per cent of the total each year. Looking more carefully at this trend, there is a strong relationship between net forest regeneration and both income and measures of governance and the protection of property rights. For example, no country ranked in the top 10 in the Heritage Foundation/Wall Street Journal Index of Economic Freedom has net forest loss and only two countries ranked in the bottom 10 have net forest gain. These questions of good governance, the rule of law and the protection of private property, which have featured in other discussions of Catholic social teaching throughout history, ought to be considered especially important where Catholic social teaching is informing thinking about the political structures that best promote the common good in relation to the environment.

Community management of environmental resources

In this context, one approach to environmental management that has shown particular success in some institutional contexts and which is especially congruent with Catholic social teaching is the community management of natural resources. The most famous figure in this area is Elinor Ostrom, who won the 2009 Nobel Prize for Economics for her anthropological work in this area. This work is highly regarded right across the political spectrum.

---

16 See, for example, this video on the project (https://www.youtube.com/watch
?v=rKLeOu1JFhc). The reserves are owned and governed by a mix of non-profit private institutions and government.

She argued that communities develop methods of controlling the use of environmental resources – fisheries and forests in particular – that are remarkably stable and effective and they do so from the bottom up. Communities develop their own systems of enforcement. And the main role of government is to support those systems and not to take them over. In other words, in line with Catholic social teaching, governments play a subsidiary role in helping the community manage resources, for example, by providing information to aid enforcement. Ostrom's principles include (see Ostrom 2009, 2012):

- There should be clear and locally understood boundaries between legitimate users and non-users. This clearly implies private property rights (at least rights of exclusion) even if those property rights belong informally to the community and are not individualized.
- There should be congruence with local social and environmental conditions – in other words, methods of managing environmental resources such as fish and forests should be culture and circumstance specific.
- The rights of local users to make their own rules are recognized by the government.

Ostrom's work is largely empirical. She demonstrates that community-managed natural resources such as forests and fish have better sustainability outcomes than where you have government-managed systems or individualized private property rights. Her approach aligns with the social teaching of the Church which has made the point that private property clearly allocates responsibility so people know who is responsible for what. In this case, community management also ensures that disputes can handled peacefully and provides an incentive to manage the resource sustainably because the community members, who control access, benefit from its sustainable management unlike where there is no ownership.

Some commentators might not define such forms of ownership as 'private' ownership. Indeed, Ostrom herself used a nuanced vocabulary which made her ideas accessible to and popular with a wide range of people. The semantics do not really matter. Her work demonstrates the importance of the principle of subsidiarity, the enforcement of rules that ensure exclusion from the resource and of non-individualized community rights of ownership in preserving environmental resources. The approach is congruent with the Church's social teaching in a number of respects and deserves greater consideration in the development of that teaching.

Trade-offs, prices and markets

A final issue on which dialogue might be useful is the question of trade-offs and the role of prices and markets in regulating consumption and spurring investment in alternatives.

Laudato si' was correct to say that the scientific consensus is that there will be damaging man-made climate change. However, there is still a question more suited to the domain of economics about whether action to stop climate change will cause more harm than good. Making energy more expensive or less reliable may inhibit economic development and reduce our ability to innovate or be resilient in the face of extreme weather events. As noted above, deforestation has slowed dramatically in many countries and this is often related to increases in incomes.[17] *Laudato si'* noted that: 'The earth, our home, is beginning to look more and more like an immense pile of filth' (21). But in many developed countries, environmental indicators are improving dramatically. When a community is choosing between malnutrition and deforestation, it is much harder to take a decision to preserve the environment. To put it in economic terms, conservation is an income elastic good. It is worth noting, for example, that since 1970 in the US, combined emissions of major particulates have reduced by 77 per cent.[18] Such improvements are much more difficult to achieve in poorer countries.

---

17 Though also with other trends that are related to increasing income such as better governance.
18 https://gispub.epa.gov/air/trendsreport/2020/#introduction

A good example of this is the use of air conditioning, which was strongly criticized in paragraph 55 of *Laudato si'*. However, air conditioning has led to a reduction of 80 per cent in deaths from heat in the US and is becoming more important in hospitals in countries such as India where it will, if it becomes more widely adopted, hugely reduce deaths from heat. Air conditioning has also facilitated significant population movements to the hotter south of the US which would otherwise not have taken place – keeping hot places cool through air conditioning is very much less carbon intensive than warming up cold places, such as Chicago, in winter (see Barecca et al. 2013). Thus, there is a trade-off between a technology that emits carbon and forsaking the role of that technology in reducing deaths in general and facilitating adaptation to climate change.

None of this discussion is intended to minimize the importance of problems caused by climate change. Pope Francis stressed the urgency of this problem in *Laudate deum*. However, nobody proposes reducing emissions to zero next year. And the vast majority of people believe that reductions should take place over some timescale. The extent of reductions, the timescale over which they take place and the mechanism by which reductions are brought about are important questions for dialogue and prudential discernment.

CONCLUSION

The issues discussed in this chapter are most acute in the world's poorest communities for whom the Church has particular care. *Laudato si'*, Pope Francis's major encyclical on the environment, was developed and united the moral teaching of the Catholic Church with modern economics and science.

The insights about human nature and why we should care for the environment were well expressed and should be taken to heart by all people of goodwill. However, Pope Francis invited dialogue and there is room for discussion about how the Church's long-held views on private property can be married with concern for the environment, especially given modern developments in economics. It is also important to emphasize how important the fundamental institutions of governance, including internal and external peace, are for environmental outcomes.

REFERENCES

Barreca, A., Clay, K., Deschenes, O., Greenstone, M., and Shapiro, J. S. (2013) Adapting to climate change: the remarkable decline in the U.S. temperature–mortality relationship over the 20th century. NBER Working Paper 18692. Cambridge, MA: National Bureau of Economic Research.

Alves, A. A., and Moreira, J. (2010) *The Salamanca School*. London: Continuum.

Aquinas, T. (1963) *Summa Theologiae*. London: Blackfriars.

Araujo, C., Araujo Bonjean, C., Combes, J.-L., Combes, M. P., and Reis, E. J. (2009) Property rights and deforestation in the Brazilian Amazon. *Ecological Economics* 68(8–9, June): 2461–68.

Bergida, J. (2019) Patristic socialism? Ambrose of Milan and Catholic social teaching on private property. *Journal of Markets and Morality* 22(2): 263–80.

Booth, P. M. (2017) Property rights and conservation – the missing theme of *Laudato si'*. *Independent Review* 21(3): 1-20.

Booth, P. M., and Nakrosis, S. (2019) Government debt, inter-generational justice and Catholic social teaching. *Bible in Transmission* Autumn/Winter, pp. 16–19 (https://www.biblesociety.org.uk/explore-the-bible/bible-in-transmission/the-bible-in-transmission-autumn-2019/).

Catholic Church (1994) *Catechism of the Catholic Church*. London: Geoffrey Chapman.

Charles, R. (1998) *Christian Social Witness and Teaching*, vol. II. Leominster: Gracewing.

Chroust, H., and Affeldt, R. J. (1951) The problem of private property according to St Thomas Aquinas. *Marquette Law Review* 34(3): 152–82.

Gissurarson, H. N. (2015) *The Icelandic Fisheries: Sustainable and Profitable*. Reykjavik: University of Iceland Press.

Hardin, G. (1968) The tragedy of the commons. *Science* 162: 1243–48.

Lawson, S. (2014) *Consumer Goods and Deforestation: An Analysis of the Extent and Nature of Illegality in Forest Conversion for Agriculture and Timber Plantations*. Forest Trends Report Series, Washington, DC: Forest Trends.

Ostrom, E. (2009) Beyond markets and states: polycentric governance of complex economic systems. Nobel Prize Lecture, 8 December, Stockholm University.

Ostrom, E. (2012) *The Future of the Commons: Beyond Market Failure and Government Regulation.* Occasional Paper 148. London: Institute of Economic Affairs.

Pontifical Council for Justice and Peace (2005) *Compendium of the Social Doctrine of the Church.* London: Burns & Oates.

Sundstrom, A. (2016) Understanding illegality and corruption in forest governance. *Journal of Environmental Management* 181: 779–90.

United Nations Environment Program (2013) *Haiti–Dominican Republic Environmental Challenges in the Border Zone.* Nairobi: United Nations Environment Program.

PAPAL ENCYCLICALS AND OTHER CHURCH DOCUMENTS

Francis (2023) *Laudate deum*, apostolic exhortation (https://www.vatican.va/content/francesco/en/apost_exhortations/documents/20231004-laudate-deum.html).

Francis (2020) *Fratelli tutti*, encyclical letter (http://www.vatican.va/content/francesco/en/encyclicals/documents/papa-francesco_20201003_enciclica-fratelli-tutti.html).

Francis (2015) *Laudato si'*, encyclical letter (https://www.vatican.va/content/francesco/en/encyclicals/documents/papa-francesco_20150524_enciclica-laudato-si.html).

Benedict XVI (2009) *Caritas in veritate*, encyclical letter (https://www.vatican.va/content/benedict-xvi/en/encyclicals/documents/hf_ben-xvi_enc_20090629_caritas-in-veritate.html).

John Paul II (1991) *Centesimus annus*, encyclical letter (https://www.vatican.va/content/john-paul-ii/en/encyclicals/documents/hf_jp-ii_enc_01051991_centesimus-annus.html).

John Paul II (1987) *Sollicitudo rei socialis*, encyclical letter (http://www.vatican.va/content/john-paul-ii/en/encyclicals/documents/hf_jp-ii_enc_30121987_sollicitudo-rei-socialis.html).

John Paul II (1981) *Laborem exercens*, encyclical letter (http://www.vatican.va/content/john-paul-ii/en/encyclicals/documents/hf_jp-ii_enc_14091981_laborem-exercens.html).

John Paul II (1979) *Redemptor hominis*, encyclical letter (https://www.vatican.va/content/john-paul-ii/en/encyclicals/documents/hf_jp-ii_enc_04031979_redemptor-hominis.html).

John XXIII (1963) *Pacem in terris*, encyclical letter (http://www.vatican.va/content/john-xxiii/en/encyclicals/documents/hf_j-xxiii_enc_11041963_pacem.html).

Paul VI (1971) *Octogesima adveniens*, apostolic letter (https://www.vatican.va/content/paul-vi/en/apost_letters/documents/hf_p-vi_apl_19710514_octogesima-adveniens.html).

Leo XIII (1891) *Rerum novarum*, encyclical letter (http://www.vatican.va/content/leo-xiii/en/encyclicals/documents/hf_l-xiii_enc_15051891_rerum-novarum.html).

CHAPTER 6

The positive role of virtuous business in economic life

Martin Schlag

CATHOLIC SOCIAL TEACHING ON BUSINESS

Catholic social teaching on business is a tree rooted in the soil of the bible and the tradition of the early Church, from which it draws its nourishment. In order to grow, this tree needed additional elements: philosophy, law and the social sciences. To be understood and implemented in social life, faith requires the mediation of systematic thought (philosophy) as well as the order of practical reason that determines and makes concrete general principles in light of the common good. This is the task of law, both of canon law (the law that regulates the life and organisation of the Church on earth) and civil law (originally, in the history of the Church, Roman law). However, for law to be effective it needs to understand reality. Social sciences deliver the data and their interpretation that are necessary in order to address the real issues and concerns that beset society in each moment of history.

THE PRINCIPLES AND NORMATIVE INSIGHTS OF CATHOLIC SOCIAL TEACHING

In this chapter I cannot present the development of the whole tradition of Catholic social thought regarding business. I will therefore concentrate on the social encyclicals from their inception with Leo XIII's *Rerum novarum* in 1891 to Pope Francis's *Laudato si'* published in 2015. In preparing this chapter I have reread all the social encyclicals for the umpteenth time. I came out of this rereading with mixed feelings. On the negative side, I felt somewhat embarrassed that some unsubstantiated claims, without discussion or analysis of data, were made in the name of the Catholic magisterium. In some sections I could not avoid an acute sense of boredom and needed to force myself to work through tedious pages that have become (or always have been) at best irrelevant, if not meaningless. Some descriptions of economic affairs are so negative that the reader is left to wonder what world the author lived in. On the positive and preponderant side, I was filled with gratitude for the deep wisdom contained in the hundreds of pages of social magisterium. The principles of Catholic social teaching are well formulated and exquisitely balanced.

The principles are human dignity, the common good, solidarity, and subsidiarity. They relate to each other in tension. Human dignity supports individual freedom and flourishing through the integral development of one's personal talents and gifts. The common good potentially requires the sacrifice of individual freedom and goods in order to serve the community. Solidarity, as social principle and not as individual virtue, creates a system that collectivizes social burdens. Take public debt as an example (see chapter 10). Society as a whole shares the financial and economic burdens that have become necessary to uphold the common good (health, security, old age, unemployment benefits, etc.). Partly as a result, public debt is sky-rocketing, a tendency which is encouraged by dwindling demographics and reactions to the Covid-19 pandemic. Readily we perceive that there needs to be a check on this tendency. It is subsidiarity that delivers the check. Subsidiarity fulfils the task of reigning in free-riders and dysfunctional shrugging off of personal duties. Subsidiarity requires that those things that smaller entities can and should achieve should not be taken away from them by larger ones, nor should the smaller entities call for relief too quickly. Resilience is a prerequisite for subsidiarity.

The four mentioned principles are antagonistic and in their opposing tendencies form the social space in which we can live well. They are like the straps that are needed to erect a tent. Four straps pull in four opposite directions, thus pulling up the tent and maintaining it upright. If we capped one of the straps, the tent would collapse, we would lose our social space. If we absolutized one of the principles at the expense of the others, we would lose all. They who sacrificed freedom on the altar of equality (as communism did) ended up losing both freedom and equality. They who sacrifice equality on the altar of freedom (as libertarianism does) end up losing both. By contrast, Catholic social teaching avoids extremes and creates a social space for peaceful social life and integral human flourishing. The stability and continuity of Catholic social teaching over the centuries reveals its conformity with human nature and the deepest desires of our hearts and minds. It is a secure path forward.

Looking at the encyclicals regarding business in their entirety, we see that some stress the socioeconomic system as a whole (Pius XI 1931; Paul VI 1967). Others rather address the individual business actor (Leo XIII 1891; John XXIII 1961). Still others are a mixture of both approaches (Second Vatican Council 1965; John Paul II 1991; Benedict XVI 2009). Some encyclicals are pessimistic and somber (Pius XI 1931; Paul VI 1967), others optimistic (John XXIII 1961; John Paul II 1991). Following the development of Catholic social teaching, as formulated in the encyclicals over time, we notice that the quality and quantity of topics they deal with expand. There are ever more topics to be found. Initially, the plight of the workers was at the forefront (the workers' question), but soon the social question became that of the whole socio-economic system; then the institutional question was broached; then the anthropological; and, finally, the ecological question. There is hardly any social topic that has not been mentioned in one of the social encyclicals. In *Caritas in veritate* (Benedict XVI 2009) alone I have counted 92 different themes of concern (I am sure other readers will count differently depending on what they consider to be a theme). This inflation of Catholic social teaching has to do with the wish of the popes to bring earlier encyclicals up to date by shedding the light of the principles of the teaching on the new and rapidly evolving historical circumstances of their own times. It also has to do with the process of publication of such an encyclical: many hands are at play and add their own favourite items before the pope approves the final text. The

interaction between perennial principles and their applications to varying and diverse historical circumstances is a hallmark of Catholic social
teaching. It is characterized by continuity and reform (see *Sollicitudo
rei socialis*, 3).

What becomes apparent in reading the social encyclicals is the existence of an intermediate level between the perennial and very abstract
principles mentioned above (human dignity, common good, solidarity,
and subsidiarity) and the ebb and flow of events and circumstances (a
financial crisis, a pandemic, etc.). This intermediate level consists of
regulative ideas or normative insights that render the principles applicable on an operational level. The gap between the sublimity of human
dignity and the concrete question of whether to lay off workers in a
specific situation or not, is so wide that the human mind grasps for
something more specific to aid it in its decision. We need an intermediate level. Beauchamp and Childress (2001) report something similar for
the field of bioethics. From their work in bioethical committees they
gathered the experience that members with varying and even opposing
ethical convictions (utilitarians, Kantians, liberals, communitarians,
ethics of care) nevertheless were able to converge on certain normative
insights.[1] They were able to agree on *what* to do in a given case but not
on *why* they were to do so. In Catholic social teaching there is perennial
unity of basic values (the principles): as Christians we know *why* we do
things. However, we need also to put them into practice in an effective
way. This is where the encyclicals supply a thread of normative insights
that form a tradition.

In the social encyclicals I discern three such intermediate regulative ideas or big convictions regarding the economy and business
that form a common thread throughout the whole tradition:

- The economy is part of a bigger moral order; this implies that
  so-called economic laws are no excuse for immoral economic
  behaviour.

---

1   Beauchamp and Childress call these intermediate normative insights 'prin-
     ciples of bioethics'. This would not work for Catholic social teaching, in
     which the principles are sublime and abstract notions that require greater
     practicability.

- The human person is at the centre of the economy: as a consequence, the purpose of business is not profit maximization but human flourishing.
- The common good takes precedence over individual economic interest.

These intermediate regulative ideas or basic convictions have many theoretical implications and practical consequences. In what follows I will strive to unfold their meaning for business based on Catholic social teaching. I cannot possibly summarize all the encyclicals and list all the examples they contain but will try to give the gist of each normative insight. I will quote a few relevant texts from social encyclicals[2] and analyse possible applications for economics and business life today by tracing the lines of tradition in the social teaching of the Church.

THE ECONOMY IS PART OF A BIGGER MORAL ORDER: SO-CALLED ECONOMIC LAWS ARE NO EXCUSE FOR IMMORAL ECONOMIC BEHAVIOUR

The magisterium of the Church respects the professional expertise of economists and the technical skills of businesspeople. The magisterium is not competent in these matters and cannot venture to impose any professional or scientific judgment. It would be just as foolish for a priest or theologian (who has not studied economics) to make pronouncements on economic data and analyses, as it would be for him to try to wire or plumb his house, even though he legitimately insists on having wiring and plumbing in his abode.

The Church's authority is moral. She claims to be divinely endowed with a patrimony of moral wisdom which she is charged to share also with the world of business. All free human activity is moral activity. Its

---

2   These texts are taken from the official English translation on www.vatican
.va. However, I have corrected some of the translations where necessary to
render the English more comprehensible or convey the original meaning
with more precision.

ultimate goal is to express love for God and our fellow creatures. This is why the Church formulates a moral doctrine on economic activity (*Quadragesimo anno*, 41–42). The economy is not a purely mechanical, technical or scientific system: it is made up of human persons with bodies and souls, desires and wishes, reasonable and irrational fears and hopes. These are the people the Church is trying to illuminate with the light of the gospel and to set on fire with the Holy Spirit. In other words, the Church respects the autonomy of earthly affairs while, at the same time, reminding us that such an autonomy can only be relative: relative to God's moral law (*Gaudium et spes*, 64). This is the kind of secularity that the Church accepts. In modernity, sectors of social life have become emancipated from ecclesial tutelage and developed their own rules and governance independent from the clergy. Politics, economics, science, culture, education, even military power were, at one time, under the control and guidance of the clergy or at their service. At the Second Vatican Council the Church proclaimed the universal vocation to holiness of all the faithful, also of the laity, who are called to be leaven, salt and light in the middle of the world, building up the kingdom of God with their secular nature and mindset. In their own responsibility, guided by their well-formed conscience, with the sacramental and educational help of the clergy, the laity have to blaze the trail of what it means to be truly Christian in their own walk of life, with its infinite variations and constant ebb and flow.

In their apostolic mission in business, lay Christians frequently encounter an environment hostile to faith, including the Christian faith. Instead of good secularity a culture of secularism has spread. Secularism excludes Christian faith from public life. Christianity is tolerated as a purely private affair that must not influence public behaviour. Instead, a stance of supposed scientific neutrality that is considered the only objective truth is imposed on all. The magisterium has reacted in a threefold way to contemporary cultural currents.

Already during the Second Vatican Council, the Church proclaimed that 'Christ, the final Adam, by the revelation of the mystery of the Father and His love, fully reveals man to man himself and makes his supreme calling clear' (*Gaudium et spes*, 22). The modern moral order is a failed attempt to preserve Christian values (human dignity, equality, freedom, etc.) without faith in the Christian God. However, these values stand and fall with the conviction of the existence of a Creator and Father of all, in whose image and likeness we are created and in whom we can recognize each other as brothers and sisters. Without God we can be neighbours but not brethren. In a world and a culture that exclude God, humanism becomes inhuman. For some time perhaps people stick to the traditional values handed on to them by their believing forbears but then the rationale and the narrative are lost. The values wither like cut flowers that have been severed from their roots. The rules and norms become meaningless like the lines on a football field and the rules of the game when the goals are removed. For some time, players remember that once there were goals and where they stood but in the end the lines and rules lose their sense. People ask themselves why they are made to run after a ball. The rejection of God therefore has immediate repercussions on the vision of man, on our anthropology. Thus economics (and any science, especially social science) makes many implicit anthropological assumptions when it formulates its own theories. These assumptions can approximate truth or distort it. For this reason, John Paul II, I think rightly, posited Catholic social teaching in the field of Christian anthropology, thus of theology, more precisely moral theology. It concerns itself with the way men and women behave in society and business (*Centesimus annus*, 55, quoting *Sollicitudo rei socialis*, 41).

The second line of argument in recent magisterial pronouncements warns of the rise of a form of positivism that by absolutizing certain aspects of human life, ends up losing the capacity to understand the human person in her totality. 'This scientific reduction … mutilate[s] man' (*Octogesima adveniens*, 38). We know more and more about our bodies, we know *what* we are in a physical and chemical sense but we know less and less *who* we are and what our purpose on earth is. 'Having subdued nature by using his reason, man now finds that he himself is as it were imprisoned within his own rationality; he in turn becomes the object of science' (38). Without a holistic vision of the human being and a guiding moral order, technology, economic growth and progress turn against us: 'Progress of a merely economic and technological kind is insufficient. Development needs above all to be true and integral' (*Caritas in veritate*, 23). Progress is true and integral when it develops the moral dimension of the human person. The spectacular rise of natural and social science since the Enlightenment was partly due to specialization. Scientific disciplines made themselves independent, focused on smaller sections of reality, relying on empirical data gained through experimentation. However, when this specialization rejects metaphysics and declares faith in God irrelevant, it damages (*Caritas in veritate*, 31, quoting Benedict XVI, Address at the University of Regensburg, 12 September 2006):

> not only ... the development of knowledge, but also ... the development of peoples, because these things make it harder to see the integral good of man in its various dimensions. The 'broadening [of] our concept of reason and its application' is indispensable if we are to succeed in adequately weighing all the elements involved in the question of development and in the solution of socio-economic problems.

We end up knowing more and more about less and less, until we know everything about nothing, at least nothing that is humanly relevant. For this reason, Pope Francis too called for a more integral vision: 'We urgently need a humanism capable of bringing together the different fields of knowledge, including economics, in the service of a more integral and integrating vision' (*Laudato si'*, 141).

Building on the above, the third claim of Catholic social teaching on this subject is that 'the economy needs ethics in order to function correctly' (*Caritas in veritate*, 45). On the one hand, this sentence recalls the traditional teaching that the whole of the economy must be ethical because it is free human behaviour. On the other hand, the quoted sentence is also intended to invert the traditional line of argumentation: in order to be correct in an *economic* sense, business must be ethical. There is only one reality, one truth that can be seen from different angles and under different formal aspects, but the results of the different disciplines must converge in substantial agreement. In the case of apparent disagreement the higher, defining, discipline decides. However, where there is no disagreement, all disciplines support each other: ethics aids business, and economics supports ethics.

In *Caritas in veritate,* Benedict XVI used economic reasons to back moral claims. This is new in the magisterium and something Amartya

Sen (1987) had already proposed back in 1987.[3] Benedict XVI wrote: 'there is a convergence between economic science and moral evaluation. Human costs always include economic costs, and economic dysfunctions always involve human costs' (*Caritas in veritate*, 32).

Why should we belabour ethical or moral arguments if there are enough economic reasons for a good course of action? The difficulty that arises here, however, is that we must distinguish between human *agency* in economic *praxis* and the *methodology* of economics as *science*. The ethical dimension is not the same on the practical and epistemological levels. When it comes to human activity as a business person, it is quite clear, actually trivial, that it has to be evaluated in a moral sense. Every free action is located on the moral level by the mere fact of being free, directed by our will to an aim, and therefore either good or evil.[4] There is a vast literature on this in business ethics.

In contrast, the prevalence of ethics is not so clear when it comes to economics as a science. Should economics be value-neutral? How does ethics influence economic research? Should economic research be curtailed for moral reasons? These are difficult questions that exceed the scope of this chapter. However, I give two brief answers. First, even though there is no universally accepted definition of economics, generally speaking economics studies the efficient use of scarce resources for the attainment of alternative ends; it studies the creation of wealth, and does so either in a descriptive (positive economics) or in a prescriptive way (normative economics). I propose that economics should study certain pursuits of profit not as economic but as criminal activities. Take, for instance, the different markets and distribution systems for drugs; or human trafficking, prostitution and pornography. These activities move billions of dollars. Nevertheless, they are immoral and, in many legal systems, criminal. As economists we should study the economic aspects of these activities (formation of prices, distribution models, etc.) but signal them as evil. Otherwise, in a certain sense, we could become

---

3   Sen (1987, p. 10): 'Economic issues can be extremely important for ethical questions, including the Socratic query, "How should one live?"'

4   In this sense, the affirmation of *Caritas in veritate* (37) is incoherent: 'Thus every economic decision has a moral consequence.' No: every economic decision *is* a moral decision.

accomplices. By giving the impression of value-neutrality we would grant such activities the right to citizenship. Secondly, in economics we use expressions that are defined by other disciplines or by culture in general: person, good, service, wealth, work, production, and so on. We also are part of a value system that we have not created ourselves. In order not to be manipulated, we need to reflect and, as far as possible, make values explicit. Take, for instance, empirical studies on the impact of the liberalization of prostitution on rape (see the study by Bisschop et al. 2017) Liberalizing prostitution seems to reduce the incidence of rape. In affirming this empirical fact, we rightly presuppose that rape and prostitution are bad and undesirable, but that one is worse than the other. These are values that guide our research.

THE HUMAN PERSON IS AT THE CENTRE OF THE ECONOMY: THE PURPOSE OF BUSINESS IS NOT PROFIT MAXIMIZATION BUT HUMAN FLOURISHING

Catholic social teaching started out with the defence of the worker (*Rerum novarum*, 34):[5]

> [I]t is only by the labor of working men that States grow rich. Justice, therefore, demands that the interests of the working classes should be carefully watched over by the administration, so that they who contribute so largely to the advantage of the community may themselves share in the benefits which they create – that being housed, clothed, and bodily fit, they may find their life less hard and more endurable. It follows that whatever shall appear to prove conducive to the well-being of those who work should obtain favorable consideration. There is no fear that solicitude of this kind will be harmful to any interest; on the contrary, it will be to the advantage of all, for it cannot but be good for the commonwealth to shield from misery those on whom it so largely depends for the things that it needs.

---

5   The quoted passage paraphrases Adam Smith in *The Wealth of Nations* I.viii, 36 (Smith 1776).

Thus from the beginning we encounter the firm conviction in Catholic social teaching that the economy should serve all, not only a few. The Second Vatican Council expressed it in these words (*Gaudium et spes*, 64):

> The fundamental finality of this production is not the mere increase of products nor profit or control but rather the service of man, and indeed of the whole man with regard for the full range of his material needs and the demands of his intellectual, moral, spiritual, and religious life; this applies to every man whatsoever and to every group of men, of every race and of every part of the world.

On the other hand, the Church certainly does not defend egalitarianism (all must have and be the same) but is aware of the beneficial effect of incentivizing those who have talent and rewarding people for their hard work by defending their right to private property. Catholic social thought consistently rejects socialist attempts at abolishing private property of the means of production and of collectivizing economic output. Nothing motivates work more than the prospect of enjoying the fruits of one's labours. The social encyclicals defend private property as an extension of individual freedom and as in the interest of family independence. For the same reasons (freedom and independence), John XXIII included economic rights in his list of human rights and duties. Among these are the right to work and to entrepreneurship, but also social rights of workers in work (just wage, social protection, safety, rest, etc.) (*Pacem in terris*, 18–22). On the other hand, the popes repeat the traditional Catholic teaching that property is not an absolute and unlimited right but is under a 'social mortgage': not only is the use of property common to all in circumstances of extreme need, but private property obliges its owners to use it in the interest also of others not only in their own interests: property ennobles but *noblesse oblige*. From the first social encyclical we discover a special concern for the poor: 'when there is question of defending the rights of individuals, the poor and badly off have a claim to especial consideration' (*Rerum novarum*, 37). These words formulate a kind of 'preferential option for the poor' *ante litteram*: it will become a central term in liberation theology and in Catholic social thought after Paul VI.

As Western and other developed societies became more opulent, the popes grew increasingly concerned about the purpose of economic goods and the hierarchy of values in human life. Their commitment to the poor and the workers did not wane, but the call for the centrality of the human person in business and economy took on a new, additional note. Consumerism and practical materialism threaten to stifle higher spiritual and intellectual aspirations, enticing people to stumble into the trap of increasing desires and diminishing satisfaction. We desire more and more but get less and less from every additional possession. So many people in opulent societies seem to be on a treadmill, running and running but not getting anywhere, except into a spiritual void and human emptiness. The reason for this frustration lies in the fact that happiness is 'a matter of perfection rather than extensive accumulation (of material goods or experiences).' Perfection 'is coming to the fullness of being that is possible' (Hirschfeld 2018, p. 93).

In a Christian world view, our ultimate end is to know and to love the ultimate good, which is God. Catholic social teaching therefore underscores the instrumental character of material goods. 'Material goods are, indeed, good. But they are purely instrumental. It is not enough to be wealthy. Happiness requires that we deploy our wealth toward the worthy end of realizing our nature as fully as possible in lives ordered to God' (Hirschfeld 2018, p. 97). Economic goods are means not ends in themselves: they should help us achieve human flourishing (*Mater et magistra*, 246).

From this conviction stems the Church's teaching on the essence of integral human development. Development must be true and integral and therefore is moral in nature. Benedict XVI delineated the Church's notion of integral human development in his social encyclical *Caritas in veritate*. Integral human development requires economic growth, without which people could not enjoy the prosperity and leisure necessary for the attainment of higher ends. However, besides the material aspect, true and full human development also implies the solidity of happy families that are open to life, according to the teaching of the encyclical *Humanae vitae*. Furthermore, development in the Christian sense requires formation in the faith and evangelization. Christ the *Logos* purifies every person and culture from within and brings it to their true self (*Caritas in veritate*, 15).

For this reason, Catholic social teaching consistently condemns profit maximization as a 'structure of sin', if it is understood as an all-consuming desire for profit that leads to a quest for maximizing profit 'at any price' (*Sollicitudo rei socialis*, 37). Profit as such is an indicator of a well-functioning business both in the economic and the moral sense: when there is profit, resources are used well and put to the service of owners and workers. However, when the thirst for profit becomes the main motive of economic activity it becomes self-destructive. Profit cannot be the purpose of business just as petrol cannot be the purpose of a car. The purpose of business is the goods and services they provide. When business leaders make profit their only goal they are bound to make many practical mistakes: they lose the trust of their customers and employees; the quality of their products goes down as they are not passionate about them; they become ethically blind and morally mute about the human needs of people and society. Here we come to the deep underlying issue of the Church's insistence on the instrumental character of economic goods. We live in a society that upholds a paradigm of accumulation ('the more the better!') instead of a paradigm of perfection ('what and how much of it do I need in order to achieve excellence?') (see Hirschfeld 2018, p. 100). The paradigm of accumulation and greed is a structure of sin that leads to an absolutization of partial and subordinate goods and in consequence to 'real forms of idolatry: of money, ideology, class, technology' (*Sollicitudo rei socialis*, 37). 'The evil does not consist in "having" as such, but in possessing without regard for the quality and the ordered hierarchy of the goods one has. Quality and hierarchy arise from the subordination of goods and their availability to man's "being" and his true vocation' (*Sollicitudo rei socialis*, 28). Pope Francis is forcefully outspoken in this sense.

These deeper considerations, and not political alliances, define the Church's position on the different economic systems. The popes are consistently critical of both liberal capitalism and of Marxist socialism, if and in so far as they are dominated by a materialistic notion of the human person, and thus reverse 'the order laid down from the beginning by the words of the Book of Genesis: man is treated as an instrument of production, whereas he – he alone, independently of the work he does – ought to be treated as the effective subject of work' (*Laborem exercens*, 7). Catholic social teaching recommends socio-economic systems that combine free markets with social responsibility, at the same time repeating the principle that the magisterium does not have socio-economic programmes or technical solutions or systems to offer. After the collapse of real socialism John Paul II recommended a 'business economy', 'market economy' and 'free economy' as forms of good capitalism (*Centesimus annus*, 42), whereas Francis speaks rather of 'social market economy', 'social economy' and 'economy of communion'.[6]

Benedict XVI added an innovative aspect to the understanding of markets that has to do with the centrality of the human person in business. In the intellectual and cultural context of post-modernism, Benedict XVI approached the question of socio-economic systems in a unique way. Post-modernism rejects all universal narratives of meaning: all meaning and sense in life is subjective choice. As it were, each one of us sits on a cloud without connection to others because there is no sky in common that would allow us to communicate. Post-modernism thus implicitly rejects the notion of essential differences given by a Creator or by nature, replacing it with the notion of diversity as the result of individual choice. One's identity is defined by choice and is liquid. People have no stable profile anymore; it can change continually because no objective limits on self-definition are accepted. Without difference in the strong sense of the word, stable duality or relationships are not possible because

---

6   See both the following papal addresses: Pope Francis (2016) Address at the Conferral of the Charlemagne Prize, 6 May 2016 (http://w2.vatican.va/content/francesco/en/speeches/2016/may/documents/papa-francesco_20160506_premio-carlo-magno.html); Pope Francis (2017) Address to participants in the meeting of 'Economy of Communion,' Sponsored by the Focolare Movement, 2 February 2017 (http://w2.vatican.va/content/francesco/en/speeches/2017/february/documents/papa-francesco_20170204_focolari.html).

they presuppose objective difference of persons and qualities, and lasting commitments based on them. In this context, Benedict XVI rethinks the Holy Trinity in its social dimension. The Three Persons are subsistent relations, one in nature and at the same time different in their personhood. Analogically, human personhood does not consist in mere individuality but in communion of relationships that make possible what is truly human about us: love, compassion, friendship, gift, etc. Benedict XVI attributes the capacity to build human relationships also to the markets: 'In a climate of mutual trust, the market is the economic institution that permits encounter between persons, inasmuch as they are economic subjects who make use of contracts to regulate their relations as they exchange goods and services of equivalent value between them, in order to satisfy their needs and desires' (*Caritas in veritate*, 35).

Such a vision exceeds existing socio-economic models and finds no or little correspondence in contemporary political programmes. Using the language of the French Revolution: equality is blazoned on the banners of socialism; liberty on those of liberalism. Where is the political party that really fights for fraternity?

These last two sections on the overarching moral order and on the centrality of the human person are intimately linked. Ethics is the practical wisdom of human flourishing, and thus is essentially person-centred. The human person is relational or social in nature, and this leads us to the third section on the common good. It is intrinsically linked to all that has been said so far.

THE COMMON GOOD TAKES PRECEDENCE OVER INDIVIDUAL ECONOMIC INTEREST

That business should promote a situation in society that has been called the commonwealth, the common weal, or the common good is a mantra that Catholic social teaching repeats incessantly. This message is not always well received by business people who feel encumbered by additional burdens that make entrepreneurship excessively difficult. Entrepreneurs need few incentives. They have enough drive of their own. What they need is protection against excessive fiscal and bureaucratic strain that drains their energies. Acting in business with economic acumen and in an ethical and Christian spirit that places human flourishing at its centre (as described in the preceding sections), is a form of business that promotes the common good. What else can a business person do? What more is expected of them? In particular, what role should government play in economic life? In order to answer these questions, we need to clarify the concept of the common good as it appears in Catholic social teaching.

The common good is not the same as a public good. A public good is a good in public or common ownership that can be used by everyone individually. Examples are streets, sewage systems, public lighting, etc. Of course, public goods greatly contribute to the common good. The Second Vatican Council defined the common good as 'the sum of those conditions of social life which allow social groups and their individual members relatively thorough and ready access to their own fulfillment [*perfectionem*]' (*Gaudium et spes*, 26 and 74).

This definition conceives of the common good as something external to the person or the group itself, like a framework, in which persons as individuals or groups can develop their potentialities. It reminds one rather of the notion of public good than of the authentic common good; and has therefore also been called an 'instrumental common good' (Bradley Lewis 2019, p. 254). Benedict XVI therefore complemented this notion with a more relational outlook. In his social encyclical he wrote: 'It is the good of that "all-in-one,"[7] made up of individuals, families and intermediate groups who together constitute society. It is a good that is sought not for its own sake,[8] but for the people who belong to the social community and who can only really and effectively pursue their good within it' (*Caritas in veritate*, 7).

---

7   The official English translation says: 'the good of "all of us,"'. However, the Italian version is more incisive: '*il bene di quel "noi-tutti"*'. This would be translated better as: 'the good of that "all-in-one"'. '*Quel "noi-tutti"*' substantiates the communal aspect of the common good.

8   Here the official English translation says 'its'. However, I propose that 'one's' would be a better expression. Any good that is truly good must be sought for 'its own sake', because this is what makes it good. Here the encyclical wishes to stress that we are seeking a good not for ourselves but for the community as a whole. It is the shared good of togetherness.

The innovation that Benedict XVI made explains the common good as the good of being and acting together. The common good is not the sum of individual goods nor is it the outer framework for individual action, it is the good of communality. The common good is a shared good in the strong sense of the word. It cannot be achieved alone by oneself, or by divvying up an object held in common property. If we divide a pie and each one takes a piece to their room and eats it alone, we have divided a shared object but we have destroyed the common good. Whereas when we share the same pie in a common meal we have created the common good of a meal and the conversation during it. Having a beer by oneself is a pleasurable experience but drinking one together creates so much more community. From the framework definition in *Gaudium et Spes* (26), Benedict XVI has moved to the notion of the common good as a product. We all know the difference between a product and a sum. In a sum, any addend can be a zero without the sum changing $(2 + 2 + 0 = 4)$. In a product, if one factor is reduced to zero, the product is zero, even though all other factors are high numbers $(2 \times 2 \times 0 = 0)$. If one person in a community is violated in her human dignity, the community as a whole has lost its common good.

This conception of the common good has led Catholic social teaching to refer to the business firm as a community of persons (*Centesimus annus*, 35). A firm is a productive unit, an entity submitted to necessities of the market and of efficiency. However, in its operations there must be room for personal relationships and friendship. Otherwise it would lack cohesion and motivation. This has important consequences both for employers and employees. On the side of the employees, concern for the common good of the firm increases the sense of responsibility, motivation and cohesion that stimulates us to go beyond and above the call of duty. In times of crisis, employees understand that pay cuts might be inevitable and sacrifice must be shared. Lack of resources increases tensions. This is when strong ties among colleagues save an enterprise. On the side of the employers, understanding their business firm as a community of persons, will give them a heightened sense of responsibility for their workers. It will lead them to avoid layoffs as long as possible, finding alternatives that do not endanger the life of a family. When pay cuts are inevitable, then the leader of a community of persons takes a pay cut him or herself. Understanding the business as a community leads to reinvest some of the profit in the firm. This may be through the finance of research and development and through programmes that enhance the security of employees or the well-being of workers. There are examples of successful businesses which act in this way. Their voluntary commitment has been rewarded.

However, as stated above, the crux of the Church's discourse on the common good is government involvement. How much can and should government intervene in economic affairs? Since *Quadragesimo anno*, published in 1931, Catholic social teaching has insisted on the need for social justice, without fully defining this expression. Most reliable authors understand social justice as a modern way of referring to legal or general justice in the terminology of Thomas Aquinas (Calvez and Perrin 1961, pp. 133–61; Gregg 2019, pp. 93–98; Kennedy 2019; Booth and Petersen 2020). In a nutshell, what this means is the following. General justice is the general ordering of all individual acts, both of the two species of particular justice (commutative and distributive justice) as well as the acts of all other virtues, towards the common good. It must not be confused with a mere obligation of fulfilling existing laws, but it obliges us in conscience to contribute to the common good even if there are no laws forcing us to do so. General justice is also called legal justice by Aquinas, because the common good is the aim of all law. Thomas, needless to say, did not reduce law to positive law.

As true as this interpretation of Aquinas might be, this understanding of social justice by the authors mentioned above misses, I think, the crucial point of the social encyclicals' use of the term social justice. From Pius XI to Paul VI, Catholic social teaching placed the task of creating a socially just (and charitable) society on the shoulders of the state, the government and public authorities. This precisely was the novelty of the expression. Up to the beginning of the twentieth century the Church had strenuously defended the Church's monopoly on charity. Leo XIII still wrote in favour of rejecting forms of state-organized relief of the poor: 'Charity, as a virtue, pertains to the Church' (*Rerum novarum*, 30). With mounting social tensions, masses of unemployed and after the carnage of World War I among Christian nations, Pope Pius XI changed course, calling on public authorities to exercise the functions the Church could no longer fulfil because she was overwhelmed by the needs of the time.

In more recent magisterium, the popes have become warier in their appeals to state intervention. John Paul II spurns what he terms the 'social assistance' state, which may become bloated. He criticizes the suffocation of economic initiative by totalitarian governments and calls for freedom of all kinds in the name of Christ. Benedict XVI and Francis have continued this tendency, most notably Francis. Benedict XVI called for a rediscovery and revaluation of civil society with its logic of reciprocity, gift and fraternity, to act alongside the logic of exchange (markets) and the logic of duty (state). This made him write of a great challenge: 'to demonstrate, in thinking and behaviour … that in commercial relationships the principle of gratuitousness and the logic of gift as an expression of fraternity can and must find their place within normal economic activity' (*Caritas in veritate*, 36). This does not disenfranchise or discredit the government but does remove its monopoly on the preservation of the common good. Francis goes even further.

Contrary to general perception, Francis is not in favour of big government and of government handouts except in situations of humanitarian crises. He has used the expression 'social justice' very rarely in his pontificate. Instead he speaks of the preferential option for the poor. This is not merely a terminological shift. Social justice traditionally assigns the role of actor to the public authorities. The preferential option for the poor is a duty incumbent on all of society and on each of its members. In his own words (*Laudato si'*, 158):

> In the present condition of global society, where injustices abound and growing numbers of people are deprived of basic human rights and considered expendable, the principle of the common good immediately becomes, logically and inevitably, a summons to solidarity and a preferential option for the poorest of our brothers and sisters … We need only look around us to see that, today, this option is in fact an ethical imperative essential for effectively attaining the common good.

No pope before him has made as clear that the promotion of the common good is a task and a duty for all of us. This is also true for business people. In his message to the World Economic Forum of 2014, he urged the business community to use their high intelligence which made them rich to find ways to include the poor in the market economy. When the human person is at the centre, money serves, it does not rule.[9]

CONCLUSION

As has become clear in this chapter, the tradition of Catholic social teaching sees virtuous business in a distinctly positive light. The Church affirms what exists with a vision informed by faith, justice and charity. In order to evangelize persons who live in a culture or system, we must love them. In a second and necessary step, Catholic social teaching calls Christians and all persons of good will to purify the existing systems and foremost their own personal behaviour from anything sinful. In particular, the tradition warns against unethical acts in business justified by 'economic laws'; against any attitude that would lead those in business to succumb to the lures of profit maximization at any price; and against placing their own interest before the common good in a selfish and short-sighted way. All these normative insights are based on the perennial principles of Catholic social teaching: human dignity, common good, solidarity and subsidiarity. It is up to each individual to use their well-formed conscience to find the Christian way forward in a world that is in great need of the light and warmth of Christ.

REFERENCES

Beauchamp, T. L., and Childress, J. F. (2001) *Principles of Biomedical Ethics*, 4th edn. Oxford University Press.

---

9   Pope Francis, Message to the Executive Chairman of the World Economic Forum, 17 January 2014 (http://www.vatican.va/content/francesco/en/messages/pont-messages/2014/documents/papa-francesco_20140117_messaggio-wef-davos.html).

Bisschop, P., Kastoryano, S., and van der Klaauw, B. (2017) Street prostitution zones and crime. *American Economic Journal: Economic Policy* 9(4): 28–63 (https://doi.org/10.1257/pol.20150299).

Booth, P., and Petersen, M. (2020) Catholic social teaching and Hayek's critique of social justice. *Logos: A Journal of Catholic Thought and Culture* 23(1): 36–64.

Bradley Lewis, V. (2019) Catholic social teaching on the common good. In *Catholic Social Teaching: A Volume of Scholarly Essays* (ed. G. V. Bradley and E. C. Brugger), pp. 235–66. Cambridge University Press.

Calvez, J.-Y., and Perrin, J. (1961), *The Church and Social Justice: The Social Teaching of the Popes from Leo XIII to Pius XII (1878–1958)*, pp. 133–61. Chicago: Regnery.

Gregg, S. (2019) Quadragesimo Anno (1931). In *Catholic Social Teaching: A Volume of Scholarly Essays* (ed. G. V. Bradley and E. C. Brugger), pp. 90–107. Cambridge University Press.

Hirschfeld, M. L. (2018) *Aquinas and the Market: Toward a Humane Economy*. Cambridge, MA: Harvard University Press.

Kennedy, R. (2019) Social justice and competing visions of the common good. *Logos: A Journal of Catholic Thought and Culture* 22(2): 106–50.

Sen, A. (1987) *On Ethics and Economics*. Malden: Blackwell.

Smith, A. (1776) *An Inquiry into the Nature and Causes of the Wealth of Nations* (ed. R. H. Campbell, A. S. Skinner and W. B. Todd). Oxford University Press (1976). (Glasgow edition of the Works and Correspondence of Adam Smith in the reprint by the Liberty Fund, Indianapolis (1981).)

PAPAL ENCYCLICALS AND OTHER CHURCH DOCUMENTS

Francis (2015) *Laudato si'*, encyclical letter (https://www.vatican.va/content/francesco/en/encyclicals/documents/papa-francesco_20150524_enciclica-laudato-si.html).

Benedict XVI (2009) *Caritas in veritate*, encyclical letter (https://www.vatican.va/content/benedict-xvi/en/encyclicals/documents/hf_ben-xvi_enc_20090629_caritas-in-veritate.html).

John Paul II (1991) *Centesimus annus*, encyclical letter (https://www.vatican.va/content/john-paul-ii/en/encyclicals/documents/hf_jp-ii_enc_01051991_centesimus-annus.html).

John Paul II (1987) *Sollicitudo rei socialis*, encyclical letter (http://www.vati
can.va/content/john-paul-ii/en/encyclicals/documents/hf_jp-ii_enc_30
121987_sollicitudo-rei-socialis.html).

John Paul II (1981) *Laborem exercens*, encyclical letter (http://www.vati
can.va/content/john-paul-ii/en/encyclicals/documents/hf_jp-ii_enc_14
091981_laborem-exercens.html).

Paul VI (1971) *Octogesima adveniens*, apostolic letter (https://www.vatican
.va/content/paul-vi/en/apost_letters/documents/hf_p-vi_apl_19710514
_octogesima-adveniens.html).

Paul VI (1967) *Populorum progressio*, encyclical letter (http://www.vatican
.va/content/paul-vi/en/encyclicals/documents/hf_p-vi_enc_26031967
_populorum.html).

Vatican II (1965) *Gaudium et spes*, Pastoral Constitution on the Church in
the World (https://www.vatican.va/archive/hist_councils/ii_vatican_co
uncil/documents/vat-ii_const_19651207_gaudium-et-spes_en.html).

John XXIII (1963) *Pacem in terris*, encyclical letter (http://www.vatican.va/
content/john-xxiii/en/encyclicals/documents/hf_j-xxiii_enc_11041963
_pacem.html).

John XXIII (1961) *Mater et magistra*, encyclical letter (http://www.vatican
.va/content/john-xxiii/en/encyclicals/documents/hf_j-xxiii_enc_15051
961_mater.html).

Pius XI (1931) *Quadragesimo anno*, encyclical letter (http://www.vatican
.va/content/pius-xi/en/encyclicals/documents/hf_p-xi_enc_19310515
_quadragesimo-anno.html).

Leo XIII (1891) *Rerum novarum*, encyclical letter (http://www.vatican.va/
content/leo-xiii/en/encyclicals/documents/hf_l-xiii_enc_15051891_re
rum-novarum.html).

CHAPTER 7

Cronyism and Catholic social teaching

Jay W. Richards

The encyclicals with which Catholics identify modern Catholic social teaching, starting with Leo XIII's *Rerum novarum* in 1891, examine questions related to what we might call political economy. Leo XIII, for instance, wrote of labour, capital, capitalism, socialism, private property and the like. And we can find these terms in the latest encyclicals promulgated by Pope Francis.

Yet this tradition seems silent on what has arguably become the most common form of political economy, which we can call crony capitalism or cronyism. This system is not the small-government, free-market ideal of classical liberals and many American conservatives. Nor is it the state socialism that dominated much of the world in the twentieth century and continues in North Korea and Cuba. At its core, cronyism is a form of collusion between the administrative state and large corporate actors. It involves a concentration of power between what we often call the 'public' and 'private' spheres.

In this chapter, we will consider what light Catholic social teaching can cast on cronyism, how the Holy See could respond to this informal political economy and whether is it well-positioned to do so.

DEFINING CRONYISM

As an economic system, cronyism shares some features with twentieth-century fascism. That term, however, now carries connotations of the dictatorships, racism, anti-Semitism and militarism of Fascist Italy, Spain and Nazi Germany. It is less tendentious to describe these economic systems as 'corporatist'. This is a form of consolidation among political and business entities, including industrial cartels and cooperatives. In theory, corporatism represents a hierarchical economy run by political, business and even ecclesiastical elites cooperating, they believe, for the common good. It need not involve a literal dictatorship, racial theory or militarism – all features commonly associated with fascism.[1]

In the twentieth century, many Catholic intellectuals and clerics supported corporatism as a supposed 'third way' between liberal capitalism and socialism.[2] This is discussed further below.

Unlike corporatism, cronyism is not a political economic theory in its own right. It is, rather, what many modern economies evolve into because of incentives in both the political and economic spheres.

In a sense, the emerging Chinese system is a form of cronyism, with an especially powerful state. But an apparently more benign form is common in liberal democracies with vibrant markets, private businesses and low levels of criminal corruption. This may seem paradoxical to those who assume that private corporations always prefer to compete in a free market and so will oppose the regulatory state. In fact, cronyism would be no surprise to most champions of a free economy from Adam Smith in the eighteenth century to Thomas Sowell in the twenty-first. All these thinkers treated cronyism as a perennial danger. That is because a private company, especially a large, unvirtuous one, may be only too happy to bear regulatory burdens, if those burdens disproportionately harm current and/or potential competitors.

Collusion and cartels among competitors to fix prices or supply are almost always illegal in modern economies. But cronyism may

---

1   While Catholic-inflected corporatism and fascism have affinities, they are not identical. As Michael Pakaluk has noted (personal correspondence), an essential feature of fascism is to duplicate entities in civil society by entities of the party, and then ultimately to replace them. In this way, civil society is ultimately assimilated into an ideology.

2   See Morck and Yeung (2010) and, for a good general treatment of the forms of corporatism, Williamson (1985).

be legal. Indeed, retired regulators may have lucrative careers as lobbyists for private corporations, in part because they are experts in navigating the byzantine regulations that they previously wrote and enforced.

Economists call this classic cronyism 'regulatory capture' (Dal Bó 2006). This is how cronyism tends to start. In the late twentieth century, however, we began to witness the emergence of a new and more encompassing form. If classic cronyism involves cooperation or collusion between government and large business, full-spectrum cronyism adds non-profits and charities, cultural and media institutions, and transnational organizations such as the United Nations and the World Economic Forum.

Cronyism, then, does not look like the homogeneous socialism of the former Soviet Union, which radically curtailed private property and crowded out the private sphere with state-owned industry and agriculture and with a violent security and surveillance apparatus. In contrast, cronyism retains different institutional spheres, even as these spheres become an ever larger and more unitary machine of social control.[3]

Catholic social teaching says nothing explicitly about this cronyism, which makes our task difficult. There are, however, affinities between cronyism and corporatism which play a positive role in a few prominent social encyclicals. This requires us to ask an awkward question: how aware is the Holy See of the dangers of cronyism? Might its past and present lack of sensitivity to these dangers leave it susceptible to it?

As we will see, the principles of Catholic social teaching cast clarifying light on cronyism. To judge from recent events, however, the Holy See itself seems ill-prepared to deal with a political

---

3   Mussolini, describing his own vision of totalitarian fascism, said, 'Everything within the state, nothing against the state, nothing outside the state.' Cronyism is not a distinct political philosophy, and so would never have a motto. But as a tendency, it moves toward 'everything inside the machine, nothing against the machine, nothing outside the machine.' The machine is the amorphous sphere of social control that emerges from the collusion, behind the scenes, of powerful institutions that may remain visibly and even legally independent.

economy that does not fall into the typical categories of liberalism, capitalism or socialism. In fact, decades of sympathy to corporatism might even lead some churchmen to see in cronyism a kindred system to be nurtured rather than challenged. There are some recent signs that the Holy See is far less prepared to deal with cronyism than it should be.

CATHOLIC SOCIAL TEACHING AND ECONOMIC MODELS

Beginning with Pope Leo XIII's 1891 *Rerum novarum*, the Church has sought to apply the perennial truths of natural law and the Catholic faith to concrete social conditions.

Some claim that, in Catholic social teaching, the magisterium proposes a detailed political programme that constitutes a 'third way' between capitalism and socialism.[4] And detailed claims in encyclicals about private property, unionization, foreign aid, vocational guilds, and wage and employment policies, as well as critiques of socialism, capitalism, liberalism and 'neoliberalism' can be found.

This third way is often identified with either corporatism or distributism. Randall K. Morck and Bernard Yin Yeung, for instance, argue that 'corporatism was Roman Catholic social doctrine from the 1890s to the 1960s' (Morck and Yeung 2010, p. 2). Distributists such as Hilaire Belloc and G. K. Chesterton emphasize the widespread distribution of 'productive property' and claim that their model either is, or at least is grounded in, Catholic social teaching. These thinkers, in other words, see Catholic social teaching as a specific economic model with specific economic policies.

This is not wholly implausible. Samuel Gregg argues that the corporatist vision makes an appearance in *Rerum novarum* (1891) and becomes central in Pius XI's 1931 encyclical *Quadragesimo anno*. 'Pius XI appears to go further than his predecessor', Gregg writes, 'in formally proposing what a social order derived from Catholic Social Teaching should look like' (Gregg 2019, p. 102). His encyclical and

---

4   https://www.thecatholicthing.org/2014/08/30/the-myth-of-catholic-soc ial-teaching-2/

others encouraged corporatism in Catholic social thought especially in the German world among Christian Democrats after World War II. Earlier, it had influenced the policies of regimes such as the Vichy in France, Spain under Franco, and, as noted above, Mussolini in Italy. It is detectable in a number of Latin American countries as well.

On the other hand, John XXIII seemed to demote corporatism in *Mater et magistra*. And later encyclicals, especially *Centesimus annus* (1991), are more sympathetic to the market economy than to corporatism.

As a result, it would not be correct to identify corporatism unambiguously with the core principles of Catholic social teaching. Indeed, to identify either corporatism or distributism with Catholic social teaching is to contradict the principles of the tradition. In *Centesimus annus* (1991) John Paul II insisted that 'the Church has no models to present' and that 'the Christian faith does not presume to imprison changing sociopolitical realities in a rigid schema.' In his 1987 encyclical *Sollicitudo rei socialis*, he wrote, 'The church's social doctrine is not a "third way" between liberal capitalism and Marxist collectivism ... rather it constitutes a category of its own.'

For this reason, in 1986, the Congregation for the Doctrine of Faith (CDF) made clear that the relevant documents often include 'contingent judgments' to be distinguished from the core of the Church's social teaching. For example, in *Instruction on Christian Freedom and Liberation* (72), the CDF explained that the Church, 'offers by her social doctrine a set of *principles for reflection* and *criteria for judgment*.' Even without these statements from John Paul II and qualifications from the CDF, however, there is too much internal diversity among the documents to identify Catholic social teaching with corporatism or any single economic model.

Moreover, treating Catholic social teaching as a detailed political programme opens it up to devastating objections. It is not hard to find misguided factual and economic claims in the Catholic social teaching corpus. Philosopher John Finnis summarizes such problems in a book chapter entitled 'A radical critique of Catholic social teaching' (Finnis 2019, p. 548). According to Finnis, Catholic social teaching interpreted in this way is:

impaired by (1) ambiguity about its scope or subject matter, (2) inattention to its dependence on judgments about empirical facts and likelihoods, and/or upon the other contingent factors and diverse but not unreasonable preferences inherent in any application of the Golden Rule, and (3) inappropriate assumptions that pastors have primary responsibility for making such judgments and assessments, and for deciding and choosing how the laity should act in line with them. Much (not all) of CST should be formulated hypothetically: if you judge that such and such facts obtain, or are likely, then (unless you judge that certain other facts do not obtain or are unlikely), true moral principles and norms, confirmed by divine revelation, direct that you should choose thus-and-thus.

If it were to propose a detailed political platform, Catholic social teaching would reduce to ephemeral attempts by popes to speak about subjects on which they have no special authority or expertise. It is no surprise that Finnis advises that churchmen get out of the business of offering such advice (Finnis 2019, p. 548):

> Popes and other bishops therefore should be little involved in it, beyond reminding everyone of those true principles and norms, in season and out. Their documents or preaching need not address CST more often than other matters of morality. Organs of the Holy See or bishops' conferences dedicated to CST are unnecessary.

One alternative that accounts for these difficulties is to recognize that the authoritative remit of Catholic social teaching is quite limited. Following the CDF guidance from 1986, we should see Catholic social teaching as a tradition that seeks to apply perennial *principles* rooted in Catholic theology and the natural law to changing social and economic conditions. These are what Finnis (2019, p. 548) refers to as 'true moral principles and norms, confirmed by divine revelation'.

Alas, there is no canonical list of these principles. But they include: the intrinsic dignity of the human person from conception to natural death; marriage and family as the fundamental units of society; the common good; subsidiarity; solidarity and human equality; reason and natural law; the dignity of work and of workers; the reality of human rights and responsibilities; the right to private property; and our stewardship of the natural world. These principles have a much greater command on the Catholic conscience, than do the various ways popes and Church officials have attempted to apply them.

Framing matters in this way has its own problems, of course. As we have noted, apostolic letters, encyclicals and the like are rarely limited to abstract principles. They also contain scientific and economic assumptions and make claims based on those assumptions. This means we can and should distinguish non-negotiable questions of 'faith and morals' (over which the magisterium has divinely protected authority) from the prudential application of those questions, which are based on empirical observations and theoretical assumptions, not just normative principles. On these complex conjunctions of propositions, the magisterium has no special protection, and thus can make mistakes.

Pope Francis wrote in *Laudato si'* (188), for instance, that 'the Church does not presume to settle scientific questions or to replace politics'. Such a task is not delivered to us prepackaged by the magisterium.

In dealing with cronyism, the role of the laity is important for three reasons. Firstly, the Holy See has offered little explicit reflection on this political form. Secondly, owing in part to the support for corporatism in some Catholic social teaching documents, the Holy See is arguably vulnerable to the charge that it supports systems that can encourage cronyism, with which corporatism shares a familial resemblance. And thirdly, applications of Catholic social teaching to political economy should be grounded in economic reality (Richards 2020). No theory that ignores, for instance, the role of incentives or the relationship of supply and demand, or that fails to account for the role of prices in transmitting information, has much hope of promoting human flourishing. And any such attempt to reduce widespread poverty that ignores our knowledge of how to do so – through, for instance, the rule of law, property rights, economic freedom and innovation – is at best deficient, if not harmful.

When he was the head of the Congregation for the Doctrine of the Faith, Joseph Ratzinger called for such an effort (Ratzinger 1986, p. 4):

A morality that believes itself able to dispense with the technical knowledge of economic laws is not morality but moralism. As such it is the antithesis of morality. A scientific approach that believes itself capable of managing without an ethos misunderstands the reality of man. Therefore, it is not scientific. Today we need a maximum of specialized economic understanding, but also a maximum of ethos so that specialized economic understanding may enter the service of the right goals.

Armed with economic knowledge, the principles of Catholic social teaching can help lay analysts think as Catholics about cronyism, and perhaps help the Holy See recognize this form of political economy for what it is.

CRONYISM: HOW IT STARTS

Cronyism may start with the best of intentions. Perhaps a thought experiment illustrates the point. Imagine a crisis in private banking leads to massive unemployment and bankruptcies. In liberal democracies, elected officials feel strong pressure from voters to see them acting to alleviate suffering. So, these officials may create a regulatory agency which they claim will prevent future crises. They need experts to run the agency, and the best place to find such experts is in the banking industry where the crisis took place. The banks, for their part, now have to deal with a new regulatory body, and hire lobbyists to represent their interests. These lobbyists are part of the same peer group, and may even be former colleagues, of the new regulators.

The agency seeks to fulfil its charter, but that charter may not prevent crises. Indeed, perhaps the original crisis was itself the result of a prior well-meaning but misguided regulatory attempt to prevent a previous crisis. And so, when some new crisis emerges, elected officials have a new incentive to add new regulatory agencies, and the regulated industries have even more incentive to lobby regulators. Large, private industries capable of navigating the regulatory terrain thus grow up alongside – they co-evolve with – an ever more expansive regulatory state.

This feedback of incentives is the seedbed from which cronyism grows. It involves rational if self-interested actions of private companies, politicians and government regulators. It can happen even without baser motives of greed and the lust for power. But these motives can catalyse the feedback. They can create a situation where it is difficult to enter the industry without the resources to navigate the regulatory landscape. So, big business thrives alongside extensive regulation while new and smaller businesses find it difficult to compete.

'Full spectrum cronyism' involves much more than this, however. Man does not live by economics and politics alone. He does not just want to amass a fortune and power. Indeed, as his wealth grows, an industrialist or entrepreneur may find more fulfilment, and even more social status, by talking about world peace, trying to eradicate hunger and disease, spreading 'sexual freedom' and 'marriage equality' and saving the planet. The businessman thus becomes a philanthropist and political lobbyist. Think of Bill Gates and George Soros. Both men amassed fortunes worth many billions of dollars in the private sector. They then spent decades as equally powerful and influential philanthropists. Of course, philanthropy is, in itself, virtuous. But some kinds of philanthropy can be connected with political lobbying which feeds the development of global elites.

Any robust account of cronyism in the early twenty-first century must account for this shifting of roles, and the social institutions that encompass it.

A CASE STUDY IN CRONYISM: THE 2008 FINANCIAL CRISIS

The 2008 financial crisis in the US provides a quintessential example of full-spectrum cronyism. The media focused on stereotypical villains: Wall Street greed, deregulation and unfettered competition. These culprits were blamed in the 2010 Dodd–Frank Act putatively designed to prevent another crisis.

The widely accepted story, however, is far from the mark. I describe the real story in detail in my book *Infiltrated* (Richards 2013). The simplest way to distil it is to ponder a simple question: in a free market – fettered by a reliable rule of law but little political micromanaging – would 'NINJA' loans exist? Would they be common? These notorious loans were available to borrowers with 'no income, no job or assets' as late as 2007. Even if we assume that lenders are fuelled by avarice, would they be likely to give out loans that they doubt will be repaid? Not normally. Something clearly had scrambled the normal market incentives, including price signals, in the mortgage bazaar. That something was a wide range of 'affordable housing goals', enacted over several decades across many government departments, all designed to increase home ownership among lower-income Americans.

Thanks to the work of Edward Pinto and Peter Wallison, and later to the US Securities and Exchange Commission, we know that, as a result of these efforts to expand homeownership, by 2008 there were about 27 million 'non-traditional', 'subprime' and otherwise risky loans.

The government-sponsored enterprises Fannie Mae and Freddie Mac held 12 million of those loans – which they bought on the secondary market under stiff quota requirements from Congress. The Federal Housing Administration (FHA) and other federal agencies held 5 million while the Community Reinvestment Act and HUD programmes had another 2.2 million. That makes a total of 19.2 million risky loans held by entities controlled by or within the federal government. Only for 7.8 million loans did the risk lie entirely with private lenders.

Alongside this market for risky loans grew an implicit understanding that the large financial institutions, at least collectively, would enjoy a government-sponsored safety net if they got into trouble. They came to believe that they would be 'too big to fail'. Or rather, they acted as if they were too big for the government to allow them to fail. This attitude led to severe moral hazard in which banks were willing to take on far more risk than they would if they knew they would bear the full consequences of failure. A report by the Federal Reserve Bank of Richmond in 2013 (republished as Haltom and Lacker 2015) stated (ibid., p. 3):

> In a series of incidents beginning in the 1970s, the Fed, in cooperation with the Federal Deposit Insurance Corporation, intervened to limit bank failures' effect on creditors. Early interventions were

relatively small, but they established precedents that led potential creditors to expect to be rescued in future instances of financial distress, weakening their incentives to limit borrower risk-taking and vulnerability. Government-lending programs often appeared to stabilize markets because they confirmed hopes of intervention, and so have been hailed as successes. But this has come at the cost of moral hazard, greater risk-taking, and greater instability down the road.

This form of government support for financial markets is a particularly prominent feature of the US financial system, which was the seat of the financial crisis.

The crisis was not the fruit of deregulation or an 'unfettered' free market that lacked government oversight. After all, two-thirds of all risky loans in the system 'were held by the government or entities acting under government control' (Wallison 2011, p. 453), and they existed largely because of aggressive government housing policy spanning several decades. And it encouraged behaviour by private institutions that would have been unthinkable without the possibility of a government-sponsored back stop. This was the *sine qua non* of the 2008 financial crisis.

One effect was a meltdown in the financial sectors involved in mortgages and mortgage-backed securities. It is a perfect illustration of what can happen when governments interfere with the coordinating power of prices in a properly functioning, competitive market.

Unfortunately, rather than unwinding itself from the private housing market, government doubled down on its role. Firstly, it effectively nationalized 'government-sponsored enterprises' Fannie Mae and Freddie Mac, thus providing government subsidies to private investors. Then, it orchestrated buy-outs among key financial institutions and forced loans on the nine largest US banks.

Then came the 2010 Dodd–Frank Act – named after two members of Congress who had been ardent champions of government housing policy – Chris Dodd and Barney Frank. Among the many provisions of this law was a call to designate large banks and financial firms as 'systemically important financial institutions'. In other words, the law made 'too big to fail' explicit government policy. The 848-page act also created a new regulatory agency, the Consumer

Financial Protection Bureau, with expansive powers over the entire financial sector of the economy – including industries that had nothing to do with the financial crisis. Federal agencies under the Act's direction now add over six million new words of regulation every year (McLaughlin 2014). No elected legislator plays a role in these regulations. Regulators, and corporate lobbyists, do.

The financial crisis should have provided a lesson in what can happen when market discipline is distorted by regulatory incentives. This is not to say that there will never be failures in financial markets without the interventions described above – our human nature ensures that there will be. However, every significant intervention by the government in these markets arguably made the financial crisis more likely or its effect worse.

The failure of every intervention then becomes an excuse for more intervention. In a healthy market economy, the costs are linked to the benefits of enterprise. Entrepreneurs who invest their savings in a business may enjoy success or failure. This fact helps focus and discipline the risks they accept. Cronyism, in contrast, tends to detach costs and benefits. At its worst, it privatizes profits and socializes costs. Failures tend to reinforce the business–regulator relationships, which are problematic to begin with.

The aftermath of the crisis

Some noticed the cronyism between government and large banks that received loans or bailouts. But few observers noticed cronyism outside the business and political spheres. It included actors in the media, non-profit and philanthropic world, all of which had excessive influence in the crisis and its legislative aftermath. This full-spectrum cronyism was a harbinger of the future.

For example, in August 2010, housing activist Martin Eakes boasted to a gathering of MBA students at Duke University that the ideas hatched in the non-profits that he founded, called Self-Help, were now the law of the land. He was referring to provisions in the Dodd–Frank Wall Street Reform and Consumer Protection Act, which had passed the month before. Regulatory ideas have to hatch somewhere, of course. But Eakes's statement revealed that cronyism can reach beyond business and government. Firstly, he and his Self-Help non-profits were key players in subprime lending and cheerleaders for the government's 'affordable housing' goals. Indeed, Eakes played an important role in mediating risky loans from unwilling private banks to an initially squeamish Fannie Mae. Secondly, he claimed in the same speech that Self-Help's national lobbying arm, the Center for Responsible Lending (CRL), had 'hired fifty lawyers, PhDs, and MBAs to basically terrorize the financial services industry for any of their abusive practices nationwide' (Richards 2013, p. 65).

CRL was inspired and funded primarily by California Savings & Loan owner, Herbert Sandler, who wanted Eakes's work to have a national impact (Self-Help now owns a ten-story building in Washington, DC, a few blocks north of the White House). Sandler and his wife, Marion Sandler, made news in 2008 at the height of the financial crisis. As it happens, their bank had pioneered the 'option ARM loan' which the *New York Times* called the 'Typhoid Mary' of the housing crisis. *Time* magazine listed the couple among the twenty-five people to blame for the financial crisis.

The Sandlers, however, did not suffer irreparable harm from this temporary bad press or from the housing crisis itself. They had cashed out in 2006 – at the height of the housing bubble – by selling their company for $24.3 billion to Wachovia in North Carolina – the same bank that went bankrupt two years later. This allowed the Sandlers to engorge their charitable foundation, making it one of the thirty largest foundations in the country. They immediately began to fund media operations that provided the metanarrative of Wall Street greed and Republican deregulation that supposedly led to the financial crisis. They also continued to heavily fund the non-profit Center for Responsible Lending.

Herb Sandler appeared before the official Financial Crisis Inquiry Commission, but its final report carefully preserved his self-defence and rationalizations. The California politician who chaired that commission, Phil Angelides, had enjoyed Sandler support as California state treasurer. In that capacity, Angelides had funnelled pension money from state employee and teachers' unions to 'private equity businesses in underserved areas' and 'affordable housing'.

With so much cross-fertilization, it was inevitable that many from this web would find their way into federal bureaucracies. One example was Mark Pearce, who became Director of the Federal Deposit Insurance Corporation's (FDIC) Division of Depositor and Consumer Protection. We were told in 2010 that the US needed a new bureau – the Consumer Financial Protection Bureau – to protect consumers, since the other agencies (such as the FDIC) could not. Yet the FDIC created its own consumer protection division the same year, which now has many hundreds of employees.

Pearce was a long-time employee at Self-Help and was the first president of its Center for Responsible Lending,[5] with its horde of 'financial terrorists'. The foxes were not only hired to run the hen house: they laid its foundations.

This is only one tiny chapter of a much larger saga of the full-spectrum cronyism – some on display, some behind the scenes – that played a crucial role in both the financial crisis and its official response. It involved not just government agencies and private corporations, but philanthropists, non-profit charities and activist organizations. And it was a template for the cronyism to come.

THE HOLY SEE MISSED THE CRONYISM AT THE ROOT OF THE FINANCIAL CRISIS

The 2008 financial crisis is relevant to this chapter because the Holy See has responded to it. That response provides us with the best example of how the Church, in her teaching function, failed to respond to cronyism.

In 2018, a decade after the financial crisis, the Church published *Oeconomicae et pecuniariae quaestiones* ('Financial and economic questions', OPQ hereafter). It is the closest thing we have to an official Church interpretation of the 2008 financial crisis.[6]

---

5   https://www.fdic.gov/about/comein/biosPearce.html.

6   Though the media gave the CDF document fawning coverage, it received little serious analysis. One important response to it came from the (Catholic) Chairman of the Commodity Futures Trading Commission, along with its chief economist. The pair wrote an open letter to the Holy See, correcting what they took to be major errors and misconceptions in the CDF document involving derivatives and credit default swaps (Giancarlo and Tuckman 2018).

OPQ's indisputable moral claim is that the human person should be front and centre in any economic discussion, and that money and economics always have an ethical dimension. Human dignity and the common good are recurring themes throughout. Sections 1, 2 and 4 discuss the ethical criteria for judging markets and finance. OPQ also affirms the goodness of finance (15) and profit (23) for meeting human needs. Although it avoids sweeping attacks on finance in general, it tends to treat finance as distinct from the 'real economy' – a phrase it uses five times.

Unfortunately, the document is also marked by misconceptions about the technical causes of the financial crisis. Specifically, it argues that the crisis was caused by individual and collective greed, overly complex and avaricious financial instruments, and a lack of national and supranational regulation of financial markets. Its basic argument is that the self-sufficiency of markets is a myth (21). Therefore, there should be far more regulation of financial markets to avoid future crises.

This follows the media stereotype about the cause of the crisis. Take its invocation of greed: this vice is universal; and there's no evidence that greed was more rampant in 2008 than in, say, 1998. Pointing to greed as the cause of the crisis is like pointing to the presence of an oxygen-rich atmosphere to explain why a car exploded in front of the house of the district attorney. It fails to point to the *sine qua non* of the event.

The call for more regulation of financial markets also misses the main lessons of the financial crisis. Firstly, the 2008 financial system was already the most highly regulated sector of the US economy. And it was already shaped by international banking protocols such as Basel I and Basel II[7] and a complex web of trade agreements. There was no self-sufficient market to speak of.

Secondly, as noted above, regulation played a decisive role in the crisis. Through its housing directives, the federal government created a massive demand for housing through risky loans, and the market delivered them. OPQ mentions these loans briefly but treats

---

7   Basel II: Revised international capital framework (https://www.bis.org/pu bl/bcbsca.htm).

them as products of malicious private actors. It shows no awareness that housing policies and regulations created and incentivized these loans in the first place (25).

Thirdly, OPQ misinterprets the role of securities. It is true that securitization and sundry derivatives magnified and globalized the effects of these risky loans. The problem was aided and abetted by misleading ratings which underestimated the true risks of these products. Those misleading ratings and the use of securitization were both encouraged by the international regulatory environment by which capital requirements for banks were determined by the credit ratings of securities. In many ways, securities helped to diversify risk within the financial system, which is why the regulatory system encouraged their use. Moreover, they did not *cause* the crisis, contrary to the suggestion of OPQ (26). Without the underlying risky loans, the financial instruments would not have been a problem.

Finally, when OPQ comments on the detail of regulation, its emphasis is often misguided. One example is its claim (22) that 'systemic crisis' could have been avoided if certain 'banking responsibilities' were separated. This seems to be an oblique reference to the so-called Volcker Rule, which would separate investment and commercial banking. But there is no example of how separating these functions would have mitigated the crisis. On the contrary, had the Volcker Rule been in place in 2008, the damage may have been even worse. At the peak of the crisis, Bank of America, a commercial bank, bought Merrill Lynch, an investment bank. That kept Merrill Lynch from failing. And in March 2008, Bear Stearns, the first investment bank to get in trouble, was bought out by JP Morgan Chase, a commercial bank. So, if the OQP-recommended barrier between commercial and investment banks had been in place, it could well have made the crisis more rather than less severe.

This is an example of what John Finnis refers to as the frequent 'dependence' in Catholic social teaching 'on judgments about empirical facts and likelihoods'. And, in this case, the judgement is mistaken. In short, although the Holy See had ten years of hindsight, it failed to discern the forms of cronyism on display in the 2008 financial crisis, and instead relied on popular, but misleading, stereotypes.

THE RISK OF CRONY CAPTURE AT THE VATICAN

'Rome call for AI ethics'

The hierarchy's lack of sensitivity to the dangers of cronyism also seems to be on display in its recent initiative on artificial intelligence. On 28 February 2019, the Pontifical Academy for Life sponsored a conference to launch the initiative. The opening document, 'Rome call for AI ethics', reiterates moral truths that no Catholic will dispute. The gist of the statement is that artificial intelligence (AI) must be developed to serve humanity and the common good. Indeed, other than adding a few theological truisms, the statement does not provide any new insight or add a fresh Catholic take on the topic. Instead, it calls for AI to help people, to improve education, to respect privacy and not to discriminate against people.

Why was the statement so generic? Perhaps the reason is that Archbishop Paglia was joined as a signatory by Brad Smith, President of Microsoft; John Kelly III, Vice President of IBM; Dongyu Qu, General Director of the UN's Food and Agriculture Organization (FA); and Italian government official Paola Pisano. David Sassoli, President of the European Parliament, also participated in the event. Earlier Vatican events have included other such corporate luminaries. And a 2018 Vatican hackathon enjoyed support from the likes of Google, Salesforce and Microsoft.

These are the partners for this ongoing initiative. So, what can we expect beyond conventional wisdom? How likely is it, for instance, that we'll get a robust critique of materialist metaphysics and of the false view of man as machine so common in the AI literature and community?

One danger is that these relationships between business, transnational organizations and the Vatican on such specific initiatives encourage cronyism more widely. A statement signed by the heads of IBM and Microsoft which insists that 'new forms of regulation must be encouraged to promote transparency and compliance with ethical principles' could easily lead to giant corporate actors colluding with government to prevent small competitors from entering the market. This might look like government holding private companies accountable. In reality, the relevant government agencies can be captured by the large, well-established industries they claim to be regulating. These agencies do not so much regulate as craft regulations that hinder future competitors.

Of course, these actions are always defended for virtuous reasons – public safety, public health, transparency and the common good. But should the Church, and, in particular, the Pontifical Academy for Life, partner with IBM and Microsoft to make pronouncements on tech regulation? Given the financial interests of these organizations, it might serve to provide large tech companies with moral cover in their calls to regulate competition to the benefit of large and, potentially, monopolistic businesses.

Council for inclusive capitalism

There is a further, even more worrying, example from December 2020. To much fanfare, the Vatican announced that it was partnering with global titans to support a new organization called the Council for Inclusive Capitalism.[8] The opening meeting included finance ministers from several countries, as well as the head of the International Monetary Fund. According to Pope Francis, the effort is supposed to reduce poverty and inequality.

Members of the council are called 'Guardians' who 'at their respective companies, have said they plan to hire and promote more women, increase diversity hires, commit to clean energy by purchasing 100% renewable electricity, reduce greenhouse gas emissions, promote the reuse and recycling of water and other initiatives' (Kelly 2020). It is not clear how all of these initiatives will solve poverty or reduce inequality. Represented among the Guardians include the following: the president and CEO of Mastercard; the executive chairman of Dupont; the chairman of the board and CEO of Johnson & Johnson; the CEO of BP; the chairman of the board and CEO of Bank of America; and the president and CEO, State Street Corporation.

We can assume that these initiatives are well-intentioned and, indeed, they may be appropriate. But it is important to proceed

---

8   https://www.inclusivecapitalism.com

with caution. On the one hand, it may be possible to help corporate organizations be more ethical by cooperating with them in this way. On the other hand, this approach could provide corporations with window-dressing as they use connections in global organizations and in government to promote their own interests.

THE PATH FORWARD: THE IMPORTANCE OF IDENTIFYING CRONYISM

The Vatican has not connected cronyism with the financial crisis and has often given tacit support to models of cooperation between big business and government that might encourage cronyism, though with good intentions. Still, Pope Francis did identify the risk of cronyism very starkly in *Laudato si'*. In this chapter, we have emphasized the form of cronyism whereby private sector interests can capture regulatory systems and use them to their own advantage. In *Laudato si'*, Pope Francis identifies a different form of cronyism in which corporations corruptly avoid the law to benefit their own private interests and those of politicians. He is, perhaps, the first pope to mention these problems consistently. Pope Francis wrote in *Laudato si'* (197):

> Often, politics itself is responsible for the disrepute in which it is held, on account of corruption and the failure to enact sound public policies. If in a given region the state does not carry out its responsibilities, some business groups can come forward in the guise of benefactors, wield real power, and consider themselves exempt from certain rules, to the point of tolerating different forms of organized crime, human trafficking, the drug trade and violence, all of which become very difficult to eradicate.

Corrupt relationships between business and government are common in many countries. Experience of this problem in South and Central America may explain Pope Francis's example. Given the fallen nature of man and the resources that are at the disposal of government and business, there is a real danger that close relationships between both can give rise to opportunities for enrichment, which harm the common good.

An example in South America is the 'carwash' scandal.[9] This saga involved a nationalized business, private businesses and politicians. The total amount of money misdirected to personal interests is not known, but it is probably over $2 billion. The unwinding of the scandal contributed to a sharp recession and inflation in Brazil and, arguably, the loss of trust in government and the rise of populism criticized in Pope Francis's most recent encyclical *Fratelli tutti*.

Catholic social teaching does provide guidance on cronyism. Catholics, and the Holy See itself, would do well to draw on its resources in developing Catholic social thought and teaching about this subject. Many Catholic social teaching principles – private property, the common good, solidarity, equality and subsidiarity – bear on cronyism. There is also the wider content of Christian theology itself. Any full treatment would go beyond a single chapter. Let us focus here on subsidiarity and original sin.

A proper account of subsidiarity

In *Quadragesimo anno*, Pius XI summarizes the principle of subsidiarity while defending the existence of non-state institutions. He refers to it as 'that most weighty principle, which cannot be set aside or changed, remains fixed and unshaken in social philosophy' (79):

> Just as it is gravely wrong to take from individuals what they can accomplish by their own initiative and industry and give it to the community, so also it is an injustice and at the same time a grave evil and disturbance of right order to assign to a greater and higher association what lesser and subordinate organizations can do. For every social activity ought of its very nature to furnish help to the members of the body social, and never destroy and absorb them.

Subsidiarity implies a normative judgment about the jurisdictions and responsibilities of various institutions. Some institutions should have primary jurisdiction or responsibility over some domains and functions. Others should have secondary or tertiary, and so

---

9   https://www.britannica.com/event/Petrobras-scandal

on, responsibility. And some should not have responsibility over a jurisdiction.

A complete account of how subsidiarity applies in a society, then, should answer, for each institution or social sphere, the following: Does this institution have proper jurisdiction over X, where X is some domain or function?

Examples would include raising children, buying a house, growing vegetables, selling used cars, declaring war, and establishing a speed limit on a side road. If an institution has, or should have, proper jurisdiction over X, then that institution must, in principle, be competent to exercise that responsibility. Competence is a necessary condition for proper jurisdiction.

If the answer to (1) is 'no', then that institution should, simply put, not have responsibility over X.

If the answer is 'yes', then the next question is: Does this institution have primary, secondary, tertiary, etc., jurisdiction over X?

How (1) and (2) are answered may depend in part on the political philosophy held by the person answering the question. But answers should also depend on observation and experience. We know, for instance, that mothers and fathers should have primary responsibility for raising children. Why? By reflecting on human nature, by a careful reading of Holy Scripture and Sacred Tradition, and by observing that most cultures throughout history have recognized this fact.

Defining subsidiarity, which Catholic social teaching does, is one thing. Answering (1) and (2) precisely is more difficult. So, the question arises, which institution should have primary jurisdiction when it comes to determining the terms on which people trade, including prices, in the economy?

It can be argued that the principle of subsidiarity and human reason and experience suggest that no human institution has literal jurisdiction for determining these things. The state should, though, ensure that the market be governed by the general rule of law, including robust property and contract rights in a setting which allows prices to change freely based on the interactions of buyers and sellers, following their own subjective assessments and incentives.

When states try to exercise more direct control over markets – by fixing prices, setting quotas and the like – they scramble the information-bearing function of prices, which leads to distortions such as shortages and surpluses or waste. In this way, states show that they do not have the competence to determine prices. If a state lacks competence to determine prices, then it cannot have responsibility for them. Furthermore, intervening in markets in this way draws business into close proximity to the state and provides the opportunities for cronyism that we have discussed.

This way of thinking would seem to accord with *Centesimus annus* paragraph 42, which expressed the view that a free economy was the desirable form of economic organization, but that the state should ensure that the market operated in a well-functioning legal framework. In this way, prices in a competitive market emerge from countless interactions of actors in a marketplace. The state plays a role that is essential and that is within its competence. Businesses and individuals, in turn, are able to do what only they can do.

This also helps us see one of the problems with cronyism. A properly functioning market allows firms to compete for customers, investors and employees according to the same legal rules. 'Competition' here has no Darwinian connotations. If two people want the same gallon of petrol, their competition for the petrol is a fact. That is the nature of scarcity. The question is how to adjudicate it. We know, by long experience, that competitive markets generally improve the quality and lower the price of such goods and allocate them where they are most valued. Or, at least, they do this better than any known alternative. As a 'discovery process',[10] a market is better – for customers, employees and the common good – if it includes many firms competing for customers and employees. The alternative is not the brotherhood of man or universal cooperation. It is a monopoly.

A literal monopoly usually involves not just a single provider but also unfair barriers to entry for potential competitors usually reinforced by government often as a result of a process of cronyism. This drastically mutes the benefit of markets. Besides a literal monopoly,

---

10 F. A. Hayek described competition as a discovery process in Hayek (2002), which is a translation by Marcellus S. Snow of Hayek's 1968 lecture 'Der Wettbewerb als Entdeckungsverfahren,' sponsored by the Institut für Weltwirtschaft at the University of Kiel.

however, there are quasi-monopolies, which create similar problems. One quasi-monopoly is a cartel, when competitors collude to restrict supply, control prices and lock out competition. These are illegal in developed countries.

Cronyism is another, more protean, form of quasi-monopoly, which has much the same effect as a cartel. Cronyism disrupts the functioning of markets by breaking down the proper borders of different institutions. So, rather than, say, national regulators and powerful corporations performing complementary functions according to the principle of subsidiarity, they can come together to serve their own narrow benefit at the expense of others and to the detriment of the common good.

If government and business are allowed to play their distinct and different roles in the economy in this way, there will be a distance between them. There may be particular situations in which government may reasonably intervene, for example to ensure supplies of a vaccine on an equitable basis during a pandemic, to deal with monopoly or to prevent environmental damage. However, as the *Compendium of the Social Doctrine of the Church* puts it: 'state action in the economic sphere should also be withdrawn when the special circumstances that necessitate it end' (Pontifical Council for Justice and Peace 2005, p. 188). Though this statement is not related to cronyism, governments not intervening in the economic sphere unless it is strictly necessary makes it less likely that cronyist relationships between politics and business will develop. Business and politics have their own domain. The state should not take over the role of business. If it does, there is a danger that business will then take over the realm of politics, as Pope Francis warns in *Fratelli tutti* (77).

Original sin

Another related principle, fundamental in Christian theology, is original sin. 'Certain new theologians dispute original sin', quipped G. K. Chesterton in *Orthodoxy*, 'which is the only part of Christian theology which can really be proved.' The doctrine of separation of powers in the US Constitution is famously attributed to a widespread, Calvinist-tinted conviction that no one should be trusted with too much power over others. As James Madison put it in *Federalist* 51, exaggerating for effect:

> If Men were angels, no government would be necessary. If angels were to govern men, neither external nor internal controls on government would be necessary. In framing a government which is to be administered by men over men, the great difficulty lies in this: you must first enable the government to control the governed; and the next place, oblige it to control itself.

This conviction, that someone should watch the watchmen, is not unique to Calvinism. Still, the political importance of original sin has, at times, been less prominent in Catholic social teaching than it could have been. In *Rerum novarum*, for instance, Pope Leo XIII was right to call for harmony and cooperation between capital and labour in a hierarchal Catholic polis. But he may have been, as Randall Morck and Bernard Yin Yeung put it in their critique of corporatism in Catholic social teaching: 'overconfident in asserting that the Church possesses a power [to] bring men to act from a motive of duty, to control their passions and appetites, to love God and their fellow men.' They continue (Morck and Yeung 2010, p. 40):

> Power corrupts even devout Catholics. Elites less vulnerable to upset by takeovers, foreign competition, or the unhindered economic mobility of talented upstarts wield a more absolute power, and therefore risk a more absolute corruption. Corporatism's sanctified cartels bleach private property of its social purpose – the unleashing of market forces to effect such upsets and reallocate resources to where they are most valuable. Without conveying the freedom to change jobs, retool factories, and create new markets, private property is no more than the dead hand of entrenched privilege.

A proper account of social spheres – of subsidiarity – must include a realistic view of fallen human beings. In particular, it should recognize that counterbalancing interests between spheres is sometimes the very best way to foster cooperation and the common good. A cosy alignment of interests between power elites in government, business, non-profit organizations, philanthropy and culture is rarely a sign of harmony, but rather of concentrated and corrupt power in the hands of the few.

If the Holy See is to help faithful Catholics navigate the byzantine maze of cronyism in the twenty-first century, it will need to develop these insights, and avoid entanglements with the power elites at the centre of the maze. It will need to embrace the insight of an erstwhile critic, Lord Acton, who insisted that 'power tends to corrupt' even popes and kings, 'and absolute power corrupts absolutely.'[11]

The evidence suggests that cronyism is becoming the dominant form of political economy, so there is little time to waste.

REFERENCES

Dal Bó E. (2006) Regulatory capture: a review. *Oxford Review of Economic Policy* 22(2): 203–22.

Finnis, J. (2019) A radical critique of Catholic social teaching. In *Catholic Social Teaching: A Volume of Scholarly Essays* (ed. G. Bradley and E. Brugger). Cambridge University Press.

Giancarlo, J. C., and Tuckman, B. (2018) CFTC Chairman J. Christopher Giancarlo response to Bollettino, 21 July 2018 (https://cftc.gov/Press Room/SpeechesTestimony/giancarloresponsetobollettino072118).

Gregg, S. (2019) *Quadragesimo anno* (1931). In *Catholic Social Teaching: A Volume of Scholarly Essays* (ed. G. Bradley and E. Brugger). Cambridge University Press.

Haltom, R., and Lacker, J. M. (2015) Should the Fed have a financial stability mandate? Lessons from the Fed's first 100 years. *Economic Quarterly* 101(1): 49–75.

Hayek, F. A. (2002) Competition as a discovery procedure. *Quarterly Journal of Austrian Economics* 5(3): 9–23.

---

11   Acton wrote this in a letter to Anglican Bishop Mandell Creighton on 5 April 1887, in which he is discussing how historians should treat the corrupt actions of popes. Quoted in the *Online Library of Liberty* (https://oll.liberty fund.org/quotes/214).

Kelly, J. (2020) Pope Francis partners with corporate titans to make capitalism more inclusive and fair. *Forbes*, 9 December 2020 (https://www.forbes.com/sites/jackkelly/2020/12/09/pope-francis-partners-with-corporate-titans-to-make-capitalism-more-inclusive-and-fair-is-this-for-real-or-just-corporate-virtue-signaling).

McLaughlin, P. (2014) Measuring the Dodd–Frank Act (and other major acts) with Regdata 2.0. *Regulation*, 23 September 2014 (https://www.mercatus.org/publications/regulation/measuring-dodd-frank-act-and-other-major-acts-regdata-20).

Morck, R. K., and Yeung, B. Y. (2010) Corporatism and the ghost of the third way. *Capitalism and Society* 5(3), article 2 (https://ssrn.com/abstract=2209136).

Pontifical Council for Justice and Peace (2005) *Compendium of the Social Doctrine of the Church*. London: Burns & Oates.

Ratzinger, J. (1986) Church and economy: responsibility for the future of the world economy. *Communio* 13: 200–4.

Richards, J. W. (2013) *Infiltrated*. New York: McGraw Hill.

Richards, J. W. (2020) What economists know, believe, and debate. *Journal of Markets & Morality* 23(1): 117–30.

Wallison, P. (2011) *Official 'Dissent' to the Financial Crisis Inquiry Report, Official Government Edition*, revised 25 February 2011 (http://www.gpo.gov/fdsys/pkg/GPO-FCIC/pdf/GPO-FCIC.pdf).

Williamson, P. J. (1985) *Varieties of Corporatism: A Conceptual Discussion*. Cambridge University Press.

PAPAL ENCYCLICALS AND OTHER CHURCH DOCUMENTS

Francis (2020) *Fratelli tutti*, encyclical letter (http://www.vatican.va/content/francesco/en/encyclicals/documents/papa-francesco_20201003_enciclica-fratelli-tutti.html).

Congregation for the Doctrine of the Faith and Dicastery for Promoting Integral Human Development (2018) *Oeconomicae et pecuniariae quaestiones: Considerations for an ethical discernment regarding some aspects of the present economic-financial system* (https://press.vatican.va/content/salastampa/en/bollettino/pubblico/2018/05/17/180517a.html).

Francis (2015) *Laudato si'*, encyclical letter (https://www.vatican.va/content/francesco/en/encyclicals/documents/papa-francesco_20150524_enciclica-laudato-si.html).

John Paul II (1991) *Centesimus annus*, encyclical letter (https://www.vati can.va/content/john-paul-ii/en/encyclicals/documents/hf_jp-ii_enc _01051991_centesimus-annus.html).

John Paul II (1987) *Sollicitudo rei socialis*, encyclical letter (http://www.vati can.va/content/john-paul-ii/en/encyclicals/documents/hf_jp-ii_enc_30 121987_sollicitudo-rei-socialis.html).

Congregation for the Doctrine of the Faith (1986) *Instruction on Christian Freedom and Liberation* (http://www.vatican.va/roman_curia/congrega tions/cfaith/documents/rc_con_cfaith_doc_19860322_freedom-libera tion_en.html).

Pius XI (1931) *Quadragesimo anno*, encyclical letter (http://www.vatican .va/content/pius-xi/en/encyclicals/documents/hf_p-xi_enc_19310515 _quadragesimo-anno.html).

Leo XIII (1891) *Rerum novarum*, encyclical letter (http://www.vatican.va/ content/leo-xiii/en/encyclicals/documents/hf_l-xiii_enc_15051891_re rum-novarum.html).

CHAPTER 8

The Biblical and patristic roots of Catholic social thought on business and commerce

Martin Schlag

We often think of Catholic social teaching as an endeavour which started in 1891 with the publication of *Rerum novarum*. This would be incorrect on several levels. Teaching on matters to do with civil, social and economic life has been interwoven into communications from the Church from her earliest days. Furthermore, the formalization of Catholic social teaching in the modern social encyclicals relied not just on earlier pronouncements by the Church but on a tradition of Catholic social thought which has its roots in the early Church fathers, in the Bible and in the teaching of Christ. By way of example, no fewer than 27 of the 40 references in *Rerum novarum* are to biblical sources. And comprehensive works on Catholic social teaching, such as Rodger Charles's (1998) two-volume *Christian Social Witness and Teaching* are rooted in the teaching of the Bible, the witness of the Church Fathers and the action of the early Church.

Other chapters in this book have examined the history of Church teaching from well before 1891 in areas such as the right to own property and usury. This brief chapter examines the biblical and patristic sources that explain the Church's modern attitude towards the role of virtuous business in economic life and which have informed modern Catholic social teaching. In doing so it shows how teaching on the role of virtuous business, since *Rerum novarum*, is rooted in sacred scripture and in the living tradition of the Church.

THE BIBLE

'Isn't this the carpenter?' (Mk 6: 3). Jesus Christ was known to His fellow men by the profession He exercised throughout the hidden years of His life. Before His public ministry, Jesus did not perform any miracles but produced goods and offered services for money or in exchange for other goods and services. He might even have employed others, thus running His own small business as an entrepreneur. In any case, He was known by His role in the economy of His time. How He worked, we do not know: but we can guess that He worked with excellence, judging by the way He conducted His public life. He was undaunted by days and weeks of tiring travels; He spent nights in prayer. His miracles, besides being marvellous in themselves, aimed at excellence: the wine at Cana was so good that the chef criticized the bridegroom for not having served it first. The sick, blind, deaf and paralysed could immediately exercise the functions they had lost or never had. This excellence must also have defined the level of effort Jesus put into His work as a carpenter. His professional vocation so much shaped Him that even His redeeming death was perpetrated with hammer, wood and nails, the tools of His profession. Jesus was not beheaded with a sword, or stoned to death with masonry, or strangled in a fisher's net, or beaten to death with a banker's scales.

If Jesus Christ Himself identified with working in the business and economy of His time, how could the Church possibly have a negative attitude towards business and the economy? It is true, as we shall see below, that in the Bible we encounter a certain suspicion of commerce, merchants and their dealings but never a condemnation of the economy as such. Both John Paul II and Francis summarized the Church's stance in relation to business in a masterful way. In his encyclical *Laudato si'*, Pope Francis wrote (129): 'Business is a noble vocation, directed to producing wealth and improving our world. It can be a fruitful source of prosperity for the areas in which it operates, especially if it sees the creation of jobs as an essential part of its service to the common good.' In these lines Francis under-scores business not merely as a job or a career but as a calling to serve others through the creation of wealth. Indeed, before we can distribute wealth, somebody must create it.

John Paul II had the socio-economic system as a whole in mind rather than individual action. His experience of real socialism and the human and economic misery it produced taught him to appre-ciate the right to economic initiative, which, at his time, was still suppressed in many countries. He wrote in *Sollicitudo rei socialis* (15):

> Yet it is a right [to economic initiative] which is important not only for the individual but also for the common good. Experience shows us that the denial of this right, or its limitation in the name of an alleged 'equality' of everyone in society, diminishes, or in practice absolutely destroys the spirit of initiative, that is to say the creative subjectivity of the citizen. As a consequence, there arises, not so much a true equality as a 'leveling down' ... This provokes a sense of frustration or desperation and predisposes people to opt out of national life, impelling many to emigrate and also favoring a form of 'psychological' emigration.

Catholic social teaching upholds the virtuous and principled entre-preneur, manager and businessperson not only as contributors to the common good but as persons called to holiness in and through their work. There is continuity in this depiction of work and economic life from the Bible to modern Catholic social teaching. This is not surpris-ing if we consider that 'the Church's social teaching finds its source in Sacred Scripture, beginning with the Book of Genesis and especially in the Gospel and the writings of the Apostles and that 'human work is *a key*, probably *the essential key*, to the whole social question' (*Lab-orem exercens*, 3, emphasis in original).

From its first chapters, sacred scripture confers on the human person the task of tilling and keeping the garden in which he is placed (Gen. 2: 15), thus continuing God's work of creation through human creativity and initiative. The Bible is full of praise for diligent work and toil (Prov. 12: 11–14); whereas slothfulness is condemned (Prov. 12: 24–27). Commerce, trade and business practice, in contrast, appear in a different light. Sacred scripture differentiates. It condemns greed, foolish trust in wealth, and conceitedness based on earthly possessions (Prov. 30: 7–9). It warns against immorality in commercial affairs (Sir 27: 1–3); it deplores the use of false weights and measures and all kinds of fraud (Hosea 12: 7); and it threatens those who oppress the poor with God's punishment (Amos 8: 4–6).

Summing up the Bible's attitude towards business, we see that the Prophets and other holy authors speak unfavourably of commerce and trade when it is conducted at the wrong time or in an inappropriate place, for the wrong motives or in a dishonest, fraudulent way. They condemn the unfair exercise of power through which the rich tread upon the poor – amassing wealth by exploiting the weakness of others, thus creating great social inequality, forms of slavery and dependence. At the same time Biblical authors support the equitable creation of wealth and prosperity as a sign of God's blessing and favour.

THE CHURCH FATHERS

According to the Bible, virtuous business plays a positive role in society. Saint Paul himself worked to sustain himself and urged his fellow Christians to live off their own labour and to shun the brothers who lived in idleness (2 Thess. 3: 7–13). The Church fathers (the first academic defenders of the Christian faith) reinforced this teaching. They broke cultural moulds that assigned labour and business to slaves or freedmen. Activities such as commerce, trade and business were considered by the general culture in society to be unworthy of a free and noble person.

In contrast, the esteem in which the Church fathers held economic life is reflected in the way they explain salvation history. The language they use is commercial and monetized. They call it the 'economy' of salvation that has wrought our 'redemption' (the commercial and legal act of buying back or freeing a slave). Christ is described as the holy banker who bails out Adam's descendants from the immense debt they have foolishly incurred by sin, thus falling into the clutches of the usurious devil. The lance piercing Christ's side cut open the money bag from which flowed the price of our redemption.

All this language was not meant to endorse an economic system or theory but just goes to show how naturally these words flowed from the pens of early theologians. The Church fathers were concerned not about the economy but about the souls and bodies of the people entrusted to their pastoral care. The theory and praxis they formulate are social: they are concerned about the sick, the miserable, the outcast and those marginalized by the society of their time (such as the lepers); they appeal to the rich for help and compassion. They do not alienate the rich but call on them to share and give back, thus gathering riches for eternal life. If there were no rich, who could help the poor? Saint Augustine, the most influential of all Latin Christian authors of antiquity, defended merchants, the business people of his time. Commerce was frequently condemned wholesale because of the vices of the merchants. Augustine rejected this one-sided condemnation, attributing the vices to the individual merchants not to commerce as such (Augustine 1956, p. 954, quoted, for example, by Thomas Aquinas, *Summa Theologiae*, II.II, q. 77, a. 4 sed contra).

CONCLUSION

Thus, in summary, we see that sacred scripture and the Church Fathers differentiate: they affirm creation, human nature and work as well as commercial exchange as good. At the same time, they strive to cleanse a fallen world from sin, fraud and hardheartedness. They also distinguish between the realm of Caesar and the rights of God (Mt 22: 15–21) where Jesus tells us that we should give to Caesar what belongs to Caesar and to God what belongs to God. With these words of Jesus in mind, the Church's aim and task is not to organize the world and its economic system but to save souls.

Of course, we save our souls by living in the world and its business in a holy and upright manner. Therefore, the Church has something to say about these secular realities, but under the prism of morality and eternal life. Secular authorities, in comparison, have the duty to direct our complex pluralistic societies towards the common good during our life on earth. This too is an essentially moral activity. For Aristotle, politics was the highest, the 'architectonic', part of ethics. The contrast between Church and civil authorities does not mean that the Church alone considers morality, whereas the state can ignore moral claims and concentrate on efficiency or other technical criteria of smooth functioning. The civil authorities too exercise a moral mission. However, their aim is to create social systems that presuppose the sinfulness of mankind, our unordered passions of greed, fear, hatred and so on and do so in a way that minimizes their negative impact. Civil authorities cannot define moral good and evil; nor can they absolve from sin in the sacrament of reconciliation. Moral good and evil are embedded in our nature, recognized by human reason, revealed by God's law and taught by the Catholic Church. However, it is up to the prudential political judgement of the civil authorities to find out how to implement and protect justice in the given context of their specific society, which is always imperfect.

This is also true for business and the economy. The Church knows that we live in a sinful world. She proclaims principles that allow us to make the best of it, and she warns against the false promises of a return to paradise in this life. Utopian models that have promised heaven on earth, abundance without work, and perennial leisure tend to end in man-made hell, concentration camps and forced labour, as historical experience teaches. At the same time, the Church always points beyond what exists, calling to mind the principles of justice and charity, truth and freedom that should inspire and shape our social and economic systems. The Catholic biblical and patristic tradition in this sense is not utopian (derived from the Greek word for 'no place') but 'heterotopian' (derived from the Greek word for 'a different place'): it calls on us not to accept prevailing injustice, to improve morally as individuals and as a society and to struggle against sin where it has become part of our culture (such as in the evils of abortion, euthanasia, the death penalty, and the destruction of Christian marriage). This is the continuing vocation to holiness in the middle of the world, through the exercise of honest secular work including in business as proclaimed forcefully by the Second Vatican Council in its Dogmatic Constitution *Lumen gentium* (Second Vatican Council 1964, pp. 30–38).

REFERENCES

Augustine (1956) Ennarationes in Psalmos. In *Corpus Christianorum, Series Latina*, vol. 39. Turnholt: Brepols. Ps. 70, 17; p. 954.

Charles, R. (1998) *Christian Social Witness and Teaching*. Leominster: Gracewing.

PAPAL ENCYCLICALS AND OTHER CHURCH DOCUMENTS

Francis (2015) *Laudato si'*, encyclical letter (https://www.vatican.va/content/francesco/en/encyclicals/documents/papa-francesco_20150524_enci clica-laudato-si.html).

John Paul II (1987) *Sollicitudo rei socialis*, encyclical letter (http://www.vati can.va/content/john-paul-ii/en/encyclicals/documents/hf_jp-ii_enc_30 121987_sollicitudo-rei-socialis.html).

John Paul II (1981) *Laborem exercens*, encyclical letter (http://www.vati can.va/content/john-paul-ii/en/encyclicals/documents/hf_jp-ii_enc_14 091981_laborem-exercens.html).

Leo XIII (1891) *Rerum novarum*, encyclical letter (http://www.vatican.va/content/leo-xiii/en/encyclicals/documents/hf_l-xiii_enc_15051891_re rum-novarum.html).

Vatican II (1964) *Lumen gentium*, Dogmatic Constitution on the Church (https://www.vatican.va/archive/hist_councils/ii_vatican_council/doc uments/vat-ii_const_19641121_lumen-gentium_en.html).

CHAPTER 9

Taxation and the role of government

Robert G. Kennedy

INTRODUCTION

The question discussed in this chapter is how a system of taxation in modern government might take shape, in some respects at least, if it were informed by a Catholic vision. To do this, however, we need to be clear about the role that government ought to play in our common life and what justice means in the Catholic tradition.

The central political issue, as both a theoretical and practical problem, that has occupied Western culture in modern times (and indeed has helped to define modernity) is whether a virtuous population is a necessary condition for a just social order or whether a just social order can be designed and imposed on a population so that it becomes virtuous. The practical effects of this continuing debate have shaped most of the major conflicts and political upheavals of the last 250 years, from the American and French Revolutions of the eighteenth century, through the rise of socialism in the nineteenth century, the emergence of Fascism and the Cold War in the twentieth century and the cultural polarization of the early twenty-first century. The position one takes inevitably shapes the answer to any question about the proper role of government in society.

The debate has deeper roots than is commonly imagined and in its current manifestation it is about a great deal more than how society can more fairly distribute the benefits of modernity. The American and

French Revolutions dramatically set the stage. On the one side, the American Revolution sought to separate a small, colonial population from a great imperial power but at the same time to adapt a familiar form of government to the conditions of the New World. On the other side, the French Revolution sought to overthrow an existing social and political order and to remake the culture as thoroughly as it could. In the first case, the founders of the American republic were realists determined to craft a political structure conformed to the population and indeterminate yet hopeful about what the people would make of it. In the second, the French republicans were determined to create a new social order and to force the population to conform to it. These two approaches, one focused on realistic initial conditions, the other on an ideal end state (and ruthless about pursuing it) describe the characteristic political options of modernity.

There is an argument to be made that both choices derive from a fuller and more robust vision of society offered by the Catholic social tradition but that both also exaggerate some aspects of this tradition at the expense of suppressing other important elements.

GOVERNMENT AND THE COMMON GOODS OF SOCIETY

John Courtney Murray, a prominent Jesuit theologian in the mid twentieth century, once observed that 'civil society is a need of human nature before it becomes the object of human choice' (Murray 1960, p. 7). By this he meant that human society is not an artefact of deliberation but rather the result of a natural inclination in human beings to associate with one another and to take part of their identity from this association. That we have this inclination is one more manifestation of our nature as images of God, who is also intelligent, free and social (God is a Trinity, after all).

This civil society is the social context in which most of us live our lives. It contains within it many forms of human association, including families, voluntary associations of all kinds, government bodies and, in some respects, the Church (which is a special kind of society).

Societies are capacious. They are the most comprehensive form of common life, containing the other forms of association as if they were organs within a body. This last point is important, as it marks the distinction between a naturally healthy society and one tending toward totalitarianism.

A healthy society is much more than an aggregate of individual members, each independently pursuing his or her own vision of fulfilment. Instead, the members of society find much of their identity and fulfilment in and through their participation in a rich array of social groups. In a healthy society the principal organs – families and voluntary associations – have proper functions that directly or indirectly serve the common good. These are functions that belong to them as natural communities (families, especially) or as deliberate associations, with chosen goals and operations.

One distinctive organ of society is government. No civil society can serve the needs of its members or remain stable without government. Even poor government, to a degree, is preferable to no government at all. Contrary to a famous observation by the American revolutionary Thomas Paine, government is not a 'necessary evil' but its proper functioning *is* necessary to secure the common goods of civil society (Paine 1776, ch. 1). Paine was right, though, to observe that governments do sometimes fail to perform well and that their proper functioning is so important to human well-being that failure demands a remedy.

It is important that government should be understood as an organ of society, neither identical with society nor superior to it. It is the organ through which society exercises authority in service of the common goods of social peace and civic friendship.[1] While government must be an integral part of any civil society, it is not and cannot be the whole, or responsible for every element of private and social life. In a healthy society, there is a great deal that ought to fall outside the ordinary concerns and activities of government, to be addressed by families and voluntary associations as their proper functions.[2]

---

1   Jacques Maritain (1951, p. 42) develops the idea of government as an organ of society.

2   The principle of subsidiarity, which recognizes the organic character of society, is observed in practice, particularly by government, when the

The proper function of government

If government is an organ of society, what then is its proper function? It is to establish and secure the instrumental common good of civil society. Every human association, whether temporary or enduring, is characterized by at least two kinds of common goods, one instrumental and one final.[3] An instrumental common good is a means, or an intermediate objective, that allows the members of an association to work toward its ultimate objectives, which are final goods.

In the case of civil society, the instrumental common good, which we might also call social peace, is, in Augustine's phrase, the 'tranquility of order'. This ordering of society, in the words of Pope John XXIII, 'embraces the sum total of those conditions of social living whereby men are enabled more fully and more readily to achieve their own perfection.'[4] Of course, the goal to which this instrumental good is directed is the comprehensive flourishing of each and every member of the community, which is one of society's *final* common goods.

We must note that this instrumental common good is a set of *conditions*, not a set of *results*. It is a critical part of human dignity – as every parent of a two-year-old knows – that we exercise agency, that we are not merely passive observers of life nor always subjects of the agency of others. According to this view, which the Church

---

sound functioning of the organs of society are promoted and assistance provided when necessary. The result is a rich network of relationships and cooperation which also forms a buffer of sorts between the individual and the civil authorities, balancing the power of the state and protecting the proper freedom and independence of the individual. Subsidiarity, then, is formally a contrary of totalitarianism. It is not surprising that Pope Pius XI introduced the term in *Quadragesimo anno* (79–80), which was written in the context of the rise of Fascism and Communism.

3   Final goods are goals, the purposes for which the association exists. They provide the basis for coordinating the activities of the members. Instrumental goods are the conditions which must be in place if the association is to pursue its goals effectively.

4   Pope John XXIII, *Mater et magistra* (65). He repeated this definition in *Pacem in terris* (58), and it was taken up by the Second Vatican Council in *Gaudium et spes* (74).

has emphasized again and again, the proper and essential function of government in any society is to secure the conditions that make it possible for individuals to be agents on behalf of themselves, their families, their friends and their communities. It is not, in other words, the *proper* function of government to ensure outcomes but instead to establish justice and peace (and to provide remedies to violations of justice), to remove impediments to flourishing where possible and to provide certain kinds of support where needed.[5]

We also need to be clear about what human flourishing means. In his 1967 encyclical, *Populorum progressio*, Pope Paul VI warned against understanding human flourishing simply in material terms, as if it were no more than a matter of production, possession and consumption. Instead, influenced by the French philosopher, Jacques Maritain, he emphasized integral human development, 'the good of every man and the whole man.'[6] Some years later, John Paul II reminded us that the fundamental failure of socialism was 'anthropological in nature'.[7] That is, it was grounded in a mistaken notion of the human person and, as a consequence, the objectives and functions that were assigned to government were often destructive, not supportive, of human flourishing.

The particular errors of socialism – reducing the person to 'a molecule within the social organism', conceiving of development in strictly material terms, denying the importance of agency and freedom – are hardly the only foundational errors that a culture

---

5   See, for example, Pope John Paul II, *Centesimus annus* (11): 'If Pope Leo XIII calls upon the State to remedy the condition of the poor in accordance with justice, he does so because of his timely awareness that the State has the duty of watching over the common good and of ensuring that every sector of social life, not excluding the economic one, contributes to achieving that good, while respecting the rightful autonomy of each sector. This should not however lead us to think that Pope Leo expected the State to solve every social problem. On the contrary, he frequently insists on necessary limits to the State's intervention and on its instrumental character, inasmuch as the individual, the family and society are prior to the State, and inasmuch as the State exists in order to protect their rights and not stifle them.' See also Pope Leo XIII, *Rerum novarum* (28–29).

6   Pope Paul VI, *Populorum progressio* (14).

7   Pope John Paul II, *Centesimus annus* (13).

can make.[8] Western cultures certainly make crucial errors of their own that have severely damaging effects on real persons and also result in misaligning government functions. The recognition of this, along with millennia of experience, should lead us to adopt a certain humility about how completely any government or any society can establish the common good.

What, then, would be a better foundation for society, what would be the components of a better and more authentic vision of the person? It might begin with the conviction that every human life, without exception, has an irreducible dignity that commands respect even from the powerful. It would recognize that human persons, by nature, are intelligent, social and able to choose freely. It should acknowledge that human lives are not enriched merely by material necessities but also by things of the spirit, by truth, goodness and beauty. It would respect the indispensable contribution of families, which nurture us and prepare us to be developed and enriched by our participation in voluntary associations and political communities. And it might, in exceptional cases, admit that each person has a transcendent destiny.

Such a foundational vision would shape and inform the *proper* functions that are the basic operations of government. By proper functions, we mean those that are directly related to the preservation of peace and the common good(s) of society; are vehicles through which society legitimately exercises authority over its members, to order and coordinate their activities; and are ordinarily reserved exclusively to the state.[9] A list of these functions can be easily compiled by considering the principal division of government operations into the legislative, the executive and the judicial. Such a list would

---

8 Pope John Paul II, *Centesimus annus* (13).

9 An argument can probably be made to the effect that most, perhaps all, of the following functions could be delegated to non-governmental actors, with government retreating strictly to oversight. For example, hired arbitrators might substitute for the judiciary, mercenaries for the military, taxation contracted out to private corporations, and so on. Perhaps so, but I know of no societies in history that have done anything like this successfully and some that have found outsourcing major functions to be disastrous in the end.

include determining the laws governing the community, enforcing those laws, diplomacy, defending the community, managing public resources and adjudication.

In most societies, however, the list of government functions does not end here. In a great many cases, especially in the modern context, societies choose to delegate a variety of functions to the state that have been previously performed by private associations. These *delegated* functions might include the administration of welfare benefits, formal education, the provision of medical care, construction and maintenance of transportation infrastructure, postal services, central banking, utilities, and public safety services. Quite often, the delegation is not exclusive, so that private associations may also continue to engage in these operations. The point, though, is that these delegations are choices, made by the society or by civil authorities. Having the government take on these functions may or may not be wise or prudent, but given the democratic accountability of governments, they lie within the set of things that society, via the democratic process, can delegate to government. In this they differ from a third category of government functions.

The third category arises, in the author's judgement, because of a subtle change in our understanding of what government is about. The Catholic social tradition, as I have suggested, understands that it is the objective of government operations to establish and secure the public conditions necessary for human flourishing. The third category embraces the idea that it is the responsibility of government to ensure outcomes. As a consequence, we see the emergence of *assumed* functions of government.

The Catholic tradition, at least since Augustine in the fifth century, has long been sceptical about the possibility of perfecting the City of Man. Perhaps, Augustine speculated, if the City of Man were populated largely by saints some sort of perfection would be attainable, but since saints are never that numerous, human societies will always be corrupted.[10] As long as we are residents of the City of Man, however, we cannot be indifferent to the effects of culture on individuals.

---

10 See Augustine, *The City of God*, especially Book XIX.

In this regard, the Christian tradition has had a two-pronged strategy. It has sought, through its teaching and its sacraments, to immunize individuals against the worst of secular culture and to instil in them sound moral and spiritual habits. And through works of charity, it has sought to relieve personal suffering and to offer an example to inspire improvements in culture. In the end, the measure of its success is not in the conversion of cultures (though this would not be dismissed) but in the holiness of individuals.

In the past couple of centuries, however, a different vision has taken root in Western culture, most dramatically in the French Revolution of the eighteenth century and its imitators in the twentieth century. One of the foundational commitments in these movements was the conviction that, in spite of the weaknesses and sinfulness of individuals, society itself could be perfected through the intelligent transformation of structures and practices and that the reformation of individuals would follow. To achieve this, it would be necessary to harness the authority and power of government, which alone could assemble the resources required for the project and exercise power to ensure its execution. Naturally, once launched in this direction, government would have to assume a variety of functions related to its new duties to ensure the proper outcomes.

So, where a Catholic conception of human dignity regarded the person as intelligent, free and social, and therefore a responsible agent, this new conception of society began with an ideal social structure in mind and tasked government to build it and to fit individuals to a new order. It should be no surprise that this new order also required new forms of justice.

DISTRIBUTIVE AND SOCIAL JUSTICE

There are no more equivocal words in the field of social ethics than those associated with the concept of justice. It is no accident that Plato's *Republic* begins with Socrates asking, 'What is justice?' There have always been an array of answers to this question but the Western tradition commonly accepted the definition offered by the Roman jurist Ulpian: 'the constant and perpetual will to give to each what is his'.[11] Justice, in other words, is at root a quality of the will by which a person is disposed to give to others what they deserve to have. It is a virtue that preserves a sort of equality and harmony between persons.

In the latter half of the nineteenth century, however, an alternate conception of justice was aggressively proposed, especially among economists and legal scholars in the Anglo-American tradition. Where the classical understanding was clear that justice is principally a quality of human actions and only secondarily an assessment of results, the new thinking reversed this priority. Justice became in the first place an evaluation of situations and conditions, particularly of those evident inequalities in society, while secondarily – and inescapably – a judgement about personal and collective responsibility. The difference is subtle but powerful.

In the classical tradition, it was quite possible to distinguish between *unjust* and *unfortunate* situations. Individuals and groups who suffered a serious injustice could usually identify the persons responsible and, in principle at least, could appeal to the legal system for a remedy. But experience teaches us that it is also often the case that individuals and groups may suffer from chance events – weather, earthquakes, disease, and so on – that do not result from anyone's unjust actions.[12] The remedy for such situations in many societies is not recourse to the law but an outpouring of generosity and beneficence; a gift, not an act of reparation or restitution.

In the new way of thinking, however, differences of all sorts in society are presumed to be injustices, not merely misfortunes or the consequences of poor decisions made by the suffering themselves. Following this reasoning, such situations lead to calls for government action to supply a remedy (and often preventative measures, to guard against such situations arising again). Too often, then, challenges that could be addressed in a spirit of generosity and cooperation become occasions of conflict and accusation. In the context of our subject, this can be true with regard to issues of

---

11 Ulpian (d. *ca.* AD 223): 'Iustitia est constans et perpetua voluntas ius suum cuique tribuendi.' *Digest* 1.1.10.
12 Though various injustices, many of which may be impossible to attribute to specific individuals, may aggravate the harms caused by chance events.

distributive justice and social justice, where taxation is promoted as a remedial tool, and so a closer examination of these terms is necessary.

The contemporary Catholic moral tradition has been affected by the secular controversies about justice. In recent decades, voices in this tradition have embraced one secular definition or another but the classical moral tradition, which was generally accepted until the middle of the twentieth century, still provides the foundation for the Church's teaching on matters of justice.[13]

This classical tradition, explored by Thomas Aquinas and many others, divides justice into two broad categories by considering first, who would be the *objects* of just actions (those whose interests must be considered), and, second, the *subjects*, whose choices and actions should be shaped by the principles of justice. The first category of justice is particular justice, where the persons to whom something is owed can in principle be enumerated and identified. This could be a particular individual, the members of a distinct group, or even some of the members of a civil community.

Particular justice is further divided into two types. In the first, which is commonly called commutative justice, the persons who must act justly aim at preserving or restoring equality with others. If I receive a loaf of bread from a baker, for example, our relationship is unequal (unjust) until I give him a sum of money equal to the common value of the bread. Or if I damage my neighbour's fence, our relationship is unequal until I repair the damage or otherwise compensate my neighbour.

But persons can also act in a very different capacity, as representatives of a group (whether a family, a voluntary association, or a civil society) charged with managing the resources and demands of the group with respect to the members. For example, the managers of a business must decide how to distribute the funds available for compensating employees. In order to act justly, they must treat employees who are alike in relevant respects in the same way, while they may, and often should, treat employees who are unlike others

---

13 See Pontifical Council for Justice and Peace (2005, p. 201), hereafter referred to as the *Compendium*.

(more productive, greater responsibility) differently. This type of justice is called distributive justice.

And it is here that we encounter the first great source of confusion in contemporary discussions of justice. The classical (and we might say proper) understanding of distributive justice is that it always concerns the allocation of a benefit or burden to members of a group from what belongs to the group itself or concerning what it has a right to dispense or demand. Strictly speaking, it is never a matter of distributive justice to take what belongs to another and allocate it to third parties.

The modern problem is that, following the inversion of the understanding of justice, distributive justice has too often come to mean an attempt on the part of government to remedy or to correct an unequal distribution of a resource of some sort, which neither government nor society owns, from one group to another.[14] The simple fact of a disparity may be sufficient to demand action to restore distributive justice, even where no actual injustice can be identified as a cause of the disparity.[15]

The second broad category of justice is what the tradition calls 'general justice'. The objects that general justice serves are the

---

14 We have to acknowledge that sometimes, perhaps often, there can be a maldistribution of a resource because of actual injustices. In such cases, it is entirely appropriate for government to intervene to vindicate the rights of the victims but this would be a matter of enforcing the obligations of commutative justice, not distributive justice.

15 See the *Compendium* (353), where the document speaks about government intervention to remedy situations in which the ordinary operation of the market is 'not able to guarantee an equitable distribution of the goods and services that are essential for the human growth of citizens'. This may be a matter of distributive justice (though not here a remedy for injustice), properly speaking, as a service to the common good, in which government distributes benefits to those in need from what has become common property through lawful taxation. The key point is that it is the urgent need of particular persons that is addressed, not the mere fact of inequality. What is neglected here, though not purposely dismissed, is that private charitable activities also supplement what the market can do and in many ways may be superior to government intervention, which is better regarded as a last resort.

principal common goods of the community, not particular, identifiable individuals. Once again, two types can be distinguished.[16] The first type, often called legal justice, has as its subject civil authorities who are responsible for crafting laws and regulations binding on the community. This would include, in the first place, members of legislatures and parliaments, but also executives, regulatory agencies, and others who are empowered to make rules for society. Legal justice obliges these decision makers to enact laws and regulations that genuinely aim to serve the common goods of the society and not to favour some members at the expense of others. This same form of justice obliges those under the jurisdiction of government, as secondary subjects, to obey its just laws and rules.

It is the second type of general justice that prompts some confusion. Without going into too much detail, we might simply say that this type of justice has as its subject the members of society who have a duty, as the occasion arises, to act in support of the common goods even where no specific law or regulation explicitly requires them to do so. The idea here is that no system of laws can foresee all possible sets of circumstances but that, as social creatures, individuals have responsibilities to their communities – or more precisely to the other members of their communities, in general – that require them to attend to the common goods.

It is in the context of general (common) justice that we need to consider the idea of social justice. Social justice has become a name for an objective that should receive the support of all right-thinking members of the community – but it is an objective that has no accepted definition. For the most part, advocates of social justice seem to understand it as a name for greater equality in society or perhaps as a name for a state of affairs in which injustice is entirely eliminated. We can do better than this. We can say that in the Catholic social tradition, and in the analytic framework we have just discussed, social justice is a synonym for the instrumental common good of society. Or, as a virtue of persons, social justice is a synonym

---

16 At this point, the classical tradition becomes inconsistent, both in concept and in vocabulary (see Kennedy 2019, pp. 106–15; Calvez and Perrin 2019, pp. 116–50).

for the virtue of solidarity, as defined by John Paul II in *Sollicitudo rei socialis* (38): 'a firm and persevering determination to commit oneself to the common good'. In any event, within the context of the Catholic social tradition, social justice should be understood as a dimension of general justice, not as a new and distinct form of justice. Furthermore, while the pursuit of justice is essential to the promotion of the common good, it is never enough. Justice must be supplemented by the practice of charity,[17] by a genuine love of the other, which not only gives to others what is theirs, but also gives to them what is mine.[18]

TAX POLICY IN CATHOLIC SOCIAL THOUGHT

Our vision of the human person, the nature of human flourishing and views about the functions of government will determine our preferences in taxation. The question before us then is: what general shape might tax policies take if they were influenced by the Catholic social tradition?

The magisterium has had relatively little to say directly about taxation. When theologians have taken up the topic, it has often been to discuss the obligations of citizens to pay taxes, not to explore in detail what just and wise taxation might be.[19] However, building on our discussion of the common good, justice, and the role of government, we can effectively tease out an answer to this question.

First of all, whatever other objectives it might pursue, the collection of taxes should be just and efficient. Adam Smith's discussion in *The Wealth of Nations* is a well-known and widely accepted summary of principles (Smith 1776, book V, ch. II, part II). He proposed that tax levies ought to be clear and certain, proportionate to the ability

---

17 Note that Pope Pius XI, who first used the term 'social justice' in a papal encyclical, often coupled it with 'social charity' so that justice and charity became the two virtues essential to healing the problems of society. See *Quadragesimo anno* (88, 126) and *Divini redemptoris* (51–54); see also Pope Benedict's encyclical, *Deus caritas est* (28).

18 See *Caritas in veritate* (6).

19 The most prominent modern example of this discussion is Crowe (1944, p. 84).

of the taxpayer to pay, convenient as to timing and mode of payment, and not wasteful in method (so as not to take from taxpayers more than was necessary). It could be added add that tax levies should treat all taxpayers who are similarly situated in the same way, so as to respect distributive justice.

In broad outline, tax levies are imposed for three sorts of objectives. The first is to raise revenue to obtain resources in support of the ordinary activities of government. The second is to influence otherwise legal behaviours in accordance with legislative goals. The third is for redistribution to transfer wealth from private owners to others in the community in pursuit of greater equality. We will consider each category in turn.

Taxation and revenue raising

The revenue category is foundational and has been the focus of most of the discussions of the duty to pay taxes. Government has a duty, probably more often espoused than practised, to be cautious in its demands for funding so as to leave as much of the wealth of the nation in private hands as may be consistent with the common good.[20] The more the government takes in taxes, the less the poor have to meet the needs of their families, the less the better off have to help others and, in some cases, the longer people have to work in order to have a decent standard of living, thus potentially reducing the time they can spend with their families, looking after children and the elderly and so on.

Secondly, it is important for the health of a nation that its citizens participate in public affairs in appropriate ways (see Catholic Church 1994, 1913–15). One of these appropriate ways is by sharing in the burden of supporting the legitimate functions of government. Citizens who have no practical obligation to do so are excluded

---

20 See Pope Pius XII, On public finance, Address to delegates at the Congress of the International Institute of Public Finance, 2 October 1948, translation in *The Catholic Mind* (March 1949), pp. 189–90. Also, Pope Pius XII, On taxes, Address to the International Association for Financial and Fiscal Law, 3 October 1956, translation in *The Pope Speaks* (Summer 1957), pp. 77–80.

from this mode of participation. But they have a diminished sense of ownership in the business of governance and, indeed, little reason to be concerned that government officials moderate spending. This is particularly mischievous in a democracy because, as Aristotle observed, the dangerous temptation in a democracy is for the majority to seek to acquire the wealth of a minority. If the majority, or a near majority, have no obligation to pay taxes at some level, their judgment about public matters may be too easily swayed by leaders who promise benefits for which the bill never comes due.[21]

A third point is that any decisions about tax levies require practical wisdom and balance. There is rarely unanimity among legislators about what programmes should have priority in public spending and at what level of support. There is rarely only one right or best answer to the challenges facing a community. Communities are, and should be, free to determine for themselves what accommodations and compromises seem best to make under the circumstances. And in negotiating these compromises, citizens should remember that their neighbours may hold very different views in good faith. Indeed, it is because people legitimately hold differing views that the responsibilities of government should be limited and that many functions can be safely left to private associations to perform.

Questions about the revenue objective generally fall into four (sometimes overlapping) categories, which concern the distribution of burdens, preferences, exemptions and subsidies.

For private individuals tax burdens are generally distributed at least proportionately and often progressively. There are generally two 'tails' to the distribution of tax burdens. One tail, which is broadly endorsed, moderates (or even eliminates) tax obligations for those with modest incomes or limited resources. The other tail imposes a higher-than-average rate on individuals with greater resources. The Church approves the first tail but has said little about the second. The desire to ensure that burdens are borne by those who can afford to contribute often

---

21 We see this, for example, in the rhetoric of office seekers who promise programmes that must be funded with higher taxes, but also promising that only the wealthy will see taxes increase. This contributes to distrust between voters.

leads to a very high proportion of taxation being paid by the very rich. In the US in recent years, taxpayers with an income that places them in the top 25 per cent account for nearly 90 per cent of federal individual income tax receipts; those in the lowest 50 per cent of income pay less than 3 per cent.[22] Criticism from politicians to the effect that higher earners do not 'pay their fair share' distort this reality.[23] Now, if individuals in the higher income categories peacefully accept this greater burden, perhaps in acknowledgement that a developed society offers them opportunities that others would not, then it is hard to argue that the distribution of burdens is unfair. But we should consider whether such a skewed distribution of burdens is conducive to a society in which all parties have a shared understanding of the common good. In mitigation, it should be noted that those on lower incomes pay a greater proportion of other forms of taxes (such as value added taxes) than they do of income taxes.

In sum, from the perspective of the Catholic social tradition, the lower tail of progressive taxation is soundly endorsed (subject to good judgment in execution) but the array of regressive taxes, especially as they are more than *de minimis*, may be a challenge to the just distribution of the burden of supporting government.

Taxation to influence behaviour

When it comes to using the tax system to influence behaviour, various means are employed to encourage preferred behaviours or outcomes. It is common for those who make gifts to approved charitable

---

22 Editor's note: in the UK, there is a similar trend. The top 1 per cent of income tax payers pay 29 per cent of all income tax and the top 5 per cent pay over 50 per cent of all income tax.

23 It is really under the heading of legal justice that we find a response to the claim that some members of a society do not pay their 'fair share' in taxes. While people have a duty to obey just laws, including tax laws, they do not ordinarily have an obligation to go beyond the text of the law to comply with what they suppose (but often cannot know) to be the spirit of the law. Those who object to tax avoidance behaviours should focus their dissatisfaction first upon the legislators who either crafted the tax code badly or failed to coordinate the codes of one jurisdiction with those of another.

and non-profit organizations to be able to deduct some or all of the amount of the gift from their taxable income. The object of this is to encourage private support for such organizations. This is both in recognition of the fact that this support is often more efficient than support from government and that it may benefit many organizations that would otherwise be unlikely to receive public support. In addition, those who give their income to such causes in accordance with what they believe to be their duties to others in society do not have that income available to themselves and so it should not be taken into account when determining the tax burden. Taxes may also be designed to encourage support for industries favoured by the legislature (for example, green energy) or to penalize other forms of consumption (such as cigarettes).

If one were to assume that the government's need for resources is a constant (independent of actual revenues), then tax preferences shift some of the burden of supporting government from those who qualify for them to those who do not. No doubt the Church approves of preferences for the donations it receives but not merely for these gifts and not merely out of self-interest. The organic vision of society compels us to prefer a community in which many activities of public benefit are organized and supported by private citizens; not everything should be done by government. We also recognize the importance of the virtue of beneficence, in which individuals recognize their duty to use wealth well and are encouraged to do so.

At the same time, we must acknowledge that the power to offer preferences in service of the common good can also be misused to favour individuals and groups to the diminishment of the common good. Industries and organizations that can afford professional lobbying may be able to secure preferences that support their businesses directly by reducing their costs. This may give them an advantage over competitors which may well be unfair; it may at least shift costs to taxpayers. This one would be likely to be a violation of distributive justice but, once again, the context is important. The deciding principle is that the common good be served.

Tax exemptions or other forms of tax preferences are also often extended to the activities of approved not-for-profit organizations (for example, making higher education fees exempt from value added tax or allowing them not to pay income or corporate tax on investment returns). The objective of the exemption is to encourage the formation and operation of private associations whose purpose is to serve the common good in defined areas. Once again, Catholic teaching would approve the spirit of these exemptions, though some have been criticized in recent years. The last several decades have been particularly kind to a handful of major private universities, for example, who have been able to accumulate massive endowments.[24] Voices have been raised questioning whether the shifting of costs occasioned by these exemptions is necessary and wise. In response, many institutions have begun making voluntary payments to local municipal governments to help defray the public costs of their operations. As many Church buildings occupy valuable land in cities (which land is taken off the tax rolls), we may expect to see movements in the future pressing for their tax-exempt status to be reconsidered.

The last category here is subsidies, which share some characteristics with preferences and exemptions. Subsidies are intended to provide financial support for individuals and families or groups in consideration of the service to the common good they already provide or as compensation for burdens borne or imposed on them for the sake of the common good.

They may take several forms, such as exemptions from taxation or cash payments administered through the state's revenue service. A very common example would be benefits offered to parents as support for the contribution they provide to the common good by raising children. In connection with this, we should note that tax policies should take care not to discourage inadvertently (and certainly not deliberately) marriage and family formation. In recent decades, we have seen some tax policies that effectively penalize

---

24 The endowment of Cambridge University in the UK in 2019 was estimated to be about £6.9 billion (roughly $8.4 billion), and that of Oxford University was about £6.1 billion (about $7.4 billion). By comparison, Harvard University's endowment was estimated to be about $41 billion (£32 billion). The University of Notre Dame, the wealthiest Catholic university in the world, had an endowment of about $12 billion (£9.5 billion), larger than the next five wealthiest American Catholic universities, combined.

marriage in some cases or even deny exemptions for dependants if a family is too large. In most cases these have been unintentional but governments have not always been prompt to enact remedies. Taking into account dependents when determining the amount of tax a family pays can also be justified on the grounds of ensuring that the tax system reflects ability to pay and make a contribution for the shared services the state finances through its revenue-raising function. Though this point is contestable, arguably, a household's taxable income should reflect not just its means but the obligations that have to be met out of income, of which bringing up children is one example.

Where governments demand sacrifices for the protection of the common good or, indeed, the preservation of the state, it may also offer compensation to those affected. This reasoning can justify war pensions and the subsidization of businesses that were required to pause trading during the challenge of a pandemic such as Covid-19.

Taxation for redistribution

A third objective for tax levies is to address inequality of wealth by taking private wealth through taxation from those who have more, in order to give to those who have less. Evaluating such a policy poses a dilemma for the Catholic tradition. On the one hand, respect for private ownership is deeply embedded in the tradition but so, too, is the duty to aid the poor. However, clarifying what this right and this duty really require will help us to relieve most of the apparent tension and to reduce the issue to one of balance and judgement.

The Catholic tradition has long defended the right of ownership but at the same time it has insisted that this right has limitations.[25] The right to own property does not mean that the owners may do with their property whatever they wish. Pope John Paul II used the metaphor of a 'social mortgage' to describe the claim that the

---

25 For modern examples of papal defences of private ownership, see, for example, *Rerum novarum* (6–11); *Quadragesimo anno* (44–46); *Mater et magistra* (19) and *Pacem in terris* (21); *Populorum progressio* (22); *Centesimus annus* (6–7).

common good has on private ownership.[26] The key idea is that individuals have a right to own property sufficient for them to live out their vocations with dignity but that wealth possessed above a reasonable sufficiency ought to be at the service of the common good. If your neighbour is starving, and you have more food than you can consume, you have a duty to share.

That said, the right to own property is a natural right, not a right created and bestowed by government or society. As a consequence, government cannot suppress this right, though it may regulate it. One form of regulation may be an intervention by government in which private property is taken when this is strictly necessary to secure the common good.

When government acts in this way, there is a common presumption that it has a duty to compensate the owner for loss of the property. Intentional redistribution of wealth, however, poses a somewhat different problem. One cannot take the wealth of private parties and at the same time compensate them for the loss of that wealth. So, the argument has to be made that this coercive taking serves the common good because the continued possession of wealth or property by certain private parties is in itself a threat to the common good. This is a hard argument to make and harder still to defend such a taking as a last resort or sole option.

We might defend such a taking by showing, if it were possible to do so, that when inequality of wealth reaches a certain level in a society, unrest prompted by envy is quite likely to harm the common good severely. It can also be argued that the common good is not promoted when all people do not have sufficient resources to buy basic necessities. Government may be acting responsibly if it redistributes income and wealth in such situations. It would be better to provide incentives to wealthy individuals to induce them to use their wealth

---

26 *Sollicitudo rei socialis* (42): 'Private property, in fact, is under a "social mortgage," which means that it has an intrinsically social function, based upon and justified precisely by the principle of the universal destination of goods.' His predecessors expressed corresponding views: *Quadragesimo anno* (47–49); *Mater et magistra* (43) and *Pacem in terris* (22); *Populorum progressio* (22–23). The same view was expressed by the Second Vatican Council in *Gaudium et spes* (69–71).

effectively for the common good and to recognize their beneficence publicly.[27] Also, both the Church and governments should nurture charitable and other institutions that help ensure that poverty can be relieved and the living of a fulfilling life is promoted without the direct help of the state.[28] But if there is great need in a society and the wealthy refuse to serve the common good, then a coercive taking may be justified – but rarely.

CONCLUSION

More than 70 years ago, the French philosopher Jacques Maritain gave a lecture in Chicago in which he reflected on the challenge of drafting the United Nations' *Universal Declaration of Human Rights* (1948). His attention was captured by the fact that the various individuals who participated in the project came from diverse cultural and intellectual backgrounds.[29] While it soon became evident to them that this diversity prohibited them from arriving at a common foundation for the project, they were nevertheless in substantial agreement about the result. In other words, they found themselves agreeing on the articulation of a list of human rights but could not agree on a common set of theoretical principles on which to base these rights. They wisely decided to unite around the statement of rights and to set aside their disagreements about its foundations.

This was further evidence for Maritain, as if he needed any, that there is indeed an intuitive understanding of natural law embedded in each human heart, an understanding that may often be obscured or distorted by the wrong kind of philosophical reflection. Despite

---

27 Pope Pius XI was explicit about this when, deep in the Depression, he wrote that the investment of 'superfluous' wealth in ways that would create employment and useful goods would be an excellent use of that wealth. See *Quadragesimo anno* (50–51).

28 This point has been made strongly in *Rerum novarum*, *Quadragesimo anno* and *Centesimus annus*. It is also important that the state does not undermine such institutions thus reducing their effectiveness and increasing the burden on the state.

29 For another account of this important event, with a focus on the participation of Eleanor Roosevelt, see Glendon (2001).

the modern tendency for there to be a clouded vision of the nature and destiny of the human person, there still lingers a deep desire for justice and for a renewed respect for human dignity. What is needed, of course, is a set of constructive solutions that clarify these desires and channel them effectively. The tradition of the Church has something important to offer in this regard, with a clear vision of the human person, of justice and of the common good, and of the genuine role of government in a good society. Even if the foundations of this tradition are not shared, we have reason to be confident that the vision resonates with the human heart. We should proceed with confidence to offer this vision, and its implications for details in areas such as tax policy to a troubled world.

REFERENCES

Calvez, J. I., and Perrin, J. (2019) The expression 'social justice' before and after *Quadragesimo anno*. *Logos* 22(2): 116–50.

Catholic Church (1994) *Catechism of the Catholic Church*. London: Geoffrey Chapman.

Crowe, M. T. (1944) *The Obligation of Paying Just Taxes*. CUA Studies in Theology no. 84. Washington, DC: Catholic University of America Press.

Glendon, M. A. (2001) *A World Made New*. New York: Random House.

Kennedy, R. G. (2019) Social justice and competing visions of the common good. *Logos* 22(2): 106–15.

Maritain, J. (1951) *Man and the State*. University of Chicago Press.

Murray, J. C. (1960) *We Hold These Truths: Catholic Reflections on the American Proposition*. New York: Sheed and Ward.

Paine, T. (1776) *Common Sense*. Philadephia: W&T Bradford.

Pontifical Council for Justice and Peace (2005) *Compendium of the Social Doctrine of the Church*. London: Burns & Oates.

Smith, A. (1776) *The Wealth of Nations*. London: W. Strahan and T. Cadell.

PAPAL ENCYCLICALS AND OTHER CHURCH DOCUMENTS

Benedict XVI (2009) *Caritas in veritate*, encyclical letter (https://www.vati can.va/content/benedict-xvi/en/encyclicals/documents/hf_ben-xvi_enc _20090629_caritas-in-veritate.html).

John Paul II (1991) *Centesimus annus*, encyclical letter (https://www.vati can.va/content/john-paul-ii/en/encyclicals/documents/hf_jp-ii_enc _01051991_centesimus-annus.html).

John Paul II (1987) *Sollicitudo rei socialis*, encyclical letter (http://www.vati can.va/content/john-paul-ii/en/encyclicals/documents/hf_jp-ii_enc_30 121987_sollicitudo-rei-socialis.html).

Paul VI (1967) *Populorum progressio*, encyclical letter (http://www.vatican .va/content/paul-vi/en/encyclicals/documents/hf_p-vi_enc_26031967 _populorum.html).

Vatican II (1965) *Gaudium et spes*, Pastoral Constitution on the Church in the World (https://www.vatican.va/archive/hist_councils/ii_vatican_co uncil/documents/vat-ii_const_19651207_gaudium-et-spes_en.html).

John XXIII (1963) *Pacem in terris*, encyclical letter (http://www.vatican.va/ content/john-xxiii/en/encyclicals/documents/hf_j-xxiii_enc_11041963 _pacem.html).

John XXIII (1961) *Mater et magistra*, encyclical letter (http://www.vatican .va/content/john-xxiii/en/encyclicals/documents/hf_j-xxiii_enc_15051 961_mater.html).

Pius XI (1937) *Divini redemptoris* (https://www.vatican.va/content/pius-xi/ en/encyclicals/documents/hf_p-xi_enc_19370319_divini-redemptoris .html).

Pius XI (1931) *Quadragesimo anno*, encyclical letter (http://www.vatican .va/content/pius-xi/en/encyclicals/documents/hf_p-xi_enc_19310515 _quadragesimo-anno.html).

Leo XIII (1891) *Rerum novarum*, encyclical letter (http://www.vatican.va/ content/leo-xiii/en/encyclicals/documents/hf_l-xiii_enc_15051891_re rum-novarum.html).

CHAPTER 10

Government debt: a neglected theme of Catholic social teaching

Philip Booth, Kaetana Numa and
Stephen Nakrosis

INTRODUCTION

In recent decades, a significant number of developed countries
have accumulated high levels of government debt. Countries have
always borrowed to fight wars or to finance profligate spending.
However, the development of modern debt markets and instruments,
together with post-war thinking in economics, has changed the
nature of government borrowing and indebtedness.

Government borrowing effectively involves the transfer of the
cost of government provision of goods, services and welfare payments to future generations. There may be situations in which this
is justified. However, whether or not this is so, it is important that
Catholic social thought and teaching engages with this issue. Over
the centuries, there has been discussion of problems such as inflation
among those exploring Catholic social thought. And, in recent years,
the Catholic Church has become very involved with the question of
government debt in less developed countries. Nevertheless, there has
been relatively little discussion of government borrowing and indebtedness in developed countries. This is despite the fact that there have
been occasions when the extent of debt has severely undermined

democratic accountability and the ability of governments to undertake the key functions that are demanded of them in Catholic social teaching.

This chapter describes the evolution of government debt and some key questions that might be considered in the development of Catholic social thought and teaching on the subject.

THE RECENT EVOLUTION OF GOVERNMENT DEBT

Public attention to government debt is often sparked during difficult economic times. This was the case in the early 1980s when Latin American countries were unable to service their debt and stood on the brink of default. In 2009, the European sovereign debt crisis threatened the future of the euro zone, an episode from which it has not really recovered. Government debt was also much discussed during the Covid crisis as there had been unprecedented public spending on furlough and business support. This has led many to question whether further increases in government debt are sustainable.

However, during better economic times, problems with government debt do not disappear. Between crises, many countries have failed to reduce debt so that each new crisis leads it to grow to higher levels. Furthermore, what might be termed 'implicit debt' in the form of future pensions and healthcare liabilities accumulates regardless of economic circumstances. Individual countries also go through phases of increasing debt dramatically, but this does not necessarily reach the headlines unless it is sufficiently widespread or sufficiently serious that there is a crisis. Perhaps in this way, as in other ways that will become clear in this chapter, there are similarities with environmental crises.

Table 10.1 shows historical public debt data in five countries: the UK, the US, Japan, Greece and Brazil.

As might be expected, debt tends to rise during wartime. Indeed, the history of the UK national debt from 1700 to 2019 can, more or less, be explained by three wars, a financial crisis and a pandemic: debt increased dramatically after the Napoleonic Wars, World Wars I and II, and the financial crisis of 2008. When crises are over, government debt levels tended to fall, though that did not happen after the financial crisis. However, in recent years for a number of countries, debt has either grown or not been reduced during normal times.

Table 10.1. Government debt as a share of GDP at market prices in 1800–2025 (in %)

	1800	1820	1840	1860	1880	1900	1913	1920
UK	176.8	260.0	154.7	115.5	65.4	32.4	27.9	137.8
US	18.1	13.9	0.2	1.4	17.5	6.6	3.3	27.9
Japan	—	—	—	—	34.0	21.5	53.6	25.6
Greece	—	—	—	—	—	218.1	64.7	—
Brazil	—	—	—	—	99.0	54.9	37.7	36.2**
	1939	1950	1970	1990	2000	2010	2020	2025*
UK	149.7	216.9	73.2	28.8	37.0	75.7	108.0	117.0
US	44.0	87.5	35.7	62.0	53.0	94.7	131.2	136.9
Japan	71.2	14.0	12.0	67.0	143.8	215.8	266.2	264.0
Greece	77.8	23.6***	24.7	73.2	104.9	146.3	205.2	165.9
Brazil	30.8	10.6	—	65.7	68.5	63.0	101.4	104.4

*Projection. **Data for 1923. ***Data for 1952.
Source: IMF Data Mapper: Historical Public Debt Database for 1800–2010; IMF Data Mapper: World Economic Outlook for 2020–25.

In considering fluctuations in national debt, we should also take into account defaults and inflation. These are ways of reducing government debt without repaying it 'honestly'. And so, if debt falls for these reasons, it is, in fact, problematic. Default involves countries not paying the obligations demanded by debt contracts. Inflation leads to a country repaying debt in devalued money. In the UK, for example, the price level doubled between 1974 and 1979. Thus, in many ways, the fall in the debt to national income ratio in this period was illusory: governments were devaluing their debt using the mechanism of inflation and repaying the holders of government bonds with money that had a lower value. Japan defaulted on its debt following World War II and there were other defaults among the countries in the table.

Since 2009, Japan has been the first developed modern economy in a peaceful period to sustain a debt level above 200 per cent of GDP. Meanwhile, the Greek debt situation is probably synonymous with the debt crises in South and Central America with which we have become familiar. Although Greece managed to keep debt below 30 per cent of GDP for most of the post-war period until the 1980s, debt then rose rapidly, hovering around the 100 per cent mark from 1993, surging after the financial crisis and crossing the 200 per cent threshold. It is only as a result of bailouts, severe austerity, restructuring and intervention by outside economic agencies that the situation has been stabilized.

In the decade following the financial crisis, government debt did not return to pre-crisis levels: indeed, in many countries it rose further even after the worst of the crisis had past. Between 2007 and 2019, government debt as a share of national income doubled in the UK (from 42 per cent to 85 per cent (IMF 2020b)), with similar trends displayed in the US (rising from 65 per cent to 109 per cent), Greece (from 103 per cent to 181 per cent), Japan (from 175 per cent to 238 per cent) and Brazil (from 64 per cent to 90 per cent). Even if we take the period 2014–19, after the bailouts of banks at the height of the financial crisis, only in Germany did government debt fall.

While the snapshot and history of government debt may be a cause for concern, we should also consider the dynamics of government debt going forwards. In the UK, the Office for Budget Responsibility (OBR) projects government debt forwards for 50 years in their annual Fiscal Sustainability Report. They assume that tax and spending policies remain the same (that is, for example, that we continue to uprate pensions, tax brackets and healthcare spending in line with current policy). This demonstrates what may happen to the national debt as demographics change and, in the situation we are facing, have fewer taxpayers and more elderly people in receipt of pensions and healthcare. Even before the pandemic, government debt in the UK was forecast to reach 283 per cent of GDP by 2067 (Office for Budget Responsibility 2018). When the 2020 Fiscal Sustainability Report was produced as the pandemic was just beginning, that figure was revised to around 400 per cent of national income (Office for Budget Responsibility 2020). This figure fluctuates, but current projections are similar. To keep the debt under control, there will have to be huge cuts in government spending or increases in taxation over the next generation. Indeed, the OBR projections suggest that, even with large increases in taxation to levels a long way beyond those experienced in modern British history or in other developed countries, there would still have to be cuts in government services or transfer payments, including to those to whom promises of pensions or healthcare provision had been made. These developments in public finances are a consequence of the creation of social security systems whereby pensions and healthcare costs in respect of older people are financed by taxes from the following working generation. The implications of this will be discussed in later sections.

Figure 10.1. General government surplus as a share of GDP (%)
(negative figure is a deficit)

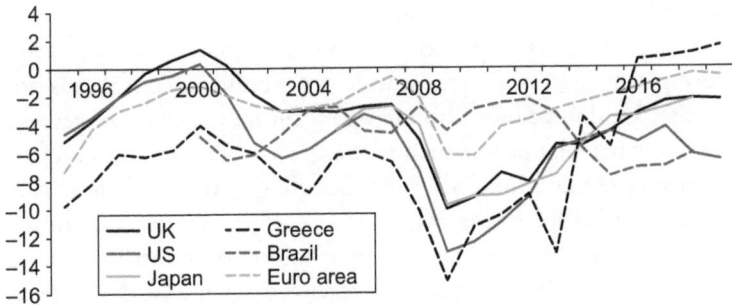

Source: OECD, General Government Debt, 2021.

In any given year, the total amount of government debt increases if there is a budget deficit: that is, if annual government spending exceeds annual revenues. Italy, for example, has had deficits every year since World War II. There are various possible reasons for running deficits (to be discussed below), and it is often argued that short-term budget deficits may be reasonable and justified if they are followed by periods of budget surplus. However, as can be seen in figure 10.1, over the last 25 years most of the countries used as examples in this section primarily ran budget deficits, with only fleeting periods of budget surplus (1999–2001 in the UK, 2000 in the US, and 2016–19 in Greece).

Government debt as a proportion of national income is often regarded as a better measure of the burden of government debt. This increases if the deficit in any year as a percentage of national income is greater than the growth in national income. This is a lower hurdle, but the increase in indebtedness as a proportion of national income in table 10.1 shows that most countries have not been clearing it for any sustained period of time.

When government debt is accumulated, there is a genuine burden: it is not merely a paper transaction. Firstly, interest has to be paid. Secondly, governments have to reduce spending or increase taxation, all other things being equal, in order for the burden of debt to be brought back down to lower levels. Currently, debt interest in the UK amounts to around nine times government spending on foreign aid and twice the level of spending on defence.

It is often suggested that government debt in developed countries is not a burden because 'we owe it to ourselves'. This is not correct. Firstly, a substantial proportion (about one-third in the UK) is owed to overseas holders of government debt. Secondly, even if that is not the case, we do not owe it to ourselves: future taxpayers in general owe it to particular people such as those who expect to receive a pension from a pension fund which has bought government bonds. This is a real burden for future taxpayers and, if governments defaulted or repaid debt with worthless money resulting from inflation, those pensioners in the future would not receive the pensions they expect.

As noted above, the Catholic Church has become interested in government debt as it relates to poorer countries which are indebted to richer countries. There has also been some discussion of government debt in middle-income countries. The national debt of Mexico was 48 per cent of national income when the country threatened to default on its debt in 1982. This brought the attention of the Catholic Church and numerous non-governmental organizations to the worsening debt situation in Latin American and African countries. By 1986, when the Pontifical Commission for Justice and Peace released a document 'At the service of the human community: an ethical approach to the international debt question', Mexico's debt had risen to 78 per cent of national income. This level is much lower than debt levels in many richer countries today. However, it still sparked a crisis. Even though debt levels in richer countries have not reached levels at which default is being threatened or feared imminent, many of the problems we discuss below, such as intergenerational justice, are even more serious in the case of today's developed countries. A country does not have to be faced with imminent disaster for its debt to be ethically problematic.

FUTURE PENSIONS AND HEALTHCARE COSTS

Official government debt is not the only obligation that a government has that could impose burdens on future generations. A feature of Western countries in the post-war period is that they have established social insurance systems whereby individuals accumulate rights to pensions and healthcare but, unlike in the private sector, no money is set aside to meet these costs. Not only that, also unlike in the private sector, governments do not have to account for these obligations. These systems can remain stable if the population structure does not change. However, if the number of young people falls relative to the number of older people, they can become a serious burden. Some countries (for example, Japan, Germany, Italy and most Central and Eastern European countries) are facing rapid population ageing. In such circumstances, the obligations increase, but the means to finance them will deplete.

These pensions and healthcare obligations are sometimes termed 'implicit government debt' as they remain hidden from public view and scrutiny. Longer life expectancy and more retirees is, of course, a welcome development. However, it poses a problem for government finances because no funding has been set aside to pay for future pension and healthcare commitments. The nature of this form of debt can easily be illustrated by policy decisions that were taken in a number of countries in the early 2000s. In countries such as Argentina, Poland and Hungary, individuals had their invested pension funds confiscated by the government which used the funds to repay government debt thus making the debt look smaller. However, the government then made pension promises to those who had their funds taken away to replace the privately invested pensions. In most private-sector contexts, such promises would have to be accounted for.

The amount of implicit debt is not simple to quantify, not least because it depends on assumptions regarding future policy decisions. One estimate placed total US debt at 500 per cent of national income in 2014 – about five times the level of explicit debt (Tanner 2015). Estimates do vary from country to country and depending on the method used to calculate the obligations. However, this estimate is quite close to the consensus across a range of countries.[1]

It could be argued that governments do not have to honour those commitments, and implicit debt could be reduced by simply changing entitlements. However, this would be like another form of debt default and offend distributive justice given the reasonable expectations of those who have made contributions to state pension schemes during their working lives.

It is worth mentioning that the Catholic former prime minister of Ireland, John Bruton, explicitly raised the issue of government debt in a lecture he gave in April 2019. He noted: 'Too often the Church takes the easy route and leaves that particular moral question to politicians … The Church should apply to fiscal policy the same sense of inter-generational justice that it applies to environmental policy'.

Bruton specifically related this to 'piling up unpayable pension obligations'.[2]

THE CAUSES AND FINANCING OF GOVERNMENT DEBT

No comment has yet been made about the causes of government debt except in passing. However, as we move on to consider the moral implications, we do need to consider why governments accumulate debt. This does help determine its moral salience. These questions of government debt management are discussed in standard public finance textbooks such as Gruber (2019). The issues relating to the incentives of democracies to have a natural bias towards voting for

---

1   See also Gokhale (2014) for a thorough discussion of this question.
2   See https://www.youtube.com/watch?v=JqARepLm888 at approximately 29 minutes.

governments that accumulate more debt are examined in Wagner (2012). The arguments can be very technical, but the basic principles are those outlined below.

As noted above, debt is often accumulated in wartime. A just war is likely to involve protecting the common good of the country (or an allied country) from being gravely imperilled. All the resources of a country might be procured to fight the war. This could involve stopping normal economic activity with the costs being met by the government. In addition, the war itself, including enemy action, might prevent normal economic activity taking place and cause a great deal of damage to infrastructure.

A situation similar to wartime might arise when there is a major catastrophic event such as a natural disaster, financial crisis or pandemic. In these situations, the government may wish to borrow to provide support so that people can maintain an adequate standard of living – this happened in many countries during the Covid pandemic. Government tax receipts will be lower and there may be direct costs to meet too (testing people in the case of the pandemic, reconstruction following an earthquake and bank rescue in the case of a financial crisis). As we have noted above, in the UK, government debt peaks have been closely related to wartime and the financial crisis, and the next peak is likely to be coincident with the evolving impact of the pandemic.

A second reason why government debt might be accumulated is that a government may simply be unwilling to raise the taxes to finance its spending. In simple terms, electorates in a democracy may demand more government spending than they will pay in taxes. The moral implications might differ somewhat where governments borrow to invest in ways that will benefit future generations – for example by investing in infrastructure. These investments might be expected to increase economic growth in future years and, perhaps, increase tax revenues as a result.

A further reason for borrowing, at least in the short term, arises because economies can go through periods of below and above average growth. When growth is below average, unemployment might also increase, profits decrease and businesses go bankrupt. When this happens, tax receipts will tend to fall and government spending on welfare payments may rise. As a result, the government may have a deficit. When growth is above average, the opposite may happen. Tax receipts may increase, government spending fall and a surplus might be generated. Rather as in the case of a household with fluctuating income, it does not make sense for the government to run a balanced budget in each individual year when its revenue and spending commitments are varying. On average, deficits arising from this effect should cancel out surpluses.

Related to this, governments often run deficits in order to try to 'stimulate' the economy when output or employment is below normal levels. This would typically be described as a 'Keynesian' policy and whether it has any beneficial effect is widely disputed. In theory, governments would run surpluses to 'cool' the economy when output or employment are above normal levels.

This chapter is discussing government debt in developed countries. In such countries, governments tend to finance their debt by selling bonds. However, government spending can also be paid for through the creation of money or, more commonly, especially since the financial crisis, by the central bank printing money in order to buy the bonds that governments have issued. This can lead to inflation. Indeed, governments printing money to finance spending has been a common cause of hyper-inflation in countries such as Zimbabwe and Venezuela.

It is easy for governments, with the support of electorates, to have a natural bias towards accumulating debt. As such, governments may run deficits when unemployment is high but not reduce them when the economy returns to normal. It may be easier for governments to spend money on infrastructure projects, even if the return is mediocre, than restrain spending, and so on. Spending without taxing allows some part of the electorate to benefit, at least in the short term, with costs being postponed to a future date. The same applies to the accumulation of implicit debts in relation to pensions and healthcare. It is easier for governments to make promises to the current workforce that they will receive pensions and healthcare in the future and not set aside the capital to finance such payments than it is to set up a fund of capital. Future generations then bear the cost.

The reasons why governments accumulate debt do matter when it comes to the moral aspects, especially in relation to distributive justice. We now move on to discuss those moral questions that are legitimately within the domain of Catholic social thought and teaching.

INTERGENERATIONAL JUSTICE AND GOVERNMENT DEBT

Though government debt is widely discussed in economics and, to a lesser degree, in other social sciences, with questions of fairness and justice being raised, it has not been discussed within Catholic social teaching documents or, for that matter, in learned discourse on Catholic social thought.

Humanity was placed at the pinnacle of Creation by God and given the responsibility to act as stewards of the earth. As it says in Genesis, God told Adam and Eve to 'Be fruitful and multiply; fill the Earth and subdue it.' (Genesis 1: 28). The principle by which the goods of this world are there for all persons to enjoy is known in Catholic teaching as the 'universal destination of goods'. It is impossible for everybody to enjoy all the goods of the world. Prudently, the Church, and governments which follow the teaching of the Church even if only implicitly, employ certain principles of distributive justice to ensure that the goods of this world are distributed peacefully and fairly. These principles will involve freedom of contract in labour markets, private property, intervention by civil society organizations, and redistribution of resources to those in serious need including by governments. These are processes in which all institutions within society, including the family, are involved.

Government indebtedness often arises from decisions that allow taxpayers in one generation to consume today with the costs being borne by future taxpayers.[3] The question is whether this is compatible with reasonable principles of distributive justice. In these matters, the exercise of prudence is important. So the answer will not be a

---

3 It is the holders of government bonds who will reap the corresponding benefit, while they sacrifice current consumption in order to lend to the government.

straightforward 'yes' or 'no': reasonable people will disagree. However, in principle, we cannot ignore future generations when it comes to distributive justice. Pope Paul VI wrote (*Populorum progressio*, 17):

> We are the heirs of earlier generations, and we reap benefits from the efforts of our contemporaries: We are under obligation to all men. Therefore, we cannot disregard the welfare of those who will come after us, to increase the human family. The reality of human solidarity brings us not only benefits but obligations.

And Pope Benedict XVI warned we are 'living in untruth' when we live at the expense of future generations (Seewald 2010, pp. 47–48): Pope Benedict was answering a question about government debt by Seewald when he made the comment. In Catholic social thought, our responsibility for the future has been recognized in terms of environmental obligations. We are compelled to 'recognize our grave duty to hand the earth on to future generations in such a condition that they too can worthily inhabit it and continue to cultivate it' (*Caritas in veritate*, 50). But little has been said about government debt.

Perhaps the first occasion on which intergenerational justice was considered systematically in Catholic social teaching was in *Laudato si'*, Pope Francis's encyclical on the environment. A section of this encyclical was titled 'Justice between the generations'. This section called for solidarity between the generations. Solidarity can be defined as the 'firm and persevering determination to commit oneself to the common good' (*Sollicitudo rei socialis*, 38). Pope Francis wrote (160): 'What kind of world do we want to leave to those who come after us, to children who are now growing up? This question not only concerns the environment in isolation; the issue cannot be approached piecemeal.' He went on to warn against a culture of instant gratification and a culture in which parents consumed too much, making it more difficult for their children to acquire a home or build the resources for starting a family.

The same principles apply to government debt. A society which is comfortable with accumulating more government debt because it is unwilling to raise in taxation from the current generation the resources necessary to fund government consumption spending is imposing an unjust burden on future generations of taxpayers as well as living in a manner that is inappropriate. If debt becomes too onerous, governments might renege on repaying debt. This too would be an injustice to those who, in good faith, have lent money to the government. It might be thought that we should have little sympathy with creditors in such a situation. But we should remember that we cannot generalize about their financial situation. They may include beneficiaries of pension funds who rely on those funds for their income in retirement or other groups of people who are not necessarily well off, both at home and overseas.[4]

If the government tries to reduce its debt burden through inflation, this will create other problems (see below) but also lead to an arbitrary redistribution of wealth from people with certain types of property (those on fixed incomes, often pensioners as well as holders of government debt) to the wider body of taxpayers and to other debtors in the economy. This, itself, is problematic from the perspective of distributive justice.

The principles of distributive justice that are normally employed in Catholic thought should make us very concerned about one generation consuming, systematically, at the expense of future generations of taxpayers except in specific circumstances which will be considered below. We would argue that this conclusion should also apply to the obligations in respect of future pensions and healthcare costs too. A generation should not vote itself entitlements without putting aside the necessary resources to provide for the future costs of those entitlements as would happen in a private sector or mutual social insurance arrangement. To do so puts society at great risk of future economic and demographic change leading to a situation where the resources may not exist to fund the obligations. This, in turn, has the potential to create tension and conflict between the generations whereas proper principles of justice should remove instances of tension and conflict. Such conflict also undermines the common good

---

4   In the UK, about 40 per cent of all government debt is held by UK insurance companies and pension funds (https://dmo.gov.uk/media/17379/oct-dec .pdf).

and so the principle of social justice is undermined as well as the principle of distributive justice.[5]

This does not mean, of course, that we should not have systems of healthcare and pension provision in old age. We would argue that such provision should largely be funded at the time the promises are made. This can happen in the context of mutual arrangements for workers sometimes organized by trades unions, commercial private arrangements or government arrangements[6] or there can be hybrid arrangements which mix these approaches.

However, there might be situations in which it is both prudent and just for a state to take on debt. A society which incurs debt to create conditions which lead to economic prosperity for both the current and future generations can rightly expect that future generations contribute to the cost of creating those conditions. This might be the case, for example, when the government funds infra-structure investment, though prudence is required to ensure that such infrastructure spending will have the expected benefits and will not simply benefit specific interests in society. Secondly, when a catastrophe hits, such as the Covid-19 pandemic, and it is prudent for the government to bear the economic costs of both treatment and actions that might be taken to prohibit economic activity, it is just for the costs to be spread over future generations, though it could also be argued that governments should accumulate resources to deal with such events rather than borrow when they happen. Also, in the event of the common good of the whole community coming under threat of destruction in war time, it would be just to borrow to defend the country if necessary. Partly, this is because future gen-erations will benefit from the action, if it is a just war. In addition, when such action is necessary for the survival of society, just as the normal principles of property rights can be overridden for the benefit

---

5   See Booth and Petersen (2020) for a discussion of the distinction between these two types of justice.

6   In the UK, for example, local government pensions are funded and the funds invested, but national government civil service pensions and general old-age pensions are not. All these pensions are provided by the state.

of a destitute person,[7] Catholic social teaching would surely accept that we should do all we can to protect the common good of society in times of war even if future generations bear part of the cost.

This chapter can only scratch the surface of the subject and perhaps lay some of the groundwork for those who follow in this area. However, we would argue that, applying the principles of distributive justice, there is a strong case for governments not to systematically accumulate debt unless the circumstances are exceptional or future generations clearly benefit. As well as being an injustice, the remaining sections consider whether such indebtedness might, in fact, prevent governments from undertaking the functions which Catholic social teaching demands of them.

THE ROLE OF GOVERNMENT IN CATHOLIC SOCIAL TEACHING

The Catechism of the Catholic Church states (Catholic Church 1994): 'every human community needs an authority to govern it' and that the authority's role is 'to ensure as far as possible the common good of society' (1898). The common good, in turn, is defined, in *Gaudium et spes*, one of the documents of the Second Vatican Council, as: 'the sum of those conditions of the social life whereby men, families and associations more adequately and readily may attain their own perfection' (74).

All organizations in society have their own responsibility in promoting the common good. And it is not the role of the state to directly require people to live a life of fulfilment and perfection. Instead, it should create the conditions whereby it is possible for all to play their part in bringing this about. It is in this context that Catholic social teaching has outlined specific functions of the state, including promoting justice, ensuring internal and external peace, protecting property rights, ensuring stable money and appropriately regulating economic life. The state should also act in accordance with what has become known as the preferential option for

---

7   See *Rerum novarum* 14. This situation was also discussed by Thomas Aquinas.

the poor, paying particular attention to the well-being of the least well off (see, for example, *Rerum novarum*, 37) because those who are richer have the means to look after their own interests. According to Hirschfeld (2018, p. 27), the government, in Thomistic thinking, should promote the cultivation of virtue – certainly it should not impede it.

The Catholic Church has supported democracy as the means of choosing the government (*Centesimus annus*, 46). This ensures that the government is accountable to the people and can be replaced peacefully.

The question arises, therefore, of whether the accumulation of government debt impairs these crucial functions of government or, indeed, the workings of democracy. In response to this question, it can be said that there are many historical examples of where debt leads to serious problems within a country that prevent governments or democracies fulfilling their legitimate functions. The examples suffice to make the point. Just because every case of excessive debt does not lead to a catastrophic outcome does not mean we should dismiss the problem.

DEBT AND THE IMPAIRMENT OF GOVERNANCE FOR THE COMMON GOOD

The accumulation of too much debt and the subsequent need to pay interest and principal on that debt has, in the past, seen governments constrained in the performance of their necessary functions. In several cases, the accumulation of debt has led to or exacerbated a total breakdown in the functioning of government and society. In the most extreme cases, the problem of too much debt resulted in the sovereign ceasing to exist. For some nations, the accumulation of debt led to a loss of control over domestic commodities and assets.

During the nineteenth century, as trade began to spread, and as the newly independent nations of the world in places such as South America and Africa sought to use borrowed money for internal development, a wave of debt crises and defaults hit the

globe. During the decade of the 1860s, Egypt borrowed exten-
sively to build roads and factories as well as to erect public and
private buildings in Cairo in imitation of Western capitals, especially Paris. The country was forced to default in 1876, with the
result that its public finances were put under the control of a joint
French–British debt administration council. The UK then invaded
Egypt in 1887, ostensibly to force the repayment of foreign debt.
However, the UK's action may also have been motivated by concern over control of the Suez Canal, with the debt issue serving as
causus belli for aggressive action against Egypt.

During the same period, many nations, including Tunisia, Ser-
bia and Greece, were forced to accept foreign debt administration
councils taking control of government revenue streams to ensure
their obligations were paid. Haiti, Nicaragua and the Dominican
Republic were forced to accept US troops on their soil in the early
years of the twentieth century and permitted US officials to take
control of customs houses so that revenue could be directed to the
repayment of foreign debt.

The fall of the Bourbon dynasty in France was accelerated by that
regime's financial woes. During the final days of Louis XVI's reign,
he was forced to call a meeting of the Estates General in an effort to
convince lawmakers to raise taxes. Once assembled for the first time
in 150 years, the Estates General sought to wrest more power from
the king, leading to the start of the French Revolution.

Debt has also been used by nations as a means to pressure a borrower to either pursue or cease national policies of which the lender
disapproves. One such example took place during the Suez Crisis of
1956. When General Gamal Abdel Nasser announced that Egypt
would nationalize the Suez Canal, the UK and France, following
Israel's invasion of Egypt in October, sent troops to occupy the Suez
Canal Zone. US President Dwight Eisenhower, fearful that this
display of military force could push Egypt into a closer relationship
with the Soviet Union, used political and economic pressure to force
the invading nations to withdraw their troops from Egypt. The US
was in a position to make such demands due to the large amounts
of UK and French debt it held which had been issued to pay for

wartime expenditure and subsequent rebuilding. The 1956 Suez Crisis serves as an example of how a creditor nation can exert pressure on those nations indebted to it.

In the most extreme cases, a nation dealing with the problem of too much debt can find itself in such dire straits that it will lose its independence and be subsumed into another nation. At the end of the seventeenth century, such an occurrence took place in Scotland. A scheme to colonize the Isthmus of Panama, under the auspices of the Darien Company, ended in complete failure. The plan essentially bankrupted Scotland and, shortly thereafter, Scotland entered into a political union with England under the Treaty of Union of 1707. While the financial fallout from the Darien scheme was not the only cause of that political union (Scotland was also suffering from famine following a series of poor harvests) the subsequent collapse of Scotland's ability to pay its debts or finance its necessary functions resulted in a loss of the nation's independence.

Similarly, in the 1930s, the financial situation in Newfoundland, at the time an independent country, resulted in the nation ultimately becoming part of Canada. The 1920s saw Newfoundland engage in deficit spending and borrowing from abroad. When the world economy contracted after the stock market collapse of 1929, Newfoundland's financial situation became perilous. In 1932, Newfoundland was forced to seek a loan from the UK and Canada to enable it to service its debt. The country gutted its civil service, closed post offices and eliminated many social assistance programmes. The collapse of its economy led to a collapse of Newfoundland's political system. The nation eventually gave up its popular sovereignty and gave control of the island's government to a commission which was appointed by and responsible to Westminster. After the end of World War II, still faced with a large debt burden, the people of Newfoundland voted to accept confederation with Canada.

The more recent history of Argentina is especially interesting because it illustrates many of the points made in this chapter. Argentina has defaulted on its debt on nine occasions. At the beginning of the 1930s, Argentina was one of the richest countries in the world. During the Peronist period of the 1950s, although state spending increased dramatically, this did not lead to the

build-up of government debt, partly because of the exception-
ally good fiscal position following World War II, but also partly
because of the printing of money to finance government spending.
However, government spending in excess of revenues eventually
led inflation to rise to over 1,000 per cent in 1976. After that point,
a huge excess of government spending over tax revenues began to
be financed by external debt, which rose by around 40 percentage
points of national income in ten years. This compounded and was
compounded by other macroeconomic difficulties and inflation
rose again to around 1,500 per cent in the mid 1980s. Inflation at
these levels is deeply damaging to the social and economic fabric
and leads to arbitrary redistribution of income and wealth as well
as encouraging financial speculation. During this period private
investment and real incomes slumped.

In the following twenty years, there was a series of events which
can be linked to economic and social dislocation. There were debt
defaults, high levels of inflation, reductions in government spending
on social programmes, a near tripling of extreme poverty in eight-
een months from May 2001, riots and a general election in which
20 per cent of the population spoilt their ballot papers. In addition,
policy autonomy (and thus the accountability of the government to
the people) was lost as the International Monetary Fund (IMF) and
creditors had a much greater say in taking political and economic
decisions. Almost every legitimate function of government was seriously impaired.

The euro crisis of 2009 saw similar problems in many southern
European countries. This crisis came, to some extent, out of the blue.
However, the already high levels of government debt in countries such
as Italy and Greece meant that they were unable to deal with the consequences of a shock which, if earlier policy had been more prudent,
would have caused much less difficulty. Both Italy and Greece went
into the euro crisis with government debt over 100 per cent of national
income. In Italy, a government entirely made up of non-elected professionals was appointed during the debt crisis. In Greece, the response
to the debt crisis involved a range of support packages by other countries and institutions. These packages have a real cost to the creditors
and, because of this, conditions are imposed, so that democratic

accountability is, in effect, lost and replaced by accountability to institutions representing creditors such as the European Union and the IMF. Extreme poverty in Greece doubled in the five years following the crisis to some of the highest levels in the EU.

An extreme case of social dislocation caused by government debt arose in the case of inter-war Germany. It is important to note that this debt did not arise as a result of German taxpayers being unwilling to fund government spending through taxes: it was imposed on the country by the allies following World War I. Nevertheless, it is the effects of indebtedness that are of interest, not the cause. The immediate effect of the high levels of debt was default and then French and Belgian occupation of the Ruhr valley. The subsequent printing of money to pay debts and finance transfers to those affected by the occupation then led to hyper-inflation and immense poverty and economic and social damage.

In the above cases, there were a number of factors at work and there is disagreement about ultimate causes of the various crises that have arisen. However, there is no doubt that the growth of government debt has been an important factor in the undermining of the key functions of government outlined in Catholic social teaching. The accountability of government to the people through democracy has been undermined. In addition, in the various examples, we have seen hyper-inflation, a huge growth in poverty, an increase in social tensions, military takeovers and riots. The basic functions of government in promoting the common good have been seriously impaired. In addition, there are also important concerns related to the government's role in promoting distributive justice. Each of default, inflation and extreme austerity lead to an arbitrary redistribution of wealth and incomes between different groups in society. Some of those groups might be able to manage the loss of incomes and wealth; others on fixed incomes or receiving pensions invested in government bonds may lose everything they own or much of their income. The same may happen to the very poorest who rely on state assistance. All citizens may face significant increases in taxes and therefore experience a reduced ability to play their part in promoting the common good through thriving business or family life.

VIRTUE IN GOVERNMENT AND CONCLUDING THOUGHTS

Following the financial crash, there has been much discussion of the importance of business ethics. The application of the virtues in government is also essential if the government is to promote the common good and distributive justice. In concluding this chapter, it is helpful to relate the problem of government debt to the practice of the virtues in government. The Pontifical Council for Justice and Peace (2005, pp. 565–74) explains the moral challenges facing governments and their electorates and these questions have been raised in a number of papal encyclicals, including, most recently, in *Fratelli tutti*.

The practice of the virtue of justice can become very difficult in situations where there is significant government debt, the accumulation of which might be regarded as an injustice in itself. Decisions may have to be taken to increase the tax burden beyond reasonable levels, to inflate away debt or to impose arbitrary costs on some groups who may be vulnerable. Alternatively, government may choose to default on debt or reduce vital social support programmes. All of these may undermine distributive justice, but the government may be in a position whereby some or all of these actions are necessary as we have seen.

Prudent judgement, whereby those who are governing soberly make difficult judgements using the information that is available, also becomes much more difficult when there are competing interests trying to avoid the costs of government debt.

A lack of the virtue of temperance may well have been responsible for the building up of debt in the first place. Once the debt reaches high levels, this virtue becomes more difficult to exercise both by government and by the electorate. There will be a temptation to pursue strategies which are attractive in the short term but which ultimately may be destructive. Such actions might include the creation of inflation or, indeed, the support for authoritarian or nationalistic political parties which try to lay the blame at the door of foreign creditors.

Finally, it should be said that the virtue of courage becomes that much more necessary in highly indebted countries. Dealing with the extremely difficult situations that arise when a country has to move from a situation in which it is spending more than it is willing to pay in taxes to one in which taxation is higher than government spending requires courage. This is true, both on the part of the electorate which could choose to continue to postpone the problem, and also on behalf of politicians who will be tempted to respond to such demands.

Ultimately, it could be said that government debt creates an occasion of sin in which virtuous behaviour becomes difficult. Indeed, government debt could be regarded as part of a structure of sin. As is discussed by Breen (2008), it is the teaching of the Catholic Church, through John Paul II, that structures of sin are ultimately the result of personal choice. It is certainly true that government debt is ultimately the result of personal choice, though, as we have noted, it may be the correct choice in some circumstances. Such structures of sin can then create conditions in political and economic life which cloud moral judgement and make virtuous behaviour more difficult. This is certainly the experience of highly indebted countries, even if many have come through the experience without the breakdown of civil society or democratic politics. The current position of many highly indebted governments suggests that those countries will face considerable challenges which will require the exercise of the virtues by governments and the electorate if there is not to be serious social dislocation and a threat to the common good in future decades. In many cases, this build-up of debt and future social insurance liabilities can be regarded as having undermined distributive justice, especially across the generations. It may also lead to governments being unable to fulfil their essential functions as demanded by Catholic social teaching.

REFERENCES

Booth, P. M., and Petersen, M. (2020) Catholic social teaching and Hayek's critique of social justice. *Logos: A Journal of Catholic Thought and Culture* 23(1): 36–64.

Breen, J. M. (2008) John Paul II, The structures of sin and the limits of the law. *St Louis University Law Review* 52: 333–35.

Catholic Church (1994) *Catechism of the Catholic Church*. London: Geoffrey Chapman.

Gokhale, J. (2014) *The Government Debt Iceberg.* Research Monograph 68. London: Institute of Economic Affairs.

Gruber, J. (2019) *Public Finance and Public Policy* 6th edition, New York:Worth.

Hirschfeld, M. L. (2018) *Aquinas and the Market: Toward a Humane Economy.* Cambridge, MA: Havard University Press.

OBR (2018) *Fiscal Sustainability Report – July 2018.* London: Office for Budget Responsibility.

OBR (2020) *Fiscal Sustainability Report – July 2020.* London: Office for Budget Responsibility.

Pontifical Council for Justice and Peace (2005) *Compendium of the Social Doctrine of the Church.* London: Burns & Oates.

Seewald, P. (2010) *Light of the World: The Pope, the Church and the Signs of the Times.* San Francisco, CA: Ignatius Press.

Tanner, M. (2015) *Going for Broke: Deficits, Debt, and the Entitlement Crisis.* Washington, DC: The Cato Institute.

Wagner, R. E. (2012) *Deficits, Debt and Democracy.* Cheltenham: Edward Elgar.

PAPAL ENCYCLICALS AND OTHER CHURCH DOCUMENTS

Francis (2020) *Fratelli tutti*, encyclical letter (http://www.vatican.va/content/francesco/en/encyclicals/documents/papa-francesco_20201003_enciclica-fratelli-tutti.html).

Francis (2015) *Laudato si'*, encyclical letter (https://www.vatican.va/content/francesco/en/encyclicals/documents/papa-francesco_20150524_enciclica-laudato-si.html).

Benedict XVI (2009) *Caritas in veritate*, encyclical letter (https://www.vatican.va/content/benedict-xvi/en/encyclicals/documents/hf_ben-xvi_enc_20090629_caritas-in-veritate.html).

John Paul II (1991) *Centesimus annus*, encyclical letter (https://www.vatican.va/content/john-paul-ii/en/encyclicals/documents/hf_jp-ii_enc_01051991_centesimus-annus.html).

John Paul II (1987) *Sollicitudo rei socialis*, encyclical letter (http://www.vatican.va/content/john-paul-ii/en/encyclicals/documents/hf_jp-ii_enc_30121987_sollicitudo-rei-socialis.html).

Pontifical Council for Justice and Peace (1986) *At the Service of the Human Community: An Ethical Approach to the International Debt Question* (http://www.iustitiaetpax.va/content/giustiziaepace/en/archivio/docu menti/at-the-service-of-the-human-community--an-ethical-approach -to-th.html).

Paul VI (1967) *Populorum progressio*, encyclical letter (http://www.vatican .va/content/paul-vi/en/encyclicals/documents/hf_p-vi_enc_26031967 _populorum.html).

Vatican II (1965) *Gaudium et spes* Pastoral Constitution on the Church in the World (https://www.vatican.va/archive/hist_councils/ii_vatican_co uncil/documents/vat-ii_const_19651207_gaudium-et-spes_en.html).

Leo XIII (1891) *Rerum novarum*, encyclical letter (http://www.vatican.va/ content/leo-xiii/en/encyclicals/documents/hf_l-xiii_enc_15051891_re rum-novarum.html).

CHAPTER 11

The financial sector in Catholic social teaching

Samuel Gregg

The love of money is the root of all evils, and there are some who,
pursuing it, have wandered away from the faith, and so given their
souls any number of fatal wounds.

1 Timothy 6: 10

INTRODUCTION

Catholicism has always stressed the potential pitfalls associated with disordered attitudes towards wealth. It has been equally clear that greed, rather than money *per se*, is the primary stumbling block. Nevertheless, many Catholics have been critical – often with good reason – of particular uses of money and capital by individuals, companies and the state.

During the Great Depression, for example, Pope Pius XI in the encyclical *Quadragesimo anno* referred to an 'accursed internationalism of finance'. He claimed that a 'dictatorship is being most forcibly exercised by those who, since they hold the money and completely control it, control credit also and rule the lending of money' (QA 109, 106). Today one does not have to look far to find similar remarks in the statements of prominent clergy and lay Catholic thinkers since the 1930s about specific financial practices.

What is curious about this situation is that the treatment of finance and banking, and money more generally, by medieval and early modern Catholic theologians was considerably more nuanced. Many such thinkers wrote at length and sympathetically, for instance, about the capital-intensive economies that first emerged in medieval Catholic Europe. Their thought played a major role in sparking the financial revolution which helped launch Europe on the path to economic prosperity.

This chapter illustrates how discussion and analysis of the issue of usury by medieval and early modern Catholic theologians opened the way to a better understanding of the nature of capital and financial systems and their role in the economy. It then outlines a framework for how Catholics might think about the finance sector's role in the economy. This is followed by an analysis of the most recent commentary about the financial sector issued by two bodies of the Roman Curia. The chapter then concludes by outlining where there is room for future development.

MONEY-AS-MONEY VERSUS MONEY-AS-CAPITAL

Finance and banking are institutions heavily associated in most people's minds with modernity and the development of modern economies. While there is a certain truth to that, in the sense that the scale and reach of such institutions accelerated in the nineteenth century, it disguises the fact that most of the tools, methods and institutions associated with modern finance attained their mature form in the Catholic world of medieval Europe. In her 2002 book *Medieval Economic Thought*, the historian Diana Wood illustrated that the intellectual explorations of the nature and use of money by medieval theologians 'sanctioned many of the monetary considerations that underlie modern economies' (Wood 2002, p. 207).

Much of this was a result of debates about the issue of usury that preoccupied many Catholic theologians and canonists throughout the medieval and early modern periods. The intensity of that analysis, however, owed something to the fact that Western Europe underwent, during the same period, what the medieval historian Robert Lopez has called the 'commercial revolution'. As Lopez describes it: 'Catholic Europe moved from stagnation at the lowest level to a social and economic mobility full of dangers but open to hope' towards the end of the tenth century (Lopez 1976, p. 31). The vicious circle of low production and consumption together with population decline that had followed the Roman Empire's slow-motion implosion was broken by what Wood describes as a 'spectacular transformation' in Western economic life (Wood 2002, p. 5). Population growth and technological innovations led to more intensive farming, which produced more products, industry, trade and, most importantly, surplus capital: capital that could be mobilized for investment and which could help move society beyond subsistence economies.

During this period, everyone believed that usury *qua* usury was sinful. In 1179, the Third Lateran Council condemned what it called 'notorious usurers', ordering them to make restitution (Lateran III 1179: Canon 25). The question, however, that Christians found themselves asking was: 'What *is* usury?' Saint Bernardine of Sienna argued, for instance, that 'all usury is profit, but not all profit is usury' (see Noonan 1957, p. 182). Reflecting upon the definition of usury was an invitation to make intellectual distinctions which addressed some of the issues noted above, but in ways that maintained Christianity's condemnation of usury. St Bernardine, for example, stated: 'Money has not only the character of money, but it has beyond this a productive character which we commonly call capital' (see Pachant 1963, p. 743). Bernardine's underscoring of the difference between money-as-money and money-as-capital opened up the possibility of distinguishing between loans of money for the purposes of consumption and loans of capital in the context of societies that invested in capital and experienced economic growth.

It was, however, the greatest medieval theologian, Thomas Aquinas, who made some of the most decisive contributions to developing Christian teaching on finance. Aquinas invested considerable effort in examining how one determined the justice of a given commercial transaction, how one measured the value of a good, and what constituted a just price. Inevitably Aquinas came face to face with the question of what, if anything, can legitimately be charged for the use of my money. Aquinas identified two titles external to the loan itself that justified a return to the lender that exceeded the principal. John Finnis (1998, p. 205) summarizes Aquinas's titles in the following way:

> (1) *Share of profits in joint enterprises.* If I 'lend' my money to a merchant or craftsman on the basis that we are in partnership [*societas*] ... so that I am to share in any overall losses or profits, my entitlement to my dividend of the profits (as well as to the return of my capital *if its value has not been lost by the joint enterprise*) is just and appropriate. (2) *Recompense or indemnity* [*interesse*] *for losses.* In making any loan I can levy a charge on the borrower in order to compensate me for whatever expenses I have outlaid or losses I have incurred by making the loan. And the terms of a loan can include a fee or charge which is payable if you fail to repay the principal on time, and is sufficient to compensate me for the losses I am liable to incur if the principal is not repaid on time.

The most striking feature of Aquinas's two titles for justly recovering something beyond the principal is its compatibility with the development of a market in loans of money at a market rate of interest. How is this so? Finnis (1998, p. 205) explains this in the following way:

> With the development of a genuine investment market, in which stocks and shares (i.e. association in the risks of productive and other commercial enterprise) are traded alongside bonds (transferable money loans), it becomes possible to identify a rate of interest on bonds and other loans which compensates lenders for what they are reasonably presumed to have lost by making the loan rather than investing their money, for profit, in shares. Indeed, an efficient market will tend to identify this indemnifying rate of interest automatically.

Many scholastic theologians quickly saw that a forgone gain could be an actual loss when people are living in an economy in which opportunities for gain are part of everyday life. The economist and historian of economic thought Joseph Schumpeter (1954, pp. 103–4) pointed out that this meant two things:

> First, merchants themselves who hold money for business purposes, evaluating this money with reference to expected gain, were considered justified in charging interest both on outright loans and in cases of deferred payment for commodities. Second, if the opportunity for gain contingent on the possession of money is quite general or, in other words, if there is a money market, then everyone, even if not in business himself, may accept the interest determined by the market mechanism.

In light of these insights, Catholic theologians and canonists identified four legitimate grounds for charging interest:

First, there was the payment of a penalty if money was not repaid in time. This was known as a *poena conventionalis*: the difference between what had been due and what was paid. Such a fine was the 'interest'. Once this was accepted, it became accepted practice to place penalty clauses against such delays into contracts.

Second, it was possible that a lender could suffer real damages because of the borrower's failure to return the capital on the schedule determined by the contract. Hence the lender could claim what was called a *damnum emergens* (actual monetary loss incurred). Significantly this title was accepted as legitimate by figures preceding Aquinas such as his master St Albertus Magnus (Divine 1959, p. 54).

Third, a lender could claim for the loss of a possible profit (*lucrum cessans*) if he missed the opportunity of making a profit as a result of lending it to others. Over time, this would become virtually synonymous with *interesse* (Divine 1959, p. 55).

Fourth, there was a legitimate payment that the lender could charge for the risk of losing his capital (*periculum sortis*) (Gilchrist 1969, p. 69). Some medieval thinkers emphasized just how damaging a borrower's failure to repay the lender's loan could be to the latter. In his *Summa Confessorum*, for instance, Thomas de Chobham presented a sympathetic portrait of a creditor who lost everything because someone to whom he lent money had defaulted (Chobham 1968: 7, 6, q. 11, ch. 7).

In all these cases, it remained wrong to charge interest on a loan by virtue of the act of making of the loan. This, however, was compatible with maintaining that moneylenders could fairly charge for other factors. These included risk of non-payment, probable inflation, taxes, the costs incurred in making and administering the loan, and the forgoing of other legitimate uses to which the money could have been put. Hence it was with little difficulty that the last ecumenical council in the West before the Reformation, the Fifth Lateran Council (1512–17), could define usury as 'nothing else than gain or profit drawn from the use of a thing that is by its nature sterile, a profit acquired *without labour, costs, or risk*' (see Gilchrist 1969, p. 115). Not only did these words imply that money was not always sterile; they also underscored the insight that risk, labour and costs provided a basis for receiving back more than the principal.

A CATHOLIC FRAMEWORK FOR FINANCE

It was on this basis that Catholicism distinguished between the difference between usury (which remains a sin) and the legitimate charging of interest. It is also necessary to address, however, the question of what is a specifically Catholic approach to the proper orientation and ends of finance.

Any such approach must take as its basis that the ultimate horizon for Christians lies in the hope of oneness with Christ at the end of time and on the day of judgement. Living out that hope in this world and thereby contributing to building up the kingdom of God that is already mysteriously present in the here and now, requires Catholics to reflect seriously upon how finance and our financial systems promote the all-round flourishing of each person and every community instead of its opposite: disintegration as persons, the dissolution of community and, ultimately, despair.

To flourish in the way that human persons are meant to flourish involves recognition that we require what are called 'instrumental goods'. These are goods that have their own value and which can be used to facilitate the pursuance of fundamental goods, but which are not in themselves fulfilling. The most obvious of such goods is the created world, of which human beings are part, but over which human beings have been charged with a type of authority. Much of the first three chapters of the Book of Genesis detail how humans exercise a genuine 'lordship' over all other created things, albeit one that is not absolute. Humans are not above God's law. In this sense, their dominion over the world is expressed through stewardship: a stewardship that gives direction to what we can choose and for which each of us will have to render an account to God at the end of our lives.

Money is a prominent example of such an instrumental good. It is not a fundamental good in the sense that goods such as life, truth and friendship are intrinsic to human persons and communities. Rather money is a good that derives its intelligibility to humans as a means of helping us to participate in fundamental goods. Through money, a husband and wife are able to obtain any number of other goods and services that help them to live out their marriage and provide for their children. Likewise, money in the form of capital enables entrepreneurs to build businesses that grow and employ people, thereby enabling others to participate in the good of work.

Problems invariably begin whenever people start to view money (or any other instrumental good) as an ultimate good, or when fundamental goods are subordinated to the pursuit of money (or any other instrumental good). While each instrumental good produced through human minds and work has its own value, it does not last. Such goods eventually corrode, malfunction or find themselves being consumed, replaced, superseded or rendered obsolete. Eventually they disappear from our lives when we die.

These limitations should not, however, distract us from the fact that money and other instrumental goods are crucial elements for the promotion of human flourishing. How then do we ensure that our use of instrumental goods, such as money, accords with the demands of human flourishing? Part of the traditional Christian answer to that question is to be found in what is called 'the universal destination of material goods'.

The origins of this idea lie in the principle that God has given the earth and all it contains to be used by and on behalf of *all* people (Grisez 1993, p. 790). In the beginning and now, God provides material goods for the use of all. The question then becomes one of *how* this common use is to be realized. The Christian response has been that it is usually realized (though not only or always) through private ownership. Private possession of property is usually necessary for realizing this goal. The commandment against theft can be understood at least partly pointing in this direction.

In his *Summa Theologiae*, Aquinas outlined three basic reasons in favour of the private ownership of economic goods. Firstly, he notes, people tend to take better care of what is theirs than of what is common to everyone, since individuals tend to shirk responsibilities that belong to nobody in particular. Secondly, if everyone were responsible for everything, the result would be confusion. Thirdly, dividing up things generally produces a more peaceful state of affairs; by contrast, sharing things in common often results in tension. Individual ownership, then – understood as the power to manage and dispose of things – is legitimate (Aquinas 1963: II.II, q. 66, a. 2).

Yet Catholic social teaching does not regard private ownership of material goods as absolute. It is a means of ensuring common use and that material goods serve man, not the other way around. A second condition that Catholicism has attached to private property is that the private nature of our property does not mean we are justified in using it exclusively for ourselves, especially in the face of others' authentic needs. Private property is not an end in itself. It is *for* something. Christianity therefore not only insists that we should use our 'surplus goods' (what each person has left over once they have used their property to meet their own and their families' needs) to assist others, but that we should be ready to use our essential wealth to serve others.

A number of qualifications need to be made here. Firstly, the precise distinction between essential and surplus property is not exactly the same for every person. Much depends, for instance, upon a person's vocation in life. The owner of a large company may have much wealth at his disposal, but very little of it may actually be surplus wealth after he has met his obligations to his family, his employees and his customers.

In his 2008 book *What Your Money Means* (Hanna 2008), Frank Hanna outlines helpful criteria that enable anyone – whatever their profession – to distinguish between essential and surplus wealth. He suggests that essential wealth consists of what is needed to pay for (1) our own bare necessities, (2) our own genuine needs, (3) our own profession-based needs, (4) the bare necessities of those who depend on me, (5) the genuine needs of those who depend on us, and (6) what he calls beneficial goods for ourselves and for those who depend upon us.

Beneficial goods, Hanna argues, are those that 'improve the life and character of the person who benefits from them; they leave us better equipped to do the good things we're called to do' (Hanna 2008, pp. 23–47). In short, it is a question of vocation. An example would be a business executive who pays for a year of foreign language training at a foreign language school in order to improve his ability to operate in business at the international level. Certainly, beneficial goods are on the borderline between essential and surplus wealth. We may, Hanna writes, still have enough wealth if we cannot pay for beneficial goods. Still, he says, it is better if we possess the resources to pay for such goods insofar as they facilitate the flourishing of ourselves and our dependants.

What then is surplus wealth? It is, Hanna states, 'money that's not demanded in any way by the obligations inherent in our circumstances and state in life' (Hanna 2008, p. 49). This is the wealth that all of us have the immediate responsibility to direct towards the common good. That doesn't mean that we are somehow required to hand it all over to the government or simply give it away willy-nilly. The responsibility to use our non-surplus wealth remains, for the most part, ours. But it does mean that any Christian should be deploying this segment of his wealth to aid the flourishing of the less fortunate. What matters is that we put our wealth to work so that the conditions that promote the flourishing of every person and each community are enhanced.

From a Catholic standpoint, the genius of private property is the manner in which it gives individuals and communities the capacity to mobilize their wealth in ways that promote the common good and the principle of common use. Some of this wealth consists of natural and manufactured products. At the same time, wealth can also be actualized in the form of capital in certain economic conditions. Some of this should certainly be used by Christians for charitable purposes – almsgiving being a constant exhortation for Christians. But another way of deploying such wealth is through investment. Herein lies the fundamental legitimacy for modern finance systems. Insofar as they help to facilitate the allocation of resources among individuals, households, entrepreneurs, businesses and governments, financial systems can help us to realize the principle of common use in ways that respect private ownership on a national and international scale. Through private finance, anyone can invest his surplus capital in investment firms that place capital in businesses whose work helps to spur economic development in numerous parts of the world at the very same time. That same person can also invest essential and surplus capital in a retirement fund that is designed to help pay for the family's retirement.

Likewise, the financial system allows government institutions to issue bonds that attract capital and use the capital raised through bond issues to invest in projects that enable government to make contributions to the common good that are beyond the capacity of private actors, such as certain kinds of public works and national defence.

On a broader scale, financial systems also create efficiencies in the investment and deployment of capital by individuals, businesses and governments that, while certainly designed to produce profit, also potentially promote a better stewardship of available capital resources, which might otherwise be wasted. Another important function is the way that modern finance enables (again, at least potentially) a better management of risk in ways that increase potential gains. They may do this in ways that distribute risks to wider segments of the population and reduce potential losses.

The financial sector also introduces more flexibility and freedom into how people match the actual and potential capital at their disposal with what they need and value at different points of time. In terms of formal economics, this is referred to as 'intertemporal choice'. This involves assessing the relative value that people assign to two or more potential payoffs at varying points in time in light of the known and unknown trade-offs of given choices. For our purposes, the point is that the enhanced potential that finance provides to borrow, lend and invest over time allows different people to exercise more control over, for instance, *when* they choose to buy a house, acquire higher education, retire, or begin and expand a business. To that extent, the scope for a person's flourishing can be widened. It is also worth noting that, by nature, the fundamental functions of the financial sector are, potentially, very 'pro-poor'. Without insurance, setting up a business might be impossible for all but the very rich. And, without the ability to buy securitized investments in a savings scheme, it is highly unlikely that anybody but the most well off in society would be able to retire and perhaps then devote more of their lives to volunteering or other wholesome pursuits. Similar arguments can be made when it comes to buying houses, the protection of widows and orphans and so on. Without modern financial systems, it is very difficult to imagine anybody but the very richest being able to move away from a mundane day-to-day existence.

The word 'potential' features significantly in the preceding paragraphs. Financial systems throughout the world are not uniform. And none are perfect. On one level, this reflects the fact that financial systems ultimately consist of fallible sinful human beings and reflect millions of daily choices by those very same fallible sinful human beings. Some of these choices – whether by individuals acting on their own behalf or in the form of a financial firm's decisions – will be based on imprudent and often reckless assessments of risk. Other financial actors will choose to commit wrongs such as fraud. And even if an action involves no choice or even an intention to do wrong, there will always be side-effects: some beneficial, some not-so beneficial, some foreseeable, and some unforeseeable.

It is also the case that all financial systems embody, at different levels and to varying degrees, various dysfunctionalities, none of which may have been intended but which have nevertheless assumed concrete form. An example of such dysfunctionality might be distorted incentives that encourage people to borrow what they are unlikely to be able to pay back.

Then there are the limitations of financial systems that reflect our innate limits as human beings. This is manifested, for instance, in the fact that even advanced economic forecasting, upon which central banks often make interest-rate decisions, often turns out to be wrong. Our inability to forecast precisely what's going to happen in the financial sector over the short, medium and long term reflects the inability of any one person or group – however wise and experienced, and no matter how much theoretical and statistical information may be at their disposal – to predict the economy's future.

OECONOMICAE PECUNIARIAE ET QUAESTIONES

Since Vatican II, various Vatican offices have produced several documents addressing the vexed topic of finance and banking. But, while these texts often set out useful principles for approaching this topic, they have sometimes reflected a selective and, at times, questionable grasp of the subject matter. This pattern was exemplified by a 2018 official statement about the financial sector issued by the Congregation for the Doctrine of the Faith (CDF) and the Dicastery for Promoting Integral Human Development.

Entitled '*Oeconomicae et pecuniariae quaestiones* [Economic and Monetary Questions]: Considerations for an ethical discernment on certain aspects of the current economic-financial system,' this text is divided into four parts. The first, second and fourth sections contain what I think is a sound set of criteria for analysing the morality of finance and financial markets. In the third section, however, the document offers what it calls 'Some clarifications in today's context'.

But the document is not always clear. Though there are some helpful observations there are also more subjective claims about the present state of financial markets, incomplete analyses of particular questions, and truncated discussions of some of the financial sector's biggest problems.

The first substantive point to note about *Oeconomicae pecuniariae et quaestiones* is that there is no demonization of capital. Indeed, the document states that money 'is a good instrument ... a means to order one's freedom and to expand one's possibilities' (OPQ 15). The financial sector likewise is presented as 'something positive' insofar as it engages in circulating capital (OPQ 15). More could have been said about the ways in which financial markets realize this goal by managing risk, engaging in the formation of prices, putting capital to work in efficient ways, correcting misallocations of resources within and between economies and, above all, establishing links between the economic present and economic futures of individuals and communities. Absent these capacities, all of us would be living materially poorer – and considerably shorter – lives.

This positive approach provides a basis for *Oeconomicae pecuniariae et quaestiones* to articulate a number of reference points useful for anyone in finance who wants to live a morally good life. These go beyond stating that money is an instrument and not an end in itself (OPQ 15). They include recognizing that good relationships, including financial relationships, are built upon people's good use of their freedom (OPQ 8) and that while economic logic has its place, it cannot capture the full meaning of human choice and action. Put another way, without the right understanding of the human person (OPQ 9), you cannot establish a sound ethics, including for finance.

For many Catholics and others, this is a given. But in a world in which many people have never had this connection explained to them, it is a point which bears repeating. The document's positive emphasis also leads it to affirm that finance has a 'primary vocation' inasmuch as 'it is called to create value with morally licit means, and to favour a dispersion of capital for the purpose of producing a principled circulation of wealth' (OPQ 16). The use of the word 'vocation' is especially important. It indicates that working in finance can be a *calling* instead of being dismissed as a necessary but disreputable occupation.

Equally noteworthy is the statement in *Oeconomicae pecuniariae et quaestiones* that 'all the endowments and means that the markets employ in order to strengthen their distributive capacity are morally permissible, provided they do not turn against the dignity of the person and are not indifferent to the common good' (OPQ 13). That is a warning against being instinctively suspicious of financial markets. Provided that a financial instrument does not in itself involve some fundamental violation of the moral law (e.g. do not steal, do not lie, etc.), it should be judged on its capacity to help financial markets grow wealth and spread capital.

These and other points contained in the first, second and fourth sections of *Oeconomicae pecuniariae et quaestiones* are helpful in identifying core principles which should be central to any sound reflection upon morality and finance. The third section, however, is a different story.

Here we find a mishmash of common-sense observations ('the market needs anthropological and ethical prerequisites that it is neither capable of giving for itself, nor producing on its own'), extensive use of arguably outmoded business school jargon ('virtuous circularity'), smatterings of different theories of the firm and some very debatable historical claims. The overall impression is one of an author or authors oscillating between offering all-encompassing macro-explanations for the way things are, while intermittingly descending into some of the micro-details of very specific questions.

The third section is not without its merits. It discusses, for instance, the problems associated with large public debt (OPQ 32), though what those have to do with offshore tax havens is not clear. That is one example of how the third section proceeds in fits and starts through a bewildering range of subjects in which the connections are not always clear. As a result, some very serious problems facing the financial sector are not given anywhere near as much attention as they need.

At one point, for instance, *Oeconomicae pecuniariae et quaestiones* mentions that 'there are often economic losses created by private persons and unloaded on the shoulders of the public system' (OPQ 32). That could have led to a thorough-going discussion of one of the biggest challenges facing the financial sector: the situation of people being insulated from the possible negative effects of their choices, which incentivizes them to take risks that they otherwise would not take. This is known as 'moral hazard'.

Moral hazard played a major role in the 2008 financial crisis. Some large financial institutions over-leveraged themselves on the premise that, if a big investment went south, governments would have no choice but to bail them out. Indeed, implicit and explicit government or central bank support for financial institutions and financial instruments has been a consistent feature of the US economy for some decades. Instead of underscoring the wrongness of financial institutions expecting others to pay for their mistakes or pointing out that allowing banks to fail would radically diminish this problem, *Oeconomicae pecuniariae et quaestiones* proceeds to enter into a discussion of the morality of everyday shopping choices.

But what is particularly missing in the document's third section is any consideration of the way that excessive regulation distorts the workings of the financial sector. In multiple places, *Oeconomicae et pecuniariae quaestiones* insists that the financial sector requires more regulations and regulators.

The difficulty is that the financial sector, especially in developed economies, is already heavily regulated. Even before 2008, the US's financial sector was subject to manifold levels of regulation. Thousands more pages of regulations were added to the statute books following the 2008 financial crisis. The 2,223-page Dodd–Frank Act signed into law in 2010 is one of many examples.

Under-regulation is not the primary problem facing today's financial markets. In the US, for example, there are no fewer than eleven federal agencies with financial regulatory responsibilities. These range from the Federal Reserve to the Commodity Futures Trading Commission. All these agencies administer and interpret thousands of regulations. Their jurisdictions also overlap in ways that truly merit the word 'Byzantine'. That does not even count the *hundreds* of regulatory bodies which function at the level of individual states. The situation in the sophisticated financial sectors of Western Europe is no different.

The negative effects of this regulation are several. Firstly, excessive regulation can encourage people to think that, as long as they comply with the endless legal requirements, they are fulfilling their moral obligations. That facilitates a legalistic approach to morality.

Secondly, excessive regulation diminishes access to capital by less-well-off segments of society and makes it harder for smaller institutions to compete. The costs associated with meeting the demands of regulatory compliance can be absorbed with greater ease by, for example, Goldman Sachs than by a small credit union.

Excessive financial regulation also works against start-up businesses. Unlike large companies, first-time entrepreneurs usually do not have the resources to hire armies of accountants and lawyers to help them navigate convoluted regulatory environments as they seek to acquire capital. If a start-up cannot obtain capital, the enterprise is unlikely to begin in the first place. The wealth and employment which could have been created thus never sees the light of day. In economic language, we can say that there are significant economies of scale in regulatory compliance.

Thirdly, over-regulation can actually contribute to further separating the financial sector from the real economy. The bigger and more extensive the regulatory environment, the greater the incentives for banks to hire very smart people to work out how to game the regulations to their advantage. Banks subsequently become distracted from their primary purpose of creating and efficiently directing capital to the economy's productive sectors. Regulators typically react by closing loopholes. But the same very intelligent people will then work out how to game the new arrangements. None of this is an argument against regulation *per se*. Nor does it excuse banks from losing sight of their primary function. But *Oeconomicae et pecuniariae quaestiones* seems unware of the many counterproductive effects upon the financial sector of excessive regulation.

A WAY FORWARD

Finance is unquestionably a sphere of life in which people are subject to specific temptations. *Oeconomicae pecuniariae et quaestiones* goes some way towards helping people make good choices in an industry upon which every single one of us is in some way reliant for our economic well-being.

But perhaps the most striking feature of *Oeconomicae pecuniariae et quaestiones* is that it makes no reference to the vast repository of knowledge on the topics of money, finance and banking developed by medieval and early modern Catholic moral theologians and canonists. This treasure of resources could have been drawn upon to produce a tightly integrated analysis of the great good produced through finance as well as its real and potential challenges and weaknesses.

In that sense, *Oeconomicae pecuniariae et quaestiones* reminds us that the Church has much work to do if it wants to make constructive contributions to the reform of a segment of modern economies that faces a number of critical challenges. Though modern Catholic social teaching says relatively little about the financial sector, or related questions such as the role of the monetary system and monetary policy, Catholics in the Middle Ages and early modern period thought and wrote about issues of money, capital and banking in detail.

Noonan goes so far as to describe the scholastic investigation of usury and money-lending as amounting to the development of 'an embryonic theory of economics' (Noonan 1957, p. 2). A noteworthy feature of their work is that scholastic theologians did not simply speculate about these matters. 'They did,' Schumpeter remarks, 'all the fact-finding that it was possible for them to do in an age without statistical services. Their generalizations invariably grew out of the discussion of factual patterns and were copiously illustrated by practical examples' (Schumpeter 1957, p. 99).

The challenge for Catholic social teaching is to recognize that, given the financial sector's prominent role in modern economies and the way in which it can fuel growth or be a cause of considerable instability, there is a need to recover this body of knowledge and build upon it. We live in a very different world from that of medieval and early modern Europe. The financial sector of our time is more sophisticated in certain respects than the banking systems which existed in those centuries. But, in addition to their insights, they also provide us with a model of how to proceed: the careful study of how banking and finance works and then the careful analysis of what is being freely chosen in order to give guidance about, firstly, how to avoid evil and then, secondly, the doing of good. Without this type of engagement, Catholic social teaching's commentary upon and analysis of the financial sector will continue to languish on the margins of reflection on these matters.

REFERENCES

Aquinas, T. (1963) *Summa Theologiae*. London: Blackfriars.

De Chobham, T. (1968) *Summa Confessorum*. In *Analecta Mediaevalia Namurcensia* 25 (ed. F. Broomfield). Louvain: Éditions Nauwelaerts.

Divine, T. (1959) *Interest: An Historical and Analytical Study in Economics and Modern Ethics*. Milwaukee, WI: Marquette University Press.

Finnis, J. (1998) *Aquinas: Moral, Political, and Legal Theory*. Oxford University Press.

Gilchrist, J. (1969) *The Church and Economic Activity in the Middle Ages.* New York: Macmillan.

Grisez, G. (1993) *The Way of the Lord Jesus,* vol. 2: *Living a Christian Life.* Quincy, IL: Franciscan Press.

Hanna, F. J. (2008) *What Your Money Means.* New York: Crossroad Publishing Company.

Lopez, R. S. (1976) *The Commercial Revolution of the Middle Ages 950–1350.* Cambridge University Press.

Noonan, J. T. (1957) *The Scholastic Analysis of Usury.* Harvard University Press.

Pachant, M. (1963) St Bernardin de Sienne et l'usure. *Le Moyen Age* 69: 743–53.

Schumpeter, J. (1954) *History of Economic Analysis.* Oxford University Press.

Wood, D. (2002) *Medieval Economic Thought.* Cambridge University Press.

PAPAL ENCYCLICALS AND OTHER CHURCH DOCUMENTS

Congregation for the Doctrine of the Faith and the Dicastery for Promoting Integral Human Development (2018) *Oeconomicae et pecuniariae quaestiones: Considerations for an ethical discernment regarding some aspects of the present economic-financial system* (https://press.vatican.va/content/salastampa/en/bollettino/pubblico/2018/05/17/180517a.html).

Pius XI (1931) *Quadragesimo anno,* encyclical letter (http://www.vatican.va/content/pius-xi/en/encyclicals/documents/hf_p-xi_enc_19310515_quadragesimo-anno.html).

Third Lateran Council (1179) (http://www.papalencyclicals.net/Councils/ecum11.htm).

CHAPTER 12

Catholic social teaching and healthcare: time for a rethink

Russell Sparkes

INTRODUCTION

Nigel Lawson, a former Chancellor of the Exchequer, stated in 1992 that: 'The National Health Service is the closest thing the English have to a religion, with those who practice in it regarding themselves as a priesthood.' Thirty years on, little seems to have changed, and the National Health Service (NHS) remains an unquestioned dogma of the British media and political classes. It was noticeable how, during the December 2019 British general election, all political parties paid obeisance to this totemic issue, swearing that the NHS would only be safe in their hands, and all promising massive spending increases for this already huge bureaucratic institution.

The aim of this chapter is to question this dogma, and to sketch out how we might rethink welfare. The focus will be on healthcare, which seems important in the wake of a pandemic. It is also an area where international comparisons can be made. The chapter will argue that the UK's current highly centralized and bureaucratic welfare system is not, as is commonly asserted, an epitome of Catholic social teaching but indeed contrary to it. There is a brief illustration of how welfare worked in practice during the Middle Ages combined with a description of how we got to the current position in the UK. Lastly, the conclusion looks at a potential revival of the hierarchy of values as presumed by Newman, and recently revived by Alasdair MacIntyre.

HEALTH AND WELFARE IN THE UK

The first question that will be considered is whether, even in the purely instrumental terms in which these questions are normally discussed, the centralized UK model of healthcare is as good as is often claimed. UK government expenditure forecasts for the fiscal year to March 2024, are shown in table 12.1. The total spending includes categories that are not listed which make up the remaining 31 per cent of government spending. This includes categories such as debt interest and transport.

Table 12.1. Planned UK government expenditure 2023–24

Programme	Cost £bn	% of total
Pensions	204	18
NHS	221	19
Social security	162	14
Education	109	9
Defence	80	5
Internal security	44	4
Total	1,145	

Most governments in the past would have been astonished that defence and the police, the core functions of government to provide internal and external security, amount to less than 10 per cent of total UK government spending. It can be further contended that the government monopoly of welfare and education, sustained by very high levels of spending, can lead to a kind of 'systemic monoculture' where the only thing that matters is meeting the government's latest set of standards and underlying values are neglected. A good example of this might be the way hospitals have turned gardens into profit-making car parks, when all the evidence suggests that the presence of a garden has a significant positive impact and therapeutic value that tends to be neglected in the current system.

In the UK, healthcare provision is essentially the monopoly of the NHS. The NHS is a government agency which is one of the largest employers in the world with 1.3m full-time equivalent staff. It is often declared to be the best healthcare system in the world. It is true that research carried out in 2017 by the Commonwealth Fund, a US think tank, ranked the NHS as the number one health system in a comparison with those of 11 leading economies. However, the Commonwealth Fund research was based upon five categories such as screening systems, speed of access, and equitable access ignoring income. The NHS fared badly on 'outcomes' such as cancer survival rates. Since one might feel that the successful treatment of major diseases is the primary purpose of healthcare, the relevance of a survey, such as that by the Commonwealth Fund, which only allocates 20 per cent of its methodology to outcomes, is surely open to question. By way of example, under the methodology of this study, a system that gave the same access to all people to a very low level of care would fare better than a system that provided a much higher level of care to everybody but where some people could access even higher standards.

The King's Fund is an independent charity working to improve health and care in England. In May 2018 it produced a detailed report analysing health data from 21 OECD countries and stated that the NHS was continuing to fall behind other comparable countries. In particular, it noted that the UK had around the lowest per capita numbers for doctors, nurses and hospital beds in the OECD. It concluded:

> Although no one would argue that the UK should make decisions about health care based solely on these international comparisons, the consistency with which the UK falls short of other countries' health care resources is striking. Dissatisfaction with the NHS is now at its highest level since 2007.

Indeed, peer-reviewed studies of cancer survival rates show that England and Wales lag well behind the rest of Europe. It generally ranks 19th or 20th out of 29 countries, with lung cancer survival rates so poor that they are next to bottom, above only Bulgaria. In September 2019, the medical journal *The Lancet* published a study, based upon research on some four million patients in seven leading economies by the World Health Organization (WHO) carried out over 20 years. The study showed that patients in Britain had the lowest survival rates for five out of seven common cancers. It was ranked bottom for bowel, lung, stomach, pancreatic and rectal cancer; next to bottom for oesophageal disease; and third from bottom for ovarian cancer. Further, while all countries had seen absolute improvements in survival rates since the 1990s, the UK's relative position was significantly worse than at the study's inception, when it was bottom for three out of seven cancers.

A hundred years ago, the sociologist Max Weber argued that bureaucracies have a tendency to follow their own agendas of self-preservation and expansion, while increasingly ignoring the purpose for which they were originally established of helping others. Does the NHS fit Weber's criticism? In December 2019 the OECD produced an international study showing that British GP partners now earn more than three times as much as the average UK employee, so that the UK ratio of doctors' pay to average earnings is among the highest in the world. Yet there was growing dissatisfaction among patients in the UK with the amount of time they were given for appointments, with Britain lagging in the bottom half of the league table. The study also showed that the UK had the second lowest number of doctors in Europe compared with its population – overall 2.8 doctors per 1,000 people, compared with an OECD average of 3.5 doctors per 1,000.

There is also evidence of weak accountability in the system. For example, for several years there had been public complaints alleging poor care at the maternity unit of the Shrewsbury and Telford Trust, with the Health Secretary ordering an inquiry in 2017 following concerns about infant deaths. Nevertheless, the Trust was awarded £1 million by NHS Resolution for good maternity care in September 2018. Within a few weeks of this award, however, the independent regulator, the Care Quality Commission (CQC), rated the trust's maternity care as 'inadequate' and by December 2019 CQC reported that services at the midwife-led unit at the Royal Shrewsbury Hospital were suspended.

THE NHS AND THE COVID PANDEMIC

In this section, there is a brief discussion of how the UK has done compared with other countries in coping with the Covid-19 pandemic – obviously a thorough analysis would require a paper of its own and a final verdict will not be possible for a number of years. The initial public response certainly confirmed Lawson's point about the NHS as a state religion. The British public were exhorted to come out into the street every Thursday evening at 8 p.m. and *Clap for Heroes,* i.e. NHS staff.

The government promoted the slogan 'Protect the NHS!' This was little questioned by the British media. It was only the foreign press that objected that the slogan was the wrong way round: i.e. that it was the job of the health service to protect the public, not vice versa. Likewise, stringent criticism tended to only be made overseas. The lead headline of the Australian *Sydney Morning Herald* (3 May 2020) was 'Biggest failure in a generation: Where did Britain go wrong?' The article quoted Dr Richard Horton, editor in chief of *The Lancet*: 'The handling of the Covid-19 crisis in the UK is the most serious science policy failure in a generation.'

The following facts are especially pertinent:

- When the pandemic broke out, hospitals were advised to discharge elderly patients back into care homes even though it quickly became that clear that Covid mortality rates were much higher in the elderly. There were 28,186 excess deaths recorded in English care homes from 2 March to 12 June 2020, 18,562 of which were attributed to Covid.
- At the same time, the NHS found its stocks of personal protective equipment (PPE), such as breathing equipment and face masks for front-line healthcare workers, were not fit for purpose. This led to an extremely expensive global scramble to find PPE while NHS staff were left poorly protected.
- When the government decided to make 'track and trace' a key policy objective, NHS England adopted a plan based upon centralizing testing in its own facilities, rejecting the use of private sector laboratories as had been used in Germany. This proved impossible to do at scale, and the whole track-and-trace system had to be redesigned again from the beginning, with valuable time having been lost.
- One of the key metrics in judging the healthcare system's effectiveness in controlling the pandemic was that of excess mortality.

There were nearly 697,000 deaths in the UK in 2020, 85,000 more than would normally be expected based on statistical patterns. In May 2020 the European Centre for Disease Prevention and Control (ECDC) produced a 'z-score' to compare excess mortality rates across countries, taking into account factors such as population size and pre-existing mortality issues. The higher the z-score, the higher the number of excess deaths, with a score higher than z = 15 classified as 'extremely high excess'. Peak excess z-scores in spring 2020 were: 44.1 in England, 34.7 in Spain and 22.7 in Italy.

The UK's poor performance in tackling the Covid pandemic was all the more surprising given that the British state imposed greater restrictions on individual freedom than any other major economy. Table 12.2 rates countries 1–100 (100 being the most stringent), taking into account workplace and school closures, restrictions on public gatherings, international travel controls and stay-at-home requirements, among others.

Table 12.2. Lockdown stringency index

Country	%
US	45
France	64
Australia	65
Italy	82
Germany	83
UK	86

Source: University of Oxford, Blavatnik School of Government Response Stringency Index.

Table 12.3 summarizes the economic and medical consequences of the pandemic in 2020. It is limited to the world's leading seven economies, the so-called 'G7'. It uses data produced by the OECD in December 2020, as well as data produced by the United Nations for the Covid death rate per 1 million people in each of the G7 countries as at 20 January 2021.

Table 12.3. Impact of Covid-19 on G7 countries 2020

Country	2020 GDP change (%)	Covid-19 death rate per 1m population
Canada	−5.4	491
France	−9.1	1,102
Germany	−5.5	609
Italy	−9.1	1,394
Japan	−5.3	38
UK	−11.2	1,389
US	−3.7	1,266

Sources: GDP OECD World Economic Outlook December 2020.
Death rate: United Nations Data January 2021.

The table shows that the UK had by far the worst economic contraction, with the economy forecast to decline by 11.2 per cent combined with the joint worst death rate (that is, similar to Italy).

The NHS did have one undoubted positive achievement: fast and effective mass vaccination. However, it is telling that this was accomplished by the government establishing an independent Vaccination Taskforce, outside the normal NHS operational structures. It was led by Kate Bingham, a venture capitalist with particular expertise in medical companies, with other leaders recruited from the private sector, the voluntary sector and the army. It also used many staff from general practice, which is the one part of the NHS which operates semi-autonomously with GPs generally being self-employed and being partners in their practices. The Vaccination Taskforce had the following achievements:

- It took entrepreneurial risks by identifying a number of the most promising vaccines in the summer of 2020, when it was not known whether any of them would work, and making legally binding purchase orders on a massive scale.
- It ensured that large-scale pharmaceutical manufacturing facilities were available to make these vaccines in the UK, so that

other countries such as those in the EU could not divert them to their own populations.

- With the help of the army logistics team, it set up a large-scale and effective mass inoculation system.

Nobody denies the skill and dedication of front-line NHS staff who worked tirelessly to try and save lives in difficult conditions and at the risk of their own lives. But it can certainly be argued that the system in which they are working has let them, and us, down. The success of the Vaccination Taskforce shows that effective leadership and a system permitting it to function are what is required. We do have limited data and the analysis here is insufficient to draw strong conclusions. However, it can certainly be said that there is no evidence that the NHS has performed better than other forms of health provision and there would seem to be a prima facie case that it has performed relatively poorly.

WELFARE AND CATHOLIC SOCIAL TEACHING

Let us move on and examine the guidance given to us by Catholic social teaching on welfare issues. The Second Vatican Council of the early 1960s, which renewed the working of the Catholic Church, calls upon people to work together for the 'common good'. This was defined, for example in *Gaudium et spes* (26): 'The common good, that is, the sum of the conditions of social life which allow social groups and their individual members relatively thorough and ready access to their own fulfilment.'

That the Church should take care of the poor and sick is highlighted in paragraph 42 of the same document: 'When circumstances of time and place create the need, [the Church] can and indeed should initiate activities on behalf of all men. This is particularly true of activities designed for the needy, such as the works of mercy and similar undertakings.'

It is striking how the first great Catholic social encyclical, *Rerum novarum* (published in 1891), contains much material on how a Catholic alternative to state welfare provision might be constituted, although this is often ignored by commentators. In paragraph 36, it strongly endorses the establishment of mutual self-help groups: that is, workplace institutions which offer help to those in need, such as relief to those who cannot work through illness or injury or those left widowed. The document reminds us of the medieval guilds which offered such support: 'History attests what excellent results were affected by the Artificer's Guilds of a former day ... such associations should be adapted to the requirements of the age in which we live.'

However, it also notes (39) that the Church has created charities and facilitated alms-giving throughout its history but warns that these bodies have been appropriated or 'nationalized' by governments, a theme to which we shall return: 'In our own times, the State has laid violent hands upon them, taken away their rights as corporate bodies, and robbed them of their property.'

Two principles seem particularly relevant when examining welfare issues. The first is *Christian anthropology*, the point that the Church's understanding of humanity is based upon the person defined in relation to others and fulfilled through small associations. The second is *subsidiarity*, the principle that decisions should be taken by the lowest and most local level, rather than by a central authority.

The most basic principle of Christian anthropology, following Genesis, is that man is made in the image of God – *imago dei*. Hence the teaching repeatedly reminds us that 'individual human beings are the foundation, the cause, and the end of all social institutions' (*Mater et magistra*, 219). Indeed, *Gaudium et spes* bases the idea of the 'common good' on the nature of the person (25):

> For the beginning, the subject and the goal of all social institutions is and must be the human person, which for its part and by its very nature stands completely in need of social life. This social life is not something added on to man. Hence, through his dealings with others, through reciprocal duties, and through fraternal dialogue he develops all his gifts and is able to rise to his destiny.

It is important to stress this point. The human person is the starting point for the Church's social teaching. We have freedom so that we may be capable of love. To be a person, to be called to love, implies that we are also part of a society. There is a further point: persons do not exist in isolation. To be a human person is similarly to be part of a society, beginning with the family into which one is born. To love others is to serve them, to do them good. And in working to fulfil ourselves and each other, we work together: hence the repeated advocacy of 'small associations'. The importance of small associations reflects the limits of a human person – we cannot possibly have deep relationships necessary for active service and love with large numbers of people.

Hence it is important to keep in mind the distinction between the *person*, defined in relation to others, and the *individual*, defined in isolation from others. Individuality is what marks somebody from everybody else: in its essence it is a principle of division or even isolation. Personality on the other hand is social, and it is only in social relationships that someone can be a person. The richer the personal relationships, the more fully 'personal' someone will be.

Probably no pope has done more to develop the Church's social thinking than Pope John Paul II, who wrote three great encyclicals on the subject. Gregg (1999) shows how, through his intellectual life, John Paul II consistently expanded and deepened Catholic social teaching's understanding of human anthropology as a major foundational theme. Humanity is the conscious subject of moral acts, but, at the same time, it is also a person, the *imago dei*, a creature who possesses the spiritual properties of reason and free-will. 'It is these attributes of personhood which endow the human subject's work-acts with their creative character and moral-spiritual significance', Gregg argues (p. 218). Gregg further comments, that a fundamental error in much modern thought lies in its propensity to conceptualize humanity in materialistic terms – a faulty anthropology of man (p. 231):

> John Paul's development of social teaching underlines a central point for anyone who wishes to study and/or develop Catholic social thought in a way faithful to authoritative teaching … [that] is profoundly anthropological in its orientation, in as much as it stresses that everything must be considered in terms of what man really is: a fallible spiritual creature called to an other-worldly destiny; a chooser; a knower; and the subject of moral acts, alone and

in association with others. In this sense, John Paul's teaching may be understood as constituting a call for Catholic social thinkers to 'return to the person', and ground their thoughts in a correct anthropology of man.

Gregg's book was published six years before John Paul II's death in 2005. But his insights are confirmed by what the pope said himself on this topic in his last book, *Memory and Identity*, about the need for authentic freedom and a true anthropology: in particular, see chapter 7, 'Towards a just use of freedom', and chapter 18, 'The positive fruits of the Enlightenment'.

The concept of subsidiarity was first explicitly developed by Pope Pius XI in *Quadragesimo anno*, the encyclical commemorating the fortieth anniversary of *Rerum novarum* in 1931. However, the basic idea of restricting state power as much as possible is already found in *Rerum novarum*, particularly 9–10 on the primacy of the family as compared with the state, and 28–29 on the role of government. *Quadragesimo anno* defines subsidiarity thus (79–80):

> Just as it is gravely wrong to take from individuals what they can accomplish by their own initiative and industry and give it to the community, so also it is an injustice and at the same time a grave evil and disturbance of right order to assign to a greater and higher association what lesser and subordinate organizations can do. For every social activity ought of its very nature to furnish help to the members of the body social, and never destroy and absorb them. The supreme authority of the State ought, therefore, to let subordinate groups handle matters and concerns of lesser importance, which would otherwise dissipate its efforts greatly.

Gregg (2014) also discusses why Catholic social teaching implies limited government. In particular, the principle of subsidiarity confers upon people the moral autonomy necessary if people are to freely make moral choices. Further, given that persons reach fulfilment through relationships with other people, then it affirms the priority of the family and other local associations above the state. Booth (2014, pp. 40, 41) makes the following, related, observation:

The market economy appears much shallower than it really is, or should be, because of the expansion of the remit of the state ... For over 90 per cent of the population decisions in relation to health-care and education are taken by the state ... We should ask whether taking away responsibility from families for essential services such as education, healthcare, savings, insurances and housing actually undermines the development and flourishing of the human person.

RESPONSIBILITY AND VIRTUE

In his influential book *After Virtue*, the moral philosopher Alasdair MacIntyre (1981, p. 2) argued that in the modern world: 'The language of morality is in a state of grave disorder ... We have – very largely, if not entirely – lost our comprehension, both theoretical and practical, of morality'. His point was that, while modern society continues to use moral language, it does so in ignorance of the traditional understanding of the meaning of moral concepts. Therefore, the language is used in defiance of its normally understood universal applicability. MacIntyre contends that, while there is intense public and private debate about the ethical issues of our time, such as the morality of going to war, or access to education or healthcare, these debates are 'interminable': that is, they never come to a conclusion, since their apparent rationality is false. McIntyre concluded that the only way to have productive discussions about healthcare, for example, was to return to the ancient concept of the virtues, as developed by the Ancient Greek philosopher Aristotle, and expanded and integrated in Catholic thought by Thomas Aquinas. This is, in my opinion, a hugely important point, and one that, from the point of view of Catholic social teaching, deserves to be more widely understood.

Aristotle used the term *'phronesis'* (φρονησισ) to mean 'practical wisdom'. This is a type of skill which can be acquired through good education, and which guides a person to analyse and make an accurate judgement about the right thing to do in a particular situation. It is also called 'practical virtue' and its practice will lead to a development of a morally good character. I wonder if the colossal impoverishment of our moral thinking, which MacIntyre describes, may not, in part at least, be due to the fact that the need to exercise phronesis, in many of the most important parts of our lives, has been taken away from us.

In other words, areas such as the care of the sick and the aged, help for the poor and the education of our children are, in the UK, overwhelmingly the monopoly of a rigid, bureaucratic state which leaves us, morally speaking, in a state of undeveloped infantilism: there are no meaningful decisions for the individual to take. If this is so, it would imply that the modern bureaucratic state impedes human flourishing or the 'common good' and is therefore in conflict with Catholic social teaching. This is not a point commonly found in Catholic social teaching exegesis. However, consider *Centesimus annus* (48):

> In recent years the range of such intervention has vastly expanded, to the point of creating a new type of state, the so-called 'Welfare State' ... excesses and abuse, especially in recent years, have provoked very harsh criticisms of the Welfare State, dubbed the 'Social Assistance State'. Malfunctions and defects in the Social Assistance State are the result of an inadequate understanding of the tasks proper to the State. Here again the principle of subsidiarity must be respected: a community of a higher order should not interfere in the internal life of a community of a lower order, depriving the latter of its functions, but rather should support it in the case of need and help to coordinate its activity with the activities of the rest of society, always with a view to the common good.

And we can relate this to paragraph 13 of the same encyclical:

> Socialism likewise maintains that the good of the individual can be realized without reference to his free choice, to the unique and exclusive responsibility which he exercises in the face of good or evil. Man is thus reduced to a series of social relationships, and the concept of the person as the autonomous subject of moral decision disappears, the very subject whose decisions build the social order ... This makes it much more difficult for him to recognize his dignity as a person, and hinders progress towards the building up of an authentic human community.

Pope John Paul II was writing about the general principle of socialism here, but would the point not apply to those parts of our lives where decisions have been socialized, such as healthcare in the UK, and, to a lesser extent, education? The fact that we are deprived of making moral choices guided by practical wisdom in these areas impoverishes us, in certain ways, as human persons.

Exponents of Catholic social teaching sometimes use the language of human rights, for example when advocating universal access to healthcare. In my view we need to be very cautious about using such terminology, as human rights are essentially political. In the UK, in the formal sense, they date back to the Bill of Rights 1689, following the overthrow of the absolute Stuart monarch James II, which set out certain basic civil rights and laid down limits to the powers of the monarch. This, in turn, inspired the American Declaration of Independence in 1776, and the use of rights language reached global recognition with the UN Declaration of Human Rights in 1948.

The problem then arises that, since human rights are political devices, any question about human rights implies that the solution lies in political action through the government. This is not consistent with the Church's social teaching. Indeed, the modern assertion, codified in law, of 'rights' to abortion, assisted suicide and some sexual rights are surely incompatible with traditional Catholic doctrine and in fact the magisterium has repeatedly clarified that what it means by human rights is very different from the modern secular understanding. For example, in *Centesimus annus* (47):

> Among the most important of these rights, mention must be made of the right to life, an integral part of which is the right of the child to develop in the mother's womb from the moment of conception; the right to live in a united family and in a moral environment conducive to the growth of the child's personality; the right to develop one's intelligence and freedom in seeking and knowing the truth … In a certain sense, the source and synthesis of these rights is religious freedom, understood as the right to live in the truth of one's faith and in conformity with one's transcendent dignity as a person.

It is also striking that in *After Virtue* MacIntyre highlights the term 'human rights' as something which at first sight looks like an ethical concept, but which, in fact, is not. He argues that theories of natural rights lack the kind of clear criteria for their application which are standard in major religious and ethical theories such as Aristotle's virtue ethics.

To conclude this section, it is worth quoting Fr Robert Sirico (2014, pp. 86–87), who argues that it is the sheer importance of welfare that requires us to challenge the current orthodoxy:

> Many have come to believe that the only way to ensure a flourishing of such support is through an elaborate state apparatus ... But the question as to whether these systems ought to be rethought entirely is hardly ever raised. We are at the first stages of considering a very radical question: whether the care of the poor ought to be treated in the same way that religion in society ought to be treated: that is, as something to be kept out of politics and immunised from political intervention, not because it is a lesser social priority but rather because it is of such high social priority that we dare not permit the state to dominate this area.

THE MEDIEVAL GUILDS

So how might we try and implement Fr Sirico's suggestion of rethinking the current orthodoxy of state welfare provision? Rebuilding civil society would seem a good start, in particular by a revival of mutual self-help groups, inspired by spiritual values, which we might call by their old medieval name of 'guilds'. Of course, we cannot return to the exact model of medieval guilds, any more than we can return to speaking Chaucerian English. Nevertheless, it is worthwhile summarizing what those organizations achieved in this area.

Some people conceive the guilds as a kind of proto trade union; others conceive them as a kind of business cartel. Both ideas are anachronistic. Trades unions grew up as a mass movement, an essentially reactive phenomenon responding to the industrial revolution. In contrast the guilds were associations of freemen, of craftsmen working together to sustain each other and, through apprenticeship and training, to ensure the quality of what they produced. They were not communes: each workshop was led by a Master who worked for his own profit.

Note, however, that the guilds had a variety of interlocking functions: religious, economic, mutual support and works of charity. Indeed, it is important not to forget that the guilds were primarily religious fraternities, based upon a desire to sanctify their work, and to bring honour to themselves within the community as a religious brotherhood. In *Religion and Rise of Western Culture* Dawson (1950, p. 207) noted:

> One of the most remarkable features of medieval guild life was the way in which it combined secular and religious activities in the same social complex. The guild chantry, the provision of prayers and masses for dead brethren, and the performance of pageants and mystery plays on the great feasts were no less the function of the guild than the common banquet, the regulation of work and wages, the giving of assistance to fellow-guild members in sickness or misfortune.

One common aim of all guilds was to arrange prayers in their guild church, particularly for the souls of deceased members. Duffy (1992, p. 143) writes about England on the eve of the Reformation in his book *The Stripping of the Altars*:

> With some variations all late medieval guilds were modelled along the (same) lines – the maintenance of lights before images and the Blessed Sacrament, the procurement of attendance by the whole guild at funerals of deceased members, and finally the exercise of sociability and charity at a communal feast associated with the saint's day.

Economists tend to be negative about the guilds, seeing them as cartel-like and bureaucratic obstructions to economic growth. This was true during the development of capitalist economies from the seventeenth century onward. (It is worth noting that guilds were essentially extinct in England by 1700, but lingered on in much of

Europe until the second half of the nineteenth century.) However, the opposite was true during the Middle Ages. The guilds emerged in Europe simultaneously with the revival of towns and cities, around the year 1100, in a society that had very low population density, poor transport links and a small economic surplus over subsistence levels. It was also a world with little mechanical power, where most capital lay in training human skill, i.e. the seven years it took to train an apprentice to be a craftsman. In this situation, where trade was inherently local and small scale, the guild system assisted in the efficient allocation of capital and restricted the growth of local monopolies. As economic historian Pollard (1981, p. 59) put it:

> Guilds, at first, had numerous functions that favoured progress. They organized the training of apprentices, preserved standards of skill and quality, guaranteed the integrity of its members and found them a market, and above all, freed them from feudal exactions and let them share in the town government ... As the centuries passed however, the system which had once been progressive increasingly came to impose rigidity on the economy until ultimately it became a fetter on progress.

The guilds also promoted works of charity in a poor society where the destitute would otherwise have starved. These ranged from direct alms-giving to the running of hospitals and schools. As Renard (1919, p. 42) noted in *Guilds in the Middle Ages*, there was a genuine attempt to integrate the ideals of brotherhood into their economic role, with the ties of unity strengthened at regular intervals by guild feasts and banquets:

> The merchant or craftsman found in his craft guild security in times of trouble, monetary help in times of poverty, and medical assistance in case of illness ... Apart from the obligatory assistance at certain offices and at the funerals of its members, the fraternity owned a chest, that is to say a fund maintained out of the subscriptions and voluntary devotions of the members, as well as the fines which they incurred.

Hence the guilds were just one part of an interconnected system of Christian aid and welfare, linked as they were to great churches and hospitals, the latter providing both alms and medicine in this period. However, while alms-giving was a major social function of the guilds, perhaps their most distinctive feature was that of a mutual self-help group. Indeed, the guild chest or fraternal treasury had a close resemblance to modern friendly societies, as there was not only help for when somebody was unable to work, but a pension for the infirm. As such, they enabled ordinary workmen and their families to receive payment in case of sickness or old age. Indeed, the earliest known example of a pension scheme comes from the Guild of St James Garlickhythe in 1375:

> If any of the forsaid brotherhood falls into such mischief that he hath nought for old age or able to help himself, and have dwelled as the brotherhood for 8 years and have done thereto all duties within the time, every week after he shall have of this common box 13 pence for the term of his life or he be recovered of his mischief.

Sadly, the wealth the guilds had accumulated attracted the attention of a greedy and self-willed king, Henry VIII, who confiscated their property at the Reformation. In the words of Scarisbrick's *The Reformation and the English People* (p. 31):

> When the royal commissioners went out in 1546, and again in 1548 to survey the colleges, chantries, obit land, guilds and fraternities which the crown was about to seize, they were interested in institutions with permanent endowments of land and property – that was what the government was after.

A flourishing network of local hospitals, schools and alms-giving was abolished. Henry VIII pledged to use the money to refound such institutions on a 'purer basis', but he totally failed to do so. Medieval England had some 500 hospitals, all of the assets of which were confiscated at the Reformation. However, as Whelan (1996, p. 3) observed in *The Corrosion of Charity*, political influence saved the London hospitals:

Henry VIII promised to replace the monastic hospitals with other foundations, paid for by the government, but this promise remained unfulfilled. Only three of the medieval hospitals (which were as much for the care of the poor and the elderly as the sick) survived the Reformation to be re-constituted as secular organisations, all of them in London: St Bartholomews, St Thomas', and Bethlehem (Bedlam). There was no further hospital building in London until the eighteenth century.

BUREAUCRATIC INCURSION UPON FLOURISHING LOCAL INITIATIVES

Earlier in this chapter, *Rerum novarum*'s complaint about the state's confiscation of Catholic charity foundations in the nineteenth century was noted. In the late nineteenth century this was particularly true of France and Italy, but, sadly, this is a recurrent feature of Church history. And history repeated itself yet again in the UK with the state's nationalization of local hospitals and, in effect, friendly societies in 1948.

Supporters of the current system of health provision rarely, if ever, seem aware that, when the current behemoth was created in July 1948, it replaced a vibrant, local, self-reliant system, though perhaps less brutally than 400 years earlier. Local initiatives which had worked well were abolished by force. Halsey (1986, p. 167) noted how ideology drove the abolition of local initiatives:

> Democracy came to Britain from the bottom upwards. The urban working classes of the nineteenth century were uprooted newcomers to the growing provincial industrial towns who responded to their circumstances with extraordinary social inventiveness to give Britain in the first half of the twentieth century its most characteristic popular organizations – the co-operative store, the football club, and the Friendly Society. This urban proletariat created its own local, communal welfare societies ... [But] the Labour movement dominated by the statist traditions of reform as propounded by the Webbs and the Fabians, set out to nationalize democracy

and welfare; to translate fraternity, equality and liberty from the local community to the national state.

One of the fiercest supporters of top-down democratic socialism in Harold Wilson's government of 1964–70 was Richard Crossman. But, near the end of his life, Crossman lamented the way the Labour Party had replaced voluntary action by bureaucratic fiat (Crossman 1976, p. 278):

> From the 1920s on, the normal left-wing attitude has been opposed to middle class philanthropy, charity, and everything else connected with do-gooding … I am now convinced that the Labour Party's opposition to philanthropy and altruism has done it grievous harm.

As Green (1993) showed in *Reinventing Civil Society*, there was a flourishing independent network of free hospitals and friendly societies that provided insurance to their members, which were forcibly incorporated into the welfare state. Of the 3,000 or so hospitals existing at that date, 2,751 were taken over by the newly created government agencies or 'health boards'. It is striking that the 70 Catholic hospitals were the one significant group which managed to stay independent from the proposed NHS. At that time Irish (Catholic) nurses formed a high proportion of nursing staff. It is believed that Cardinal Griffin managed to overcome the resistance of NHS Minister Nye Bevan, after an intense political battle, by threatening to discourage the arrival of new trainee nurses from Ireland if Catholic hospitals were nationalized.

Yet even those who share the above criticisms seem to be inhibited from putting forward positive alternatives, as Whelan (1996, p. 1) observed twenty-five years ago:

> The realisation that something has gone badly wrong with welfare is now accepted by almost all shades of the political spectrum, and the reform of the welfare state is being seriously canvassed. However, many of those who are fully aware of its defects still feel obliged to defend the welfare state out of fear of what would happen if it were to be circumscribed … this is to assume that the alternative to state welfare is no welfare.

Halsey (1986, p. 171) comments on how we might move forward:

> Weber saw only one escape from bureaucratic tyranny – a return to small scale. Subsequent writers following this line have been dismissed as proposing economic absurdity ... but at least this type of response to the modern conditions of state power and manipulative social integration, with its recognition of the failure of emotional bonds in large impersonal structures of authority, points forward rather than backward to the possibilities of solidarity through democracy.

ETHICS AND MEDICINE

In this debate about Catholic social teaching and the provision of healthcare, there is one final, and vital, point to be made. It is an issue identified by John Henry Newman over 150 years ago in a lecture to trainee doctors on 'Christianity and medical science'. This lecture forms part of the final chapter of his *Idea of a University* (Newman 1873). In this lecture, Newman warned his audience that, as doctors, they might quite legitimately make decisions based on their professional expertise, but which were illicit when looked at from a higher – moral or religious – level. He makes the point that, when there is political unrest, a general might recommend aggressive military intervention to suppress it which is logical from his own viewpoint. However, his political superior might reject this advice on the basis of his higher-level thinking of 'statecraft', to which military judgement is just one factor to be taken into account. A doctor taking decisions about medical interventions also needs to look to higher authority.

Newman goes on to give the example of a nun, also a nurse, who is urged by doctors to leave a place where plague has broken out. Their advice is medically sound, but if the nun, who has devoted her life to caring for the sick, decides to stay, being happy to risk her life in this way, her decision is a moral one at a higher level than the purely technical advice of the doctors. Newman states (chapter 10, part 3): 'The medical man was right, yet he could not gain his point. He was right in what he said, he said what was true, yet he had to give way'.

He continues:

> A patient is dying: the priest wishes to be introduced, lest he should
> die without due preparation: [but] the medical man says that the
> thought of religion will disturb his mind and imperil his recovery ...
> I think the priest ought to have that decision, just as the politician,
> not the commander-in-chief, would have the decision, were politics
> and strategics to come into collision.

Newman is warning about the risk of what might now be called
'managerialism': in other words, the possibility that medical decisions are taken on a purely technical basis, with ethical and religious
considerations being shunted to the sidelines. The horrific murder
of Catholic MP David Amess in October 2021 is a case in point. A
priest came to the scene to administer the last rites to the dying man,
but he was prevented by police from doing so on the grounds that it
was a crime scene.

This is always a risk in any profession, but one that is perhaps
particularly apparent when medical treatment is essentially a government monopoly, and one that is therefore permeated by the
implicit political ideology of the time. Religious viewpoints can
sometimes seem to be seen as an irrelevant impediment to efficient
and cost-effective medical care in such an environment. Furthermore, in such a monopoly, people are prevented from seeking institutions that would provide care in a way that accords with their
conscience.

Newman's thinking was reiterated by Cardinal Griffin in 1946
when he issued a public statement on the Bill to take over voluntary
hospitals without compensation:

> Voluntary hospitals should have the right to contract out of the
> scheme. Many of the voluntary hospitals in this country have been
> founded for a specific purpose. That is, to enable patients using
> hospitals to observe the customs and principles of their own faith.
> That is a vital issue in the treatment of disease and sickness where
> medical practice may sometimes conflict with the moral principles
> of patients. To secure these rights it is essential that appointments

to the hospital should safeguard the principles of the patients for whose benefit the hospital has been endowed.

Though a small number of such hospitals remained, including some Catholic hospitals, the method of financing healthcare in the UK prevents the effective use of such organizations except by the most-well-off in society: hardly an 'option for the poor'.

CONCLUSION: REFORMING UK HEALTHCARE

If the above analysis is correct, it seems obvious that UK healthcare provision is in need of significant reform and the introduction of competition. This does not mean the introduction of a US-style healthcare system. One important step might be to copy Australia, which, in 1975, separated payment for healthcare from provision of healthcare. Essentially the government gives everyone a medicare card that can be presented to any accredited healthcare provider, with medical procedures paid for at a set rate. France and Germany, also provide examples of how to maintain plurality of provision, and hence competition. In Germany a substantial proportion of medical provision is by religious institutions.

There also seems a clear need to simplify the current Byzantine complexity of NHS bureaucracy, with its clear risk that staff might feel obliged to prioritize paperwork above patient care. The principle of subsidiarity is not just a political principle. Organizations should ensure that their employees have the appropriate degree of auton-omy. For example, during the pandemic 40,000 retired doctors and nurses applied to come back to work. However, only 5,000 of these were successful, with many deterred by bureaucratic requirements to provide 21 different pieces of evidence, later cut to 'only' 15, to support their application.

However, as well as practical reforms, there needs to be philo-sophical changes in the way we view healthcare. Newman's views, discussed above, rely upon the belief, largely taken for granted in his day, that there is a hierarchy of knowledge. In other words, that theology and philosophy were at a higher level than purely technical subjects such as medicine or warfare. However, from the beginning of the twentieth century, this traditional viewpoint tended to fade away as the sheer complexity and volume of academic study led to increased specialization.

Is there any way in which this hierarchy of knowledge can be reintroduced given the intense academic specialization of our era? MacIntyre (2009) notes that universities were founded in the Middle Ages to enable philosophical and theological discussion about Catholic thought and its implications for contemporary life. That they were grounded in Catholic theology helped ensure that they provided an integrating principle in which subjects could be discussed in relation to each other. MacIntyre argues that, even today, or perhaps most particularly today, Catholic philosophers are needed to provide an intellectual unifying principle which is the only way to enable a genuine and productive moral debate to proceed. As he put it (p. 176):

> One of the tasks of Catholic philosophers now, therefore, has to be that of following the injunction of John Paul II in *Fides et Ratio* to do philosophy in such a way as to address the deeper human concerns that underline its basic problems, without sacrificing rigour or depth.

Let those of us who study Catholic social thought and teaching take encouragement from MacIntyre's words and use them to analyse and to challenge the ills of contemporary society such as current modes of healthcare provision.

REFERENCES

Arnold, M., Rutherford, M. J., Bardot, A., Ferlay, J., Andersson, T. M., Myklebust, T. Å., Tervonen, H., Thursfield, V., Ransom, D., Shack, L., Woods, R. R., Turner, D., Leonfellner, S., Ryan, S., Saint-Jacques, N. De P., McClure, C., Ramanakumar, A. V., Stuart-Panko, H., Engholm, G., Walsh, P. M., Jackson, C., Vernon, S., Morgan, E., Gavin, A., Morrison, D. S., Huws, D. W., Porter, G., Butler, J., Bryant, H., Currow, D. C., Hiom, S., Parkin, D. M., Sasieni, P., Lambert, P. C., Møller, B., Soerjomataram, I., and Bray, F. (2019) Progress in cancer survival, mortality, and incidence in seven high-income countries 1995–2014 (ICBP SURVMARK-2): a population-based study. *Lancet Oncol.* 20(11): 1493–505.

Booth, P. M. (2014) Understanding Catholic social teaching in the light of economic reasoning. In *Catholic Social Teaching and the Market Economy* (ed. P. M. Booth). London: St Pauls.

Charles, R. (1998) *Christian Social Witness and Teaching: The Catholic Tradition from Genesis to Centesimus Annus.* Leominster: Gracewing.

Crossman, R. H. S. (1976) The role of the volunteer in a modern social service. In *Traditions of Social Policy* (ed. A. H. Halsey). Oxford: Blackwell.

Dawson, C. (1950) *Religion and Rise of Western Culture.* London: Sheed & Ward.

Duffy, E. (1992) *The Stripping of the Altars.* Yale University Press.

Green, D. (1983) *Reinventing Civil Society.* London: Institute of Economic Affairs.

Gregg, S. (1999) *Challenging the Modern World: Karol Wojtyla/John Paul II and the Development of Catholic Social Teaching.* Maryland: Lexington Books.

Gregg, S. (2014) Catholicism and the case for limited government. In *Catholic Social Teaching and the Market Economy* (ed. P. M. Booth). London: St Pauls.

Halsey, A. H. (1986) *Change in British Society,* 3rd edn. Oxford University Press.

John Paul II (2005) *Memory and Identity.* London: Phoenix.

Lawson, N. (1992) *The View from No. 11: Memoirs of a Tory Radical.* London: Bantam Press.

MacIntyre, A. (1981) *After Virtue: A Study in Moral Theory.* London: Duckworth.

MacIntyre, A. (2009) *God, Philosophy, Universities.* London: Continuum.

Newman, J. H. (1873) *The Idea of a University Defined and Illustrated: In Nine Discourses Delivered to the Catholics of Dublin.*

Pollard, S. (1981) *Peaceful Conquest: The Industrialization of Europe 1760–1970.* Oxford University Press.

Renard, G. (1919) *Guilds in the Middle Ages.* London: Bell.

Scarisbrick, J. J. (1984) *The Reformation and the English People.* Oxford: Blackwell.

Sirico, R. (2014) Rethinking welfare, reviving charity: a Catholic alternative. In *Catholic Social Teaching and the Market Economy* (ed. P. M. Booth). London: St Pauls.

Weber, M. (1947) *The Theory of Social and Economic Organization.* Oxford University Press.

Whelan, R. (1996) *The Corrosion of Charity: From Moral Renewal to Contract Culture*. London: Institute of Economic Affairs Health and Welfare Unit.

PAPAL ENCYCLICALS AND OTHER CHURCH DOCUMENTS

John Paul II (1991) *Centesimus annus*, encyclical letter (https://www.vati can.va/content/john-paul-ii/en/encyclicals/documents/hf_jp-ii_enc _01051991_centesimus-annus.html).

Vatican II (1965) *Gaudium et spes*, Pastoral Constitution on the Church in the World (https://www.vatican.va/archive/hist_councils/ii_vatican_co uncil/documents/vat-ii_const_19651207_gaudium-et-spes_en.html).

John XXIII (1961) *Mater et magistra*, encyclical letter (http://www.vatican .va/content/john-xxiii/en/encyclicals/documents/hf_j-xxiii_enc_15051 961_mater.html).

Pius XI (1931) *Quadragesimo anno*, encyclical letter (http://www.vatican .va/content/pius-xi/en/encyclicals/documents/hf_p-xi_enc_19310515 _quadragesimo-anno.html).

Leo XIII (1891) *Rerum novarum*, encyclical letter (http://www.vatican.va/ content/leo-xiii/en/encyclicals/documents/hf_l-xiii_enc_15051891_re rum-novarum.html). (Note: quotations from *Rerum novarum* in this article are from the original Manning translation, *The Tablet*, 6 June 1891.)

CHAPTER 13

Catholic social teaching and the role of the state in education

Leonardo Franchi

INTRODUCTION

The Christian is called to promote the welfare of family, friends and wider society. This commitment to the good of the other is manifested in many ways, including active involvement in community, social and cultural groups which seek to improve society.

Education is one such venture. For the Christian, authentic education (primary, secondary and tertiary) aims to form young people in virtue and promote human flourishing. All schools should work towards this ideal. In the Catholic school, the body of knowledge known as Catholic social teaching, with its concern for the welfare of individuals, families and wider society, is not just one part of the wider curriculum but should, ideally, underpin the mission, aims and objectives of the school (Grace 2013).

Catholic educational institutions operate in many different political jurisdictions. This variety of settings engenders an unavoidable diversity in the relationship between the school and the state. Nonetheless, Catholic political thought on the role of the state in human affairs revolves around the concept of the common good and on how individuals and families can be supported to live a life that is oriented towards God (Alting van Geausau and Booth 2013).

Yet, it is reasonable to ask: what is the common good? Can we agree on a broad definition for application to the multifaceted world of education? The *Stanford Encyclopedia of Philosophy* offers a valuable working definition of the common good for our purposes:

> In ordinary political discourse, the 'common good' refers to those facilities – whether material, cultural or institutional – that the members of a community provide to all members in order to fulfill a relational obligation they all have to care for certain interests that they have in common.

We find here the importance of relationships and commonality. These are key concepts in any understanding of Catholic social teaching, yet we note also the absence of references to political machinery and the notion of a state. This form of words is not far from the vision of the common good outlined in *Dignitatis humanae*, the Second Vatican Council's Declaration on Religious Freedom:

> Since the common welfare of society consists in the entirety of those conditions of social life under which men enjoy the possibility of achieving their own perfection in a certain fullness of measure and also with some relative ease, it chiefly consists in the protection of the rights, and in the performance of the duties, of the human person. Therefore the care of the right to religious freedom devolves upon the whole citizenry, upon social groups, upon government, and upon the Church and other religious communities, in virtue of the duty of all toward the common welfare, and in the manner proper to each. (6)

It is no surprise that the Council advocates religious freedom as part of the common good. A broadly similar understanding is found in Part 4 of the UNESCO publication, *Rethinking Education: Towards a Global Common Good* (UNESCO 2015). Of course, the common good is a term ripe for hijack by politicians of all stripes in support of their own agenda, with the obvious danger that this important concept becomes no more than a slogan used with little sense of nuance by public figures. This places a greater responsibility on Catholics to use the term wisely.

We also need to ask if is it possible to maintain, far less promote, authentic Catholic schooling in the context of strong *statist* tendencies to control educational processes to the extent that would be likely to lead to a clash between Church and state. In such an atmosphere, is an attachment to 'parental rights' no more than a sweet-sounding yet meaningless headline which falls short of the reality we face? By statist I refer to a sort of modern so-called liberal groupthink which appears to be emanating from a loose coalition of people who are determined to move education, culture and society in a particular ideological direction and who, crucially, have identified the state and the big institutions of society, including universities, as the drivers of this social transformation. This Gramscian tendency in the West sits ill alongside authentic liberty and the principles of Catholic social teaching, especially in the field of parental rights, where the Christian view, the bedrock of so many public institutions, is now just 'one of many religions' (Hitchens 2019).

In light of the broad issues highlighted above, the chapter is underpinned by some fundamental questions regarding the common good in education. Firstly, what are the limits of state influence on Catholic education? Secondly, to what extent can the corpus of Catholic social teaching influence in a positive way how the Church envisages and 'practises' Catholic education?

What is necessary now is to put some flesh on the proposal for Catholic social teaching to underpin Catholic education. The next sections will explore the role of the family, school and state in the provision of education. This will be followed by a discussion of some of the limitations of state intervention in Catholic education, especially in the fields of funding, admissions and curriculum. Within the chapter, 'Catholic education' refers to 'Catholic schooling' at both primary and secondary levels.

EDUCATION AND THE ROLE OF THE FAMILY

In Catholic teaching, the family is the primary setting for education. It is the non-negotiable role of parents to lead their children to knowledge of what it means to be human. As was stated in Pope Francis's apostolic exhortation *Amoris laetitia*, the family thus becomes a place of socialization where good customs, right behaviour and virtue are exemplified and taught. In this ambitious educational *programme,* so to speak, families are encouraged to be open to others and, ideally, work with other families to build supportive local and global family networks. For Pope Francis, family education is truly an 'education in hope' (*Amoris laetitia,* 275).

The Church also recognizes some limitations of the family's role as primary educators. Indeed, as far back as 1929, Pope Pius XI, in the encyclical on education, *Divini illius magistri,* noted as follows in relation to the various agents of education (12):

> In the first place comes the family, instituted directly by God for its peculiar purpose, the generation and formation of offspring; for this reason it has priority of nature and therefore of rights over civil society. Nevertheless, the family is an imperfect society, since it has not in itself all the means for its own complete development; whereas civil society is a perfect society, having in itself all the means for its peculiar end, which is the temporal well-being of the community; and so, in this respect, that is, in view of the common good, it has pre-eminence over the family, which finds its own suitable temporal perfection precisely in civil society.

This important, if little-known, text brings to the surface a number of questions concerning the correct ordering of the relationship between the family and civil society. The preceding paragraph in the encyclical locates the family and civil society firmly in the 'natural order' and the Church in the 'supernatural order'. In the following paragraphs, Pope Pius XI sets out *why* the Church has priority in education: it is 'absolutely superior therefore to any other title in the natural order' (15). This claim was one way of reminding wider society of the Church's ambitions in and for education, especially at a time of significant political and cultural challenges in inter-war Europe.

More recently, in a general audience, Pope Francis lamented the negative consequences for the Church and society of the alleged broken 'educational alliance'. The roots of this crisis are many, he claims: pressure from work, marital breakups, lack of trust between parents, to name just a few. In this intervention, Pope Francis is endorsing and developing Pope Benedict XVI's prior diagnosis of an 'educational emergency' as manifested, for example, in a genuine gap in cultural expectations between the generations. Indeed, according to Pope Benedict, the so-called 'generation gap' (of which we hear so much) is the consequence of inadequate educational processes which have failed to 'transmit certainties and values' (Pope Benedict XVI, Letter to the Diocese of Rome 2008).

In light of this problematic educational climate and the sociological challenges arising from an apparent lack of family stability, serious thought is now needed on how the Catholic school can exemplify a way of life which is rooted in Catholic tradition yet open to people from all (or no) religious traditions.

EDUCATION AND THE ROLE OF THE SCHOOL

In the first place, the Catholic school positions itself as an extension of the natural family, opening its doors to all families, including those of no particular religious affiliation. Alongside the question of how a Catholic school can successfully accommodate people of all religious traditions (which is not a theme of the present chapter), there arises the issue of the different expectations families have for their children's education. To address this, the role of the school in working with parents as 'primary educators' is extended to include the explicit education of parents. *The Religious Dimension of Education in a Catholic School*, published in 1988, states:

> Every school should initiate meetings and other programmes which will make the parents more conscious of their role and help to establish a partnership; it is impossible to do too much along these lines. (43)

Recognition of the need to support parents with their educational responsibilities is not unique to the Church. A good society cannot but support and encourage parents to work with their children to build a bright and happy future for them and others. A major challenge arises when parental expectations differ so radically from the aims of the school that we encounter the reality of the fractured educational pact alluded to above by both Pope Benedict XVI and Pope Francis. This added dimension to the role of the teacher is a salutary reminder of how the formation of teachers is a necessary prerequisite for good schools. If teachers are to be in the front line of family support, this adds impetus to the global educational community's reflections on how best to support teachers at all stages of their career (Rymarz and Franchi 2019).

Of course, the climate of the school is not solely dependent on the teachers. Ancillary and administrative staff, along with parents and pupils, make up the school community. Nonetheless, while parents remain the primary educators of children, the culture of the Catholic school can be shaped by the policy decisions and pastoral priorities of the teaching staff. To ensure that such ways of working accord with the Church's considerable expectations, further critical reflection is needed on formational processes offered to teachers. In an important document on how to deal with the inter-cultural (inter-religious) nature of Catholic schooling today, the Congregation for Catholic Education has advised that the added value to education which the Catholic school promises requires a reconsideration of how the corps of Catholic teachers can be offered the pedagogical, cultural and religious formation they require to discharge their considerable responsibilities effectively. The Congregation for Education's document, *Educating for Intercultural Dialogue in Catholic Schools: Living in Harmony for a Civilisation of Love*, published in 2013, expresses the challenge as follows:

> The formation of teachers and administrators is of crucial importance. In most countries, *the state provides the initial formation of school personnel. Good though this may be, it cannot be considered sufficient.* In fact, Catholic schools bring something extra, particular to them, that must always be recognized and developed. Therefore, while the obligatory formation needs to consider those disciplinary and professional matters typical of teaching and administrating, it must also consider the cultural and pedagogical fundamentals that make up Catholic schools' identity. (76, my italics)

Awareness of the limitations of the state processes for teacher formation is an incentive for Catholic educators to take their own formation more seriously. There is still considerable work to be done before the Catholic educational community can make the claim that its formation processes for teachers successfully incorporate what the Congregation calls the 'cultural and pedagogical fundamentals that make up the Catholic school's identity'. A start can be made at a local level if schools make the decision to prioritize engagement with the Church's rich body of material on education published by the Congregation for Catholic Education since the Second Vatican Council. Such an initiative could involve cooperation between schools and encourage Bishops' Conferences to think more deeply about how they can support higher education bodies in this important mission.

EDUCATION AND THE ROLE OF THE STATE

Like the Church, the state is not a monolith. It is important, however, to distinguish between the state and civil society. The latter is a fluid term encompassing a wide range of voluntary organizations, charities, businesses, professional groupings and such like. What seems to unite such bodies is their voluntary nature and dependence on the support of individuals and groups. The state, on the other hand, is a more centralized force, an overarching political society which seeks to control the life of its citizens and pass legislation to that end, thus potentially bringing about a situation in which 'subordinate units are merely extensions of the dominant power' (Kennedy 2014, p. 251).

The state shapes educational priorities according to the political programmes of governing parties and ways of working shaped by education professionals. It does not follow, of course, that the state will always and everywhere be opposed to the priorities of parents and the Church: the political climate can be more or less favourable to Catholic thinking on education at any given time. A serious problem arises, however, when the political and cultural priorities of the state, following and shaped by the ideology of particular governing parties, seek to limit the legitimate influence and freedom of the Catholic Church in relation to education. At its worst, the state might oppose the existence of Catholic schools or do what it can to make their existence difficult. A no less challenging situation can arise when the state gives its full support to Catholic schools but simultaneously promotes legislation which goes against Catholic teaching on issues such as marriage and the sanctity of life and which therefore undermines freedom of conscience as expressed in the life of the school. A case in point here is that of Catholic schools in Scotland. The SNP (Scottish National Party) government has offered its full support to Catholic schools on many occasions but also takes considerable pride in its self-definition as a 'progressive' government with the standard policy priorities such an ideology enshrines.

In an encyclical on Christians as citizens, *Sapientia Christianae* (1890), Pope Leo XIII declared that, essentially, the faithful Catholic is, by definition, a good citizen. Pope Leo, best known for his commitment to the promotion of the Church's social doctrine in the encyclical *Rerum novarum* (1891), nudges the believer towards full engagement with society: in fulfilling our rights as citizens, he argues, Christians are promoting the correct moral order. As such, the institutions of Catholic education are not opposed to the operation of the legitimate functions of the state.

From this firm foundation, the Congregation for Catholic Education reminded educators in 1988 of the importance of playing a visible and positive role in civic, national and international celebrations as 'traditional civic values such as freedom, justice, the nobility of work and the need to pursue social progress are all included among the school goals, and the life of the school gives witness to them' (*The Religious Dimension of Education in a Catholic School*, 45). This is a timely and gentle reminder that Catholics should avoid seeing Catholic schools as places of refuge from the influence of wider society. Instead, they should engage appropriately with the wider cultural life of the nation. Catholic schools thus work with the state and civil societies and contribute to the life of the state and civil society in multiple ways.

A key to effective Church–state relationships is dialogue. A willingness to listen to other points of view and to make friends with people from other cultures necessarily involves an openness to the possibilities for the promotion of peace and justice offered by inter-religious dialogue (*Educating to Fraternal Humanism: Building a Civilization of Love 50 Years after 'Populorum Progressio'*, 2017) and wider human interaction. Nonetheless, it is legitimate to ask how Christians, acting both as individual citizens and collectively, can make a meaningful difference to a society where the majority view might be pushing hard in a different direction. These dangers seem to be compounded when a state is unsure how to handle religious groups whose views on particular issues might not accord with some of the liberal cultural nostrums currently in fashion.

THE LIMITS OF STATE INVOLVEMENT IN THE LIFE OF THE SCHOOL

While the majority of faith schools in the West have a Christian foundation, the rise of such schools linked to other religions does raise questions about how such varied provision sits within a socially pluralist system (Parker-Jenkins et al. 2005, ch. 1, p. 18):

> Debates about Catholic schools are rooted in wider discussions about the role of religion in educational provision. Traditionally, denominational education, so-called, referred mainly to schools with a Christian foundation. The debates now include schools associated with other religions (Islam, Sikhism etc). This brings to the fore questions related to the existence of multiple forms of denominational education and their place in a plural polity.

The *United Nations Universal Declaration on Human Rights* says clearly that: 'Parents have a prior right to choose the kind of education that shall be given to their children' (United Nations 1948, p. 26, (3)). This lapidary statement reflects the order of priority expounded in 1929 by Pope Pius XI in *Divini illius magistri* (see above). It shows how the Catholic vision of education is very much integral to the developing post-war vision of education. The *Declaration,* perhaps understandably, does not elaborate on how this aim can be realized in the emerging post-war polities. From the vantage point of contemporary politics, it could almost seem to be an unrealistic and idealistic vision of the role and influence of parents in schooling. In light of this misgiving, is it possible for the state to offer educational provision which can in any way match the expectations contained in this famous and oft-quoted line from the *Declaration*?

The importance of this topic cannot, of course, be sidelined given the fundamental need to respect parental rights. The Second Vatican Council's Declaration on Religious Freedom, *Dignitatis humanae* (1965) has, unsurprisingly, something important to say about parental rights (5):

> Government, in consequence, must acknowledge the right of parents to make a genuinely free choice of schools and of other means of education, and the use of this freedom of choice is not to be made a reason for imposing unjust burdens on parents, whether directly or indirectly. Besides, the right of parents are violated, if their children are forced to attend lessons or instructions which are not in agreement with their religious beliefs, or if a single system of education, from which all religious formation is excluded, is imposed upon all.

The Second Vatican Council's Declaration on Christian Education, *Gravissimum educationis* (1965) reflected the aspirations of the 1948 *Universal Declaration*. Indeed the *Declaration* is referred to explicitly in its opening sections (footnote 3) and the right of parents to have their choices supported by the state is again expressed in unequivocal terms (6):

> Parents who have the primary and inalienable right and duty to educate their children must enjoy true liberty in their choice of schools. Consequently, the public power, which has the obligation to protect and defend the rights of citizens, must see to it, in its concern for distributive justice, that public subsidies are paid out in such a way that parents are truly free to choose according to their conscience the schools they want for their children.

This assertion, laudable in intention, intersects with the financial realities faced by the state and the wider agenda mapped out today by those who advocate that particular approaches to questions such as inclusion, equality, diversity, sex and gender must be taught in all schools. The writers of the Declaration on Christian Education were not to know of the impending wave of religious-cultural fissures which were soon to mark Western society. Their vision would be very much that of Catholic schools located within political arrangements which were more or less supportive of their right to exist but which varied in the level of support offered. It is unlikely that the Council Fathers would have anticipated the levels of hostility directed towards Catholic schools and the content of Catholic education in many traditionally Christian countries today.

To illustrate the depth and range of challenges facing Catholic schooling today, three areas of challenge arising from the relationship between the Church and state in education are identified.

Challenge 1: State funding and Catholic schools

Regarding the relationship between state funding and Catholic schools, operational models range from the state-centred funding model in Scotland to the model of Charter Schools in the US (cf. Franchi 2018; Miserandino 2018).

There are two broad arguments against state funding for Catholic schools. Firstly, it is argued that the state should not fund schools that are associated with religious belief as the existence of such schools damages social cohesion. Religion and education are not natural allies: a socially progressive policy hence would seek to remove the influence of religious bodies on education. Clearly, the issue is less about the funding of Catholic schools but their existence: the removal of funding is part of wider moves to abolish them.

Secondly, it is suggested that the existence of faith schools is broadly acceptable, but the debate should be about the provision of school places and the economic consequences of supporting different models of schooling. This 'magnification of difference' might not be conducive to the building of a society already straining to deal with the implications for social cohesion of religious and cultural pluralism (Judge 2001, p. 470).

Together, both arguments place considerable difficulties in the way of Catholic schools. They seem to be rooted in a belief that religious practice negatively affects social cohesion and thus Catholic (and other denominational) schools should be either abolished or have significant changes in the mode of finance, which could lead to closure.

Clearly, the nostrum that parents have the right to choose the education they wish for their children is not acknowledged. The state, either through heavy-handed legislation or subtle adjustments to funding formulae, is leading the development of schooling and thus limiting or ignoring the important principle of subsidiarity.

Challenge 2: Admissions

A second challenge relates to admissions policy. The factors that coalesce to help schools decide who should be given priority of access is one of the most problematic factors in Catholic schools' relationship with the state. Given the recent turn in Catholic education towards reassessing the value of inter-cultural dialogue in the life of the Catholic school,[8] the question of admissions policies, alongside issues arising from how to deal with the faith-formation of pupils, is clearly at the centre of discussion on the 'identity' of the Catholic school.

As far back as 1994, James Arthur, referring to admissions policies for Catholic schools in England and Wales, spoke of a 'disjunction between principles and practices in Catholic education'. By this he meant the challenges arising from the need to ensure that the shared values of the Catholic school could be preserved.

In essence, admissions policies for Catholic schools have to deal with the following conundrum: to what extent can a Catholic school serve the needs of the Catholic population while at the same time fulfilling its role as a public body (with funding contributed by the state) and the concomitant obligations this brings in its wake?

The Catholic Education Service in England and Wales seeks to occupy the middle ground between an openness to all people and a commitment to serving the Catholic population. It requires that schools prioritize Catholic pupils, but that they allow in

---

8   As noted in the Congregation for Catholic Education's document, *Educating for Intercultural Dialogue in Catholic Schools: Living in Harmony for a Civilisation of Love* (2013).

non-Catholics if there is spare capacity. If there are more Catholic applicants than places, Catholic practice can be taken into account which is normally certified by a priest.

From the perspective of the advocates of secularism in education, so-called discrimination in the admissions policies of denominational schools, especially when significant amounts of public money are part of the debate, is self-evidently problematic. Yet, a state's commitment to equity also has to take into account the related – and equally high-stakes – need to support diversity of provision and hence successfully navigate the complex seas where inclusion meets choice, diversity and equality. After all, Catholic parents pay taxes and it is not unreasonable that, if the state is going to require them to pay taxes for education, they are allowed to choose how their children are educated.

Challenge 3: The curriculum

The curriculum of the Catholic school is where the Catholic intellectual tradition interacts with the wells of human culture. The Catholic intellectual tradition refers to the wide paths mapped out by Catholic thinkers over the centuries in the ongoing mission to integrate revealed truth with culture and the vagaries of human life (Royal 2015).

As always, different educational jurisdictions will reflect different aspects of human culture. What unites them should be, ideally, a recognition that the curriculum itself must be rooted in a well-defined intellectual heritage: in so doing, it allows the teacher to accompany the student on the path to wisdom and right living, illuminated and challenged by the minds of the past. In *The Religious Dimension of Education*, the Congregation for Catholic Education offers rich insights on the shape of the curriculum of the Catholic school (57):

> Every society has its own heritage of accumulated wisdom. Many people find inspiration in these philosophical and religious concepts which have endured for millennia. The systematic genius of classical Greek and European thought has, over the centuries, generated countless different doctrinal systems, but it has also given us

a set of truths which we can recognize as a part of our permanent philosophical heritage. A Catholic school conforms to the generally accepted school programming of today, but implements these programmes within an overall religious perspective.

Such an idea of curriculum, of course, is not exclusive to those belonging to the Catholic tradition. There are other strong educational trends which continue to promote the underlying value of intellectual heritage. Nonetheless, there are equally strong secular trends in education which, using superficially attractive terms such as 'future-oriented' and 'creativity' (which are not in themselves alien to a Catholic view of education), significantly diminish the perceived priority of a defined intellectual heritage in favour of more process-oriented, or skills-based, curricular models. Scotland's troubled *Curriculum for Excellence*, which also applies to Catholic schools, has attracted some criticism for diminishing the importance of subject knowledge in favour of the promotion of generic skills (Paterson 2018).

It might not be immediately obvious why Catholic educators should be attracted by the priority of intellectual heritage in the construction of contemporary curricula. The focus on tradition as 'historical memory' – the story of the human person's ongoing interaction with others – is a conduit to the critical study of 'the best of what has been thought and said', raising the further question: who decides what qualifies as the best and which criteria should be used to make such decisions? For the well-intentioned Catholic educator, working within the multi-layered dramas of relativist secular politics, this brings welcome opportunities for re-presenting the nature of truth, beauty and goodness to a pupil population (and educational community more broadly) reared on less nutritious educational diets.

In any school, study of the contribution to human society of religion and associated ways of thinking has to be part of what is offered to pupils. Of course, the inclusion of religious topics in the curriculum does not presuppose any form of religious commitment. Catholic schools exist within a pluralist society and are called to engage with people of all beliefs and none. Nonetheless, a Catholic school will have a commitment to study religious topics from a particular point of view: if it is to be true to the desire of the parental body to offer an education in accordance with their wishes, it also has to be faithful to the ongoing development of Catholic thinking in education.

In recent years there have been increasingly strident calls to 'remove religion' from schools, meaning not just the abolition of faith schools but serious curricular reform designed to minimize the potential of religious education to act as a vehicle for faith transmission. What is less widely appreciated is that the Congregation for Catholic Education has recognized the challenges inherent in a religious education syllabus which is designed explicitly to catechize:

> Religious education in schools fits into the evangelising mission of the Church. It is different from, and complementary to, parish catechesis and other activities such as family Christian education or initiatives of ongoing formation of the faithful. Apart from the different settings in which these are imparted, the aims that they pursue are also different: catechesis aims at fostering personal adherence to Christ and the development of Christian life in its different aspects. (*Circular Letter to Presidents of Bishops' Conferences on Religious Education in Schools*, 17)

This shift in Catholic thinking is not simply a result of pressure from the state or other bodies to limit the Catholic content of the religious education curriculum: far from it. Rather, it is part of the Church's ongoing reflection on how the Catholic school can contribute to evangelization and promote wider cultural enrichment. Furthermore, it recognizes the prior role of the family in catechesis and thus rejects the view that catechetical activity and children's religious formation should be driven *principally* by the Catholic school.

The curricular climate in the West emphasizes a form of individualism which, arguably, has contributed to rise in what is known as 'identity politics' (Murray 2019). The Catholic Church still struggles to articulate a vision for Catholic education which, from the

intersection of ethics and identity politics, and allied to the necessary commitment to equality and diversity, looks coherent to both
outsiders and insiders. Once again, the rights of parents have been
stated clearly by the Catholic Church (*The Religious Dimension of
Education in a Catholic School*, 42):

> Partnership between a Catholic school and the families of the stu-
> dents must continue and be strengthened: not simply to be able to
> deal with academic problems that may arise, but rather so that the
> educational goals of the school can be achieved. Close cooperation
> with the family is especially important when treating sensitive issues
> such as religious, moral, or sexual education, orientation toward a
> profession, or a choice of one's vocation in life. It is not a question
> of convenience, but a partnership based on faith. Catholic tradition
> teaches that God has bestowed on the family its own specific and
> unique educational mission.

Sex and moral education encapsulates the significant cultural challenges currently facing Catholic educators. In brief, is it possible for
Catholic educational institutions to propose established Catholic
teaching to a society where such teachings run the risk not only of
landing on barren soil but of falling foul of the law?

To move this debate forward, it is vital to rediscover the roots
of Catholic teaching on human sexuality. Pope Francis has help-
fully reminded the Church of the beauty of conjugal love and of the
urgent need to return to the message of Pope Paul VI's encyclical,
Humanae vitae. In *Amoris laetitia*, 80, Pope Francis refers specifically
to paragraphs 11–12 of *Humanae vitae* in which it says:

> The reason is that the fundamental nature of the marriage act,
> while uniting husband and wife in the closest intimacy, also ren-
> ders them capable of generating new life – and this as a result of
> laws written into the actual nature of man and of woman. And if
> each of these essential qualities, the unitive and the procreative, is
> preserved, the use of marriage fully retains its sense of true mutual
> love and its ordination to the supreme responsibility of parenthood
> to which man is called. We believe that our contemporaries are

particularly capable of seeing that this teaching is in harmony with human reason.

This text succinctly *proposes* the Catholic vision of human sexuality in a way which is both challenging but fully in accord, it is claimed, with reason. A state which, in the name of tolerance and inclusion, prevents the teaching of Catholic morality on sexuality, and requires its own view to be taught as normative, is surely neither tolerant nor inclusive. It certainly isn't pluralist.

CONCLUDING REMARKS AND RECOMMENDATIONS

Catholic social teaching, if it is truly to run through the life of the Catholic school, will support a knowledge-rich curriculum. However, if parents are the primary educators of children, there is a related urgency to advance the Church's commitment to supporting parents in this mission. While the Catholic school and its teachers do have a natural professional relationship with parents, there is a need for a thorough examination of how parishes and 'family associations' can play a more active role in supporting parents as primary educators.

How the state should support families in their primary role as educators is a key question. While the democratic state has the responsibility to ensure that all children have access to schooling of high quality, it does not follow that the state must be the principal provider. This, of course, raises further questions about the essential and desirable features of a high-quality education which the state would then oversee and finance. Central to this is discussion of the role of the state in determining curriculum content and, more broadly, shaping the wider cultural atmosphere around schooling. This is where a recovery of subsidiarity could open up new pathways for schools to be places where diversity of curricular approaches (for example with a focus on technical education, or liberal arts) contribute to the common good.

Despite the many challenges facing the life of the Catholic school, a good case can be made that the Catholic school can still be a site of rich dialogue between the 'Catholic intellectual tradition' and the multiple channels which support other worldviews.

A *sine qua non* of an authentically Catholic school is the commitment of teachers to the ideals underpinning Catholic education. Satisfactory initial formation of teachers needs to be complemented by opportunities to engage seriously with the guidance offered by the Congregation for Catholic Education on how to shape the religious and cultural life of Catholic schools. How this is done will vary across local churches but there is a pressing need to study, reflect on and put into practice the aspiration contained in the underused corpus of teaching on Catholic education.

REFERENCES

Adler, M. (1984) *The Paideia Programme: An Educational Syllabus.* Los Angeles, CA: Institute for Philosophical Research.

Alting von Geasau, C., and Booth, P. M. (2013) *Catholic Education in the West: Roots, Reality, and Revival.* Grand Rapids, MI: Acton Institute.

Arthur, J. (1994) Admissions to Catholic schools: principles and practice. *British Journal of Religious Education*, 17(1): 35–45.

Franchi, L. (2018) Religious education and Catholic education: a Scottish perspective. In *Researching Catholic Education: Contemporary Perspectives* (ed. S. Whittle). Singapore: Springer.

Grace, G. (2013) Catholic social teaching should permeate the Catholic secondary school curriculum: an agenda for reform. *International Studies in Catholic Education* 5(1): 99–109.

Hitchens, P. (2019) Human dignity redefined. *First Things* (https://www.firstthings.com/web-exclusives/2019/10/human-dignity-redefined).

Judge, H. (2001) Faith-based schools and state funding: a partial argument. *Oxford Review of Education* 27(4): 463–74.

Kennedy, R. (2014) Business and the common good. In *Catholic Social Teaching and the Market Economy* (ed. P. M. Booth). London: Institute of Economic Affairs,

Miserandino, A. (2019) The funding and future of Catholic education in the United States. *British Journal of Religious Education* 41(1): 105–14.

Murray, D. (2019) *The Madness of Crowds: Gender, Race and Identity.* London: Bloomsbury.

Parker-Jenkins, M., Hartas, D., and Irving, B. (2005/2018) *In Good Faith: Schools, Religion and Public Funding*. Abingdon: Ashgate Publishing.

Paterson, L. (2018) Scotland's curriculum for excellence: a betrayal of a whole generation (https://blogs.lse.ac.uk/politicsandpolicy/curriculum-for-exc ellence/).

Royal, R. (2015) *A Deeper Vision: The Catholic Intellectual Tradition in the Twentieth Century*. San Francisco, CA: Ignatius Press.

Rymarz, R., and Franchi, L. (2019) *Catholic Teacher Education: Historical and Contemporary Perspectives on Preparing for Mission*. Bingley: Emerald Publishing Limited.

Stanford Encyclopedia of Philosophy, *The Common Good* (https://plato .stanford.edu/entries/common-good/).

United Nations (1948) *Universal Declaration on Human Rights* (https:// www.un.org/en/universal-declaration-human-rights/).

UNESCO (2015) United Nations Economic, Scientific and Cultural Organisation. *Rethinking Education: Towards a Global Common Good* (https://unesdoc.unesco.org/ark:/48223/pf0000232555/PDF/232555 eng.pdf.multi).

PAPAL ENCYCLICALS AND OTHER CHURCH DOCUMENTS

Congregation for Catholic Education (1988) *The Religious Dimension of Education in a Catholic School* (http://www.vatican.va/roman_curia/con gregations/ccatheduc/documents/rc_con_ccatheduc_doc_19880407 _catholic-school_en.html).

Congregation for Catholic Education (2009) *Circular Letter to Presidents of Bishops' Conferences on Religious Education in Schools* (http://www.vatican .va/roman_curia/congregations/ccatheduc/documents/rc_con_ccathe duc_doc_20090505_circ-insegn-relig_en.html).

Congregation for Catholic Education (2013) *Educating to Intercultural Dialogue in Catholic Schools: Living in Harmony for a Civilisation of Love* (http://www.vatican.va/roman_curia/congregations/ccatheduc/docu ments/rc_con_ccatheduc_doc_20131028_dialogo-interculturale_en .html).

Congregation for Catholic Education (2017) *Educating to Fraternal Humanism: Building a Civilisation of Love 50 years after 'Populorum Progressio'* (http://www.vatican.va/roman_curia/congregations/ccatheduc/docu

ments/rc_con_ccatheduc_doc_20170416_educare-umanesimo-soli dale_en.html).

Pope Francis (2016) *Amoris laetitia*, apostolic exhortation (https://w2.vati can.va/content/dam/francesco/pdf/apost_exhortations/documents/ papa-francesco_esortazione-ap_20160319_amoris-laetitia_en.pdf).

Pope Leo XIII (1890) *Sapientiae Christianae*, encyclical letter (http://w2.vat ican.va/content/leo-xiii/en/encyclicals/documents/hf_l-xiii_enc _10011890_sapientiae-christianae.html).

Leo XIII (1891) *Rerum novarum*, encyclical letter (http://www.vatican.va/ content/leo-xiii/en/encyclicals/documents/hf_l-xiii_enc_15051891_re rum-novarum.html).

Pope Pius XI (1929) *Divini illius magistri*, encyclical letter (http://w2.vatican .va/content/pius-xi/en/encyclicals/documents/hf_p-xi_enc_31121929 _divini-illius-magistri.html).

Vatican II (1965) *Dignitatis humanae*, Declaration on religious freedom (http://www.vatican.va/archive/hist_councils/ii_vatican_council/docu ments/vat-ii_decl_19651207_dignitatis-humanae_en.html).

Vatican II (1965) *Gravissimum educationis*, Declaration on Christian education (http://www.vatican.va/archive/hist_councils/ii_vatican_council/ documents/vat-ii_decl_19651028_gravissimum-educationis_en.html).

CHAPTER 14

Formal sources of Catholic social teaching

Philip Booth and André Azevedo Alves

INTRODUCTION

The authors of this book have cited many sources in developing their arguments. In the annex to this brief chapter, we list all the formal Church documents that have been cited as well as many of the addresses, homilies, etc. by various popes that have been mentioned. Before that, we briefly describe some of the formal sources of Catholic social teaching that have been published by the Catholic Church. These documents themselves rely on Holy Scripture. For example, Pope Francis, in his encyclical on the environment, *Laudato si'*, writes: 'We read in the Gospel that Jesus says of the birds of the air that "not one of them is forgotten before God"' (Lk 12:6) and asks, rhetorically, 'how then can we possibly mistreat them or cause them harm?' (221).

Chronologically, scripture is followed by the teaching of the early Church fathers or the patristics. They help develop and apply the teaching of scripture in the early Christian communities from which we can learn for the present day. So, we can observe how those communities lived, inspired by the teaching of Christ, and we can also observe the teaching of those communities and their learned fathers. The patristics include saints such as St Ambrose and St John Chrysostom. Modern Church teaching documents cite the Church fathers, just as they quote from scripture. A nice example is this quotation from St Gregory the Great in Pope Francis's encyclical *Fratelli tutti:* 'In the words of Saint Gregory the Great, "When we provide the needy with their basic needs, we are giving them what belongs to them, not to us"' (119).

As discussed in chapter 2, Thomas Aquinas's great work *Summa Theologica* has informed a great deal of Catholic social teaching, especially the early social encyclicals. Pope Francis quotes Aquinas at an important point in *Laudato si'*, stating: 'Saint Thomas Aquinas wisely noted that multiplicity and variety "come from the intention of the first agent" who willed that "what was wanting to one in the representation of the divine goodness might be supplied by another", inasmuch as God's goodness "could not be represented fittingly by any one creature". Hence we need to grasp the variety of things in their multiple relationships.'

Following in what is often called a 'Thomistic' intellectual framework, the late scholastics were an important group of, mainly Iberian, thinkers from the fifteenth and sixteenth centuries. They used a similar method to Aquinas and applied that method to new social, economic and political problems, especially those arising from the new world. Their work is discussed in this book, especially in chapters 2 and 3. The late scholastics are often regarded as the first serious contributors to the development of modern economic theory. Contributions also included increasing our understanding of the morality (or otherwise) of inflation, as well as its causes, and the basis of human rights.

All these sources have been important influences on the tradition of Catholic social teaching. There are, of course, many other influences. Pope Francis has often referred to local Bishops' Conferences. Aspects of liberation theology and other intellectual traditions have also been important. Indeed, there will often be a wide process of consultation with academics, not necessarily just Catholic academics, as the thinking behind a future social encyclical evolves and the popes are guided in their prudent judgement.

SOCIAL ENCYCLICALS

It is often assumed that the formal social teaching of the Catholic Church began in 1891 with the publication of *Rerum novarum*. In fact, the social teaching of the Church goes back to her origins. It would be more accurate to say that the modern encyclical tradition – that is the production of a series of authoritative documents on social concerns referring to the signs of the times and written within a general framework – began in 1891. In a sense, these present the formal social teaching of the Church, along with other categories of document discussed above. These letters, which are of varying length, have Latin names derived from the early part of the document. Many of them are published on anniversaries of *Rerum novarum* and their titles sometimes refer back to that document. There is some dispute about how their titles should be capitalized. In this book, only the first word is capitalized unless later words in the title would normally be capitalized in their own right.

An encyclical is a letter addressed by the pope, usually to the other Catholic bishops of the world or, in the case of many social encyclicals, to all people of goodwill. An important reason for addressing encyclicals to a universal audience is the original mandate given by Jesus Christ to the apostles to make believers of all nations of the earth. Social teaching is, therefore, an integral part of the Church's evangelical mission. All encyclicals are written in the pope's name, regardless of whether the pope himself is the original author of the text or whether there have been other drafters involved.

The list of social encyclicals would normally be regarded as including:

Rerum novarum (On capital and labour), Pope Leo XIII, 15 May 1891.

Quadragesimo anno (After forty years, published to mark the 40th anniversary of *Rerum novarum*), Pope Pius XI, 15 May 1931.

Mater et magistra (On Christianity and social progress), Pope John XXIII, 15 May 1961.

Pacem in terris (Peace on Earth), Pope John XXIII, 11 April 1963.

Populorum progressio (On the development of peoples), Pope Paul VI, 27 March 1967.

Laborem exercens (On human work), Pope John Paul II, 14 September 1981.

Sollicitudo rei socialis (published in the anniversary year of *Populorum progressio*), Pope John Paul II, 30 December 1987.

Centesimus annus (The hundredth year, published to mark the 100th anniversary of *Rerum novarum*), Pope John Paul II, 1 May 1991.

Deus caritas est (God is love), Pope Benedict XVI, 15 December 2005.

Caritas in veritate (Charity in truth, intended to be published in the anniversary year of *Populorum progressio* in 2007, but published following the financial crisis), Pope Benedict XVI, 29 June 2009.

Laudato si' (On care for our common home), Pope Francis, 24 May 2015.

Fratelli tutti (Brothers all), Pope Francis, 3 October 2020.

The themes of the encyclicals can be quite general in some cases. In others, they may have a strong focus. Whether an encyclical is a social encyclical is not always beyond doubt. There is a strong argument for including *Evangelium vitae* (the gospel of life on the inviolability of human life). Some commentators would not include *Deus caritas est* among the social encyclicals. This lack of definitional clarity is not surprising. Pope Francis has been keen to emphasize the interconnectedness of different facets of our lives. We saw in chapter 5 the relationship between life issues and the natural environment. Similar links can be drawn between the family and education, or between life issues and healthcare. Our need to love and care for others and design political systems that recognize the dignity of all arises from our creation in the image of God as children of God and therefore as brothers and sisters in Christ. Given this reality, it is natural that there is no clear categorization of what is and what is not a 'social' encyclical.

In addition to these encyclicals, Catholic social teaching is presented in apostolic exhortations and apostolic letters. These are less authoritative and the former do not define doctrine. Apostolic exhortations are often issued after synods and their themes can be more specific than those of encyclicals. Pope Paul VI issued an apostolic letter, *Octogesima adveniens*, rather than an encyclical, to commemorate the 80th anniversary of the publication of *Rerum novarum*.

There is a wide range of other documents, homilies and addresses that help us understand and interpret Catholic social teaching. The statements on the World Day of Migrants and Refugees and those issued on the World Day of Peace are referred to by a number of authors in this book. Pope Pius XII did not write a social encyclical but his collection of addresses, Christmas messages, and so on, reflect a strong understanding of economic and social concerns. In addition, a vast range of documents are published by the various offices of the Vatican. One such document, 'Considerations for an ethical discernment regarding some aspects of the present economic-financial system' is mentioned by chapter authors. This was published in 2018 jointly by the Congregation for the Doctrine of the Faith and the Dicastery for Promoting Integral Human Development.

VATICAN II AND OTHER DOCUMENTS

Also, among the formal publications of the Catholic Church, are the documents from Church Councils. Authors in this book have referred to various publications arising from the Second Vatican Council (Vatican II), some of which are important in presenting the teaching of the Church on social and economic issues. Key documents which are connected with social teaching are: *Gravissimum educationis* on Christian education; *Dignitatis humanae* on human dignity and the much longer document, *Gaudium et spes* – the pastoral constitution of the Church in the modern world. These documents, especially the last of those three, obviously have special significance, arising, as they do, from a Church Council following a vote by the world's bishops.

The Catholic Church has also published foundational documents that summarize her teaching. Two of these are especially relevant to Catholic social teaching: the Catechism (which has substantial sections on social, political and economic life) and the Compendium of the Social Doctrine of the Church. These will often quote papal documents as important sources (as well as scripture and the patristics). In turn, papal letters will quote these sources, especially the Catechism. The Catechism carries particular authority and is only revised infrequently.

All the Church's publications of this nature are divided into numbered paragraphs which should always be used in quotations. The paragraph numbers remain the same between translations whereas page numbers do not. Nearly all Vatican documents are translated into a number of different languages, though there can be anomalies in the translations.

ANNEX: CATHOLIC CHURCH DOCUMENTS REFERRED TO IN THIS BOOK

Below is a list of the Church documents referred to by the chapter authors in this book, excluding the Catechism and the Compendium. All the documents, in addition to the Catechism and Compendium, can be found online at the Vatican's website.

Francis (2023) *Laudate deum*, apostolic exhortation (https://www.vatican .va/content/francesco/en/apost_exhortations/documents/20231004-lau date-deum.html).

Francis (2020) *Fratelli tutti*, encyclical letter (http://www.vatican.va/con tent/francesco/en/encyclicals/documents/papa-francesco_20201003 _enciclica-fratelli-tutti.html).

Francis (2019) *Message for the 105th World Day of Migrants and Refugees* (http://www.vatican.va/content/francesco/en/messages/migration/docu ments/papa-francesco_20190527_world-migrants-day-2019.html).

Congregation for the Doctrine of the Faith and the Dicastery for Promoting Integral Human Development (2018) *Oeconomicae et pecuniariae quaestiones* (*Considerations for an ethical discernment regarding some aspects of the present economic-financial system*) (https://press.vatican.va/ content/salastampa/en/bollettino/pubblico/2018/05/17/180517a.html).

Francis (2018) *Message for the 104th World Day of Migrants and Refugees* (http://www.vatican.va/content/francesco/en/messages/migration/docu ments/papa-francesco_20170815_world-migrants-day-2018.html).

Congregation for Catholic Education (2017) *Educating to Fraternal Humanism: Building a Civilisation of Love 50 Years after 'Populorum Progressio'*: (http://www.vatican.va/roman_curia/congregations/ccatheduc/ documents/rc_con_ccatheduc_doc_20170416_educare-umanesimo -solidale_en.html).

Francis (2016) *Amoris laetitia*, apostolic exhortation (https://w2.vatican.va/ content/dam/francesco/pdf/apost_exhortations/documents/papa-fran cesco_esortazione-ap_20160319_amoris-laetitia_en.pdf).

Francis (2015) *Message for 101st World Day of Migrants and Refugees* (http:// www.vatican.va/content/francesco/en/messages/migration/documents/ papa-francesco_20140903_world-migrants-day-2015.html).

Francis (2015) *Laudato si'*, encyclical letter (https://www.vatican.va/content/francesco/en/encyclicals/documents/papa-francesco_20150524_enci clica-laudato-si.html).

Francis (2014) *Message for World Day of Migrants and Refugees* (http://www.vatican.va/content/francesco/en/messages/migration/documents/papa-francesco_20130805_world-migrants-day.html).

Francis (2013) *Evangelii gaudium*, apostolic exhortation (http://www.vatican.va/content/francesco/en/apost_exhortations/documents/papa-franc esco_esortazione-ap_20131124_evangelii-gaudium.html).

Congregation for Catholic Education (2013) *Educating to Intercultural Dialogue in Catholic Schools: Living in Harmony for a Civilisation of Love* (http://www.vatican.va/roman_curia/congregations/ccatheduc/documents/rc_con_ccatheduc_doc_20131028_dialogo-interculturale_en.html).

Benedict XVI (2013) *Message for World Day of Migrants and Refugees* (https://www.vatican.va/content/benedict-xvi/en/messages/migration/docume nts/hf_ben-xvi_mes_20121012_world-migrants-day.html).

Benedict XVI (2011) *Message for World Day of Migrants and Refugees* (https://www.vatican.va/content/benedict-xvi/en/messages/migration/docume nts/hf_ben-xvi_mes_20100927_world-migrants-day.html).

Pontifical Council for Justice and Peace (2011) Towards reforming the international and financial monetary systems in the context of global public authority (https://www.vatican.va/roman_curia/pontifical_councils/jus tpeace/documents/rc_pc_justpeace_doc_20111024_nota_en.html).

Benedict XVI (2009) *Caritas in veritate*, encyclical letter (https://www.vati can.va/content/benedict-xvi/en/encyclicals/documents/hf_ben-xvi_enc _20090629_caritas-in-veritate.html).

Congregation for Catholic Education (2009) *Circular Letter to Presidents of Bishops' Conferences on Religious Education in Schools* (http://www.vatican.va/roman_curia/congregations/ccatheduc/documents/rc_con_ccathe duc_doc_20090505_circ-insegn-relig_en.html).

Benedict XVI (2005) *Deus Caritas est*, encyclical letter (http://www.vati can.va/content/benedict-xvi/en/encyclicals/documents/hf_ben-xvi_enc _20051225_deus-caritas-est.html).

John Paul II (2004) *Message for 90th World Day of Migrants and Refugees* (http://www.vatican.va/content/john-paul-ii/en/messages/migration/documents/hf_jp-ii_mes_20031223_world-migration-day-2004.html).

John Paul II (2001) *Message for the 87th World Day of Migration* (http:// www.vatican.va/content/john-paul-ii/en/messages/migration/docume nts/hf_jp-ii_mes_20010213_world-migration-day-2001.html).

John Paul II (1999) *Ecclesia in America*, apostolic exhortation (https://www .vatican.va/content/john-paul-ii/en/apost_exhortations/documents/hf _jp-ii_exh_22011999_ecclesia-in-america.html).

John Paul II (1998) *Message for World Day of Migration* (http://www.vati can.va/content/john-paul-ii/en/messages/migration/documents/hf_jp -ii_mes_09111997_world-migration-day-1998.html).

John Paul II (1998) *Fides et racio*, encyclical letter (http://www.vatican.va/ content/john-paul-ii/en/encyclicals/documents/hf_jp-ii_enc_14091998 _fides-et-ratio.html).

John Paul II (1993) *Message for World Day of Migration* (https://www.vati can.va/content/john-paul-ii/it/messages/migration/documents/hf_jp-ii _mes_19930806_world-migration-day-93-94.html).

John Paul II (1991) *Centesimus annus*, encyclical letter (https://www.vati can.va/content/john-paul-ii/en/encyclicals/documents/hf_jp-ii_enc _01051991_centesimus-annus.html).

Congregation for Catholic Education (1988) *The Religious Dimension of Education in a Catholic School* (http://www.vatican.va/roman_curia/con gregations/ccatheduc/documents/rc_con_ccatheduc_doc_19880407 _catholic-school_en.html).

John Paul II (1987) *Sollicitudo rei socialis*, encyclical letter (http://www.vati can.va/content/john-paul-ii/en/encyclicals/documents/hf_jp-ii_enc_30 121987_sollicitudo-rei-socialis.html).

Congregation for the Doctrine of the Faith (1986) *Instruction on Christian Freedom and Liberation* (http://www.vatican.va/roman_curia/congrega tions/cfaith/documents/rc_con_cfaith_doc_19860322_freedom-libera tion_en.html).

Pontifical Council for Justice and Peace (1986) *At the Service of the Human Community: An Ethical Approach to the International Debt Question* (http:// www.iustitiaetpax.va/content/giustiziaepace/en/archivio/documenti/ at-the-service-of-the-human-community--an-ethical-approach-to -th.html).

John Paul II (1981) *Laborem exercens*, encyclical letter (http://www.vatican .va/content/john-paul-ii/en/encyclicals/documents/hf_jp-ii_enc_14091 981_laborem-exercens.html).

John Paul II (1979) *Redemptor hominis*, encyclical letter (https://www.vatican
.va/content/john-paul-ii/en/encyclicals/documents/hf_jp-ii_enc_04031
979_redemptor-hominis.html).

John Paul II (1978) *Letter 'To the People of Poland'* (http://www.vatican
.va/content/john-paul-ii/en/letters/1978/documents/hf_jp-ii_let_1978
1024_polacchi.html).

Paul VI (1971) *Octogesima adveniens*, apostolic letter (https://www.vatican
.va/content/paul-vi/en/apost_letters/documents/hf_p-vi_apl_19710514
_octogesima-adveniens.html).

Paul VI (1967) *Populorum progressio*, encyclical letter (http://www.vatican
.va/content/paul-vi/en/encyclicals/documents/hf_p-vi_enc_26031967
_populorum.html).

Vatican II (1965) *Gaudium et spes*, Pastoral Constitution on the Church in
the World (https://www.vatican.va/archive/hist_councils/ii_vatican_co
uncil/documents/vat-ii_const_19651207_gaudium-et-spes_en.html).

Vatican II (1965) *Dignitatis humanae*, Declaration on Religious Freedom
(http://www.vatican.va/archive/hist_councils/ii_vatican_council/doc
uments/vat-ii_decl_19651207_dignitatis-humanae_en.html).

Vatican II (1965) *Gravissimum educationis*, Declaration on Christian Education (http://www.vatican.va/archive/hist_councils/ii_vatican_council/
documents/vat-ii_decl_19651028_gravissimum-educationis_en.html).

Vatican II (1964) *Lumen gentium*, Dogmatic Constitution on the Church
(https://www.vatican.va/archive/hist_councils/ii_vatican_council/docu
ments/vat-ii_const_19641121_lumen-gentium_en.html).

John XXIII (1963) *Pacem in terris*, encyclical letter (http://www.vatican.va/
content/john-xxiii/en/encyclicals/documents/hf_j-xxiii_enc_11041963
_pacem.html).

John XXIII (1961) *Mater et magistra*, encyclical letter (http://www.vatican
.va/content/john-xxiii/en/encyclicals/documents/hf_j-xxiii_enc_15051
961_mater.html).

Pius XII (1942) *Con Sempre Nuova Freschezza*, radio message (https://www
.vatican.va/content/pius-xii/it/speeches/1942/documents/hf_p-xii_spe
_19421224_radiomessage-christmas.html).

Pius XI (1937) *Divini redemptoris*, encyclical letter (https://www.vatican.va/
content/pius-xi/en/encyclicals/documents/hf_p-xi_enc_19370319_divi
ni-redemptoris.html).

Pius XI (1931) *Quadragesimo anno,* encyclical letter (http://www.vatican
.va/content/pius-xi/en/encyclicals/documents/hf_p-xi_enc_19310515
_quadragesimo-anno.html).

Pope Pius XI (1929) *Divini illius magistri,* encyclical letter (http://w2.vatican
.va/content/pius-xi/en/encyclicals/documents/hf_p-xi_enc_31121929
_divini-illius-magistri.html).

Leo XIII (1891) *Rerum novarum,* encyclical letter (http://www.vatican.va/
content/leo-xiii/en/encyclicals/documents/hf_l-xiii_enc_15051891_re
rum-novarum.html).

Pope Leo XIII (1890) *Sapientiae Christianae,* encyclical letter (http://w2.vati
can.va/content/leo-xiii/en/encyclicals/documents/hf_l-xiii_enc_1001
1890_sapientiae-christianae.html).

Leo XIII (1878) *Aeterni Patris,* encyclical letter (http://www.vatican.va/con
tent/leo-xiii/en/encyclicals/documents/hf_l-xiii_enc_04081879_aeter
ni-patris.html).

Third Lateran Council (1179) (http://www.papalencyclicals.net/Councils/
ecum11.htm).

Contributors

Andre Azevedo Alves is director of research at the Catholic University of Portugal's Institute for Political Studies and an associate professor at St Mary's University. He was a visiting professor at Rio de Janeiro State University in November 2011 and at Pontifícia Universidade Católica do Rio Grande do Sul (Brazil) in October 2012. He is co-author of the book *The Salamanca School* (Bloomsbury, 2013).

Philip Booth is professor of finance, public policy and ethics at St Mary's University, Twickenham. He is also director of Catholic Mission at St Mary's University and is director of policy and research at the Catholic Bishops' Conference of England and Wales. He has previously held positions at the University of Buckingham, the Institute of Economic Affairs, Cass Business School and the Bank of England. He is adjunct professor in the school of law at the University of Notre Dame, Australia. Philip is a fellow of the Royal Statistical Society and a fellow of the Institute of Actuaries.

Hugo Chelo holds a PhD in political science and international relations from the Institute of Political Studies of the Catholic University of Portugal and a degree in philosophy from the faculty of human sciences of the Catholic University of Portugal. He has been an assistant professor at the Institute of Political Studies at the Catholic University of Portugal. His research interests focus on the areas of contemporary political thought, classical and Christian thought, moral philosophy and the social doctrine of the Catholic Church.

Leonardo Franchi is a lecturer in education at the University of Glasgow. He is a member of the Executive of the Association of

Catholic Institutes of Education and a council member of the Scottish Catholic Historical Association. He is a series editor for "Catholic Education Globally – Challenges and Opportunities" (Springer) and for "Education and Integral Human Development" (Catholic University of America Press). Leonardo is also a professor of Catholic education at the University of Notre Dame Australia.

Samuel Gregg is an affiliate scholar at the Acton Institute and he serves as the Friedrich Hayek Chair in Economics and Economic History at the American Institute for Economic Research. He has a DPhil in moral philosophy and political economy from Oxford University. He is the author of sixteen books, including, most recently, *The Essential Natural Law* (Fraser Institute, 2021) and *The Next American Economy: Nation, State and Markets in an Uncertain World* (Encounter Books, 2022).

Inês Gregório works as a research assistant at the research centre of the Institute for Political Studies at the Catholic University of Portugal (CIEP-UCP), where she is responsible for the executive coordination of ongoing research projects. Additionally, she is a teaching assistant at CIEP-UCP. Her main research interests include education policy and alternative educative models. Inês holds a PhD in political science and international relations. She also has an MA in politics, philosophy and economics from the University of York.

Robert Kennedy is a full professor in the Department of Catholic Studies at the University of St Thomas, Minnesota. He received his PhD in mediaeval studies from the University of Notre Dame, and he also holds master's degrees in biblical criticism and business administration. Robert has published widely in the area of Catholic social thought and teaches courses on the church and culture and on St Thomas Aquinas. He is a member of the American Philosophical Association.

Stephen Nakrosis is a journalist from New Jersey and a PhD candidate at St Mary's University, Twickenham. He has written about Catholic social teaching and hagiography for a number of publications. He is currently employed by a major financial news-wire based in New York City.

Kaetana Numa is a research fellow at the Centre for the Study of Governance and Society at the department of political economy at King's College London, where she completed her PhD in political economy in 2021. Prior to her PhD research, she worked at a think tank in Lithuania for almost a decade. Kaetana graduated with a BA in economics and international relations (cum laude) from Tufts University, and she also holds an MA in religious studies from Vilnius University.

Jay Richards is director of the Richard and Helen DeVos Center for Life, Religion, and Family and the William E. Simon Senior Research Fellow in American Principles and Public Policy at the Heritage Foundation. He is a senior fellow at the Discovery Institute and executive editor of *The Stream*. Jay is the author or editor of more than a dozen books, including the *New York Times* bestsellers *Infiltrated* (McGraw Hill, 2013) and *Indivisible* (Ignatius Press, 2012). He is also creator and executive producer of several documentaries, including three that have appeared widely on PBS.

Mgr. Martin Schlag holds the Alan W. Moss endowed chair for Catholic Social Thought of the John A. Ryan Institute in the Center for Catholic Studies at the University of St. Thomas, Minnesota, where he is full professor with dual appointment in the department of Catholic Studies and the Opus College of Business. Mgr. Schlag has authored more than 80 publications, among them *Humanism in Economics and Business: Perspectives of the Catholic Social Tradition* (Springer, 2015; together with Domènec Melé), *The Handbook of Catholic Social Teaching: A Guide for Christians in the World Today* (Catholic University of America Press, 2017) and *The Business Francis Means: Understanding the Pope's Message on the Economy* (Catholic University of America Press, 2017).

Russell Sparkes is a visiting research fellow at St Mary's University, Twickenham. He has previously worked as a fund manager, pioneering the concept of ethical investment. He has written widely in the academic literature, especially on distributism and ethical investment.

Andrew M. Yuengert is a professor of economics in Seaver College at Pepperdine University. He received his PhD in economics from Yale University, and he has been the William E. Simon Visiting Fellow in Religion and Public Life at Princeton University, an assistant professor of economics at Bates College, and a research economist at the Federal Reserve Bank of New York. Andrew is a former president of the Association of Christian Economists. He is the author of *The Boundaries of Technique: Ordering Positive and Normative Concerns in Economic Research* (Lexington, 2004) and *Inhabiting the Land: The Case for the Right to Migrate* (Acton Institute 2004).